www.wadsworth.com

wadsworth.com is the World Wide Web site for Wadsworth and is your direct source to dozens of online resources.

At *wadsworth.com* you can find out about supplements, demonstration software, and student resources. You can also send email to many of our authors and preview new publications and exciting new technologies.

wadsworth.com
Changing the way the world learns®

Slaughterhouse Blues

The Meat and Poultry Industry in North America

Donald D. Stull
The University of Kansas

Michael J. Broadway
Northern Michigan University

With a Foreword by Eric Schlosser

 Case Studies on Contemporary Social Issues: John A. Young, Series Editor

Australia • Canada • Mexico • Singapore • Spain
United Kingdom • United States

Anthropology Editor: *Lin Marshall*
Assistant Editor: *Analie Barnett*
Editorial Assistant: *Amanda Santana*
Marketing Manager: *Diane Wenckebach*
Project Manager, Editorial Production:
  Rita Jaramillo
Print/Media Buyer: *Rebecca Cross*
Permissions Editor: *Sarah Harkrader*

Production Service: *Mary E. Deeg,*
  Buuji, Inc.
Copy Editor: *Pam Suwinsky*
Cover Designer: *Rob Hugel*
Cover Image: Meat&Poultry *magazine*
Text and Cover Printer: *Webcom*
Compositor: *Buuji, Inc.*

The logo for the Contemporary Social Issues series is
based on the image of a social group interacting around
a central axis, referring both back to a tribal circle and
forward to a technological society's network.

Printed in Canada
1 2 3 4 5 6 7 06 05 04 03

For more information about our products,
contact us at:
Thomson Learning Academic Resource Center
1-800-423-0563

For permission to use material from this text,
contact us by:
Phone: 1-800-730-2214   **Fax:** 1-800-730-2215
Web: http://www.thomsonrights.com

Library of Congress Control Number: 2003100340

ISBN 0-534-61303-9

Wadsworth/Thomson Learning
10 Davis Drive
Belmont, CA 94002-3098
USA

Asia
Thomson Learning
5 Shenton Way #01-01
UIC Building
Singapore 068808

Australia/New Zealand
Thomson Learning
102 Dodds Street
Southbank, Victoria 3006
Australia

Canada
Nelson
1120 Birchmount Road
Toronto, Ontario M1K 5G4
Canada

Europe/Middle East/Africa
Thomson Learning
High Holborn House
50/51 Bedford Row
London WC1R 4LR
United Kingdom

Latin America
Thomson Learning
Seneca, 53
Colonia Polanco
11560 Mexico D.F.
Mexico

Spain/Portugal
Paraninfo
Calle/Magallanes, 25
28015 Madrid, Spain

For our families, who sustain us in all things,
for the men and women who make our meat,
and for the communities that sustain them

My gal she bring me chicken,
My gal she bring me ham,
My gal she bring me everything,
An' she don't give a damn.

"Chain Gang Blues," Howard Odum and Guy Johnson,
Negro Workaday Songs, 1926

But he said unto them, I have meat to eat that ye know not of.

John 4:31

You have just dined, and however scrupulously the slaughterhouse is concealed in the graceful distance of miles, there is complicity.

Ralph Waldo Emerson, "Fate," *The Conduct of Life*, 1860

Contents

Figures and Tables

FIGURES

TABLES

Series Foreword

ABOUT THE SERIES

This book series explores the practical applications of anthropology in understanding and addressing problems faced by human societies around the world. Each case study examines an issue of socially recognized importance in the historical, geographical, and cultural context of a particular region of the world, while adding comparative analysis to highlight not only the local effects of globalization, but also the global dimensions of the issue. The authors write with a readable narrative style and include reference to their own participation, roles, and responsibilities in the communities they study. Their engagement with people goes beyond observation and research, as they explain and sometimes illustrate from personal experience how their work has implications for advocacy, community action, and policy formation. They demonstrate how anthropological investigations can build our knowledge of human societies and at the same time provide the basis for fostering community empowerment, resolving conflicts, and pursuing social justice.

ABOUT THE AUTHORS

Donald D. Stull is professor of anthropology at the University of Kansas, where he has served on the faculty since 1975. He received his doctorate from the University of Colorado, Boulder, in 1973, and a master's degree in public health from the University of California, Berkeley, in 1975. Stull is editor of *Human Organization*, the journal of the Society for Applied Anthropology, and a past coeditor of *Culture & Agriculture*. Since 1987, his research has focused on meat and poultry processing's impact on workers and host communities. In 1995, he received the Omer C. Stewart Memorial Award for exemplary achievement from the High Plains Society for Applied Anthropology. Stull was made an honorary citizen of Garden City, Kansas, in 2001 and was presented with the key to the city in recognition of the value of his work for that community. He was presented with the Irvin E. Youngberg Award for Research Achievement in the Applied Sciences by the Kansas University Endowment Association in 2002.

Michael Broadway is professor and head of Northern Michigan University's Department of Geography. He holds degrees in education and geography from Nottingham University and London University and received his Ph.D. in geography from the University of Illinois at Urbana-Champaign in 1983. Before joining the faculty at Northern Michigan in 1997, Broadway taught at the State University of New York at Plattsburgh, Wichita State University, and the State University of New York at Geneseo. It was during his time in Kansas that Broadway developed his interest in the meat industry, and he has gone on to study its impact upon communities and the environment in the United States, Canada, and Great Britain. Broadway was an expert witness in a court case against one of the leading meatpacking companies in the late 1990s. His research was the subject of a Canadian Broadcasting Corporation documentary that aired on *The National* in 1998.

Stull and Broadway have written numerous journal articles and book chapters together. With David Griffith, they edited *Any Way You Cut It: Meat Processing and Small-Town America,* published by the University of Kansas Press in 1995.

ABOUT THIS CASE STUDY

The relationship of food production to other aspects of culture has always attracted the attention of social scientists. This case study tells how the modern system of meat and poultry production has altered our very way of life. The authors take the reader on a journey through factories, farms, and communities to explore how corporate-driven forces cause air and water pollution, threaten the health and safety of workers, deny farmers the means to control their own livelihood, and alter the ethnic makeup and class structure of rural towns. They also recount how their work has helped communities resist and mitigate the negative impacts of rural industrialization, and illustrate how your own food choices have far-reaching political, economic, and social consequences.

John A. Young
Series Editor
Department of Anthropology
Oregon State University
jyoung@oregonstate.edu

Foreword

The story of meatpacking in America is a tragedy. It defies our traditional belief in progress. It shows that things don't always get better in this country—and indeed can get much worse. When Upton Sinclair wrote *The Jungle* in 1906, a corporate monopoly called the Beef Trust controlled most of the meat production in the United States, setting the prices that ranchers and farmers received for their livestock. At America's slaughterhouses the sanitary conditions and the working conditions were appalling. Spoiled meat was routinely adulterated with chemicals and sold to unsuspecting consumers. Immigrant meatpacking workers earned low wages, had little job security, often suffered debilitating injuries, and expected to be fired after getting hurt. The public outrage sparked by *The Jungle* led to swift passage of food safety laws, and antitrust enforcement broke the stranglehold of the Beef Trust after World War I. It took decades of union organizing, however, for wages and working conditions to improve. But they did, eventually. By the late 1960s meatpacking workers enjoyed one of the highest-paid industrial jobs in the United States, with one of the lowest turnover rates. Although working in a slaughterhouse was still a tough, dangerous job, it had finally become a good one, too. It provided a decent, middle-class life. At some slaughterhouses there were waiting lists for jobs.

In many respects the past 30 years have witnessed a return to the jungle. Unions were broken; wages were slashed; benefits were eliminated; and armies of recent immigrants were recruited by the meatpacking industry in order to gain cheap, docile labor. Today meatpacking workers have one of the lowest-paid industrial jobs in the United States, with one of the highest turnover rates. Slaughterhouses now tend to be understaffed, and they remain one of the nation's most dangerous workplaces. Meatpacking communities have become enclaves of rural poverty. The recent centralization and industrialization of the industry have not only created these problems, but have also facilitated the spread of newly emerged pathogens, such as *E. coli* O157:H7. Millions of pounds of contaminated meat can now be unwittingly shipped throughout the United States in a matter of days. At the height of the Beef Trust's influence and power, the five largest meatpacking companies controlled about 55 percent of the American market for beef. Today four companies control about 85 percent of that market. Ranchers are once again complaining about unfair prices and other monopolistic practices.

Slaughterhouse Blues looks at how the North American meatpacking industry has been transformed since the early 1970s—without most people realizing it. Slaughterhouses are now located in rural areas that rarely get much attention from the national media. The vast majority of meatpacking workers are impoverished Latino immigrants who don't get much attention, either. Nor do they wield much influence in Congress. Most Americans live in cities or suburbs and have little idea where their food comes from. They purchase shrink-wrapped meat at supermarkets and eat inexpensive meat at fast food restaurants and hardly give it a second thought. The profound changes in meatpacking over the past three decades have not been widely advertised. On the contrary, they have been carefully hidden. You do not find pictures of industrial hog farms on packages of American bacon.

Donald Stull and Michael Broadway have spent 15 years investigating the complex systems that now produce our meat. *Slaughterhouse Blues* is the culmination of their work, of research conducted not just in the library, but literally in the field. They have visited ranches, farms, feedlots, poultry houses, slaughterhouses, and the homes of injured workers. One of the authors tended a bar in Garden City, Kansas, to spend time with meatpacking workers and observe the changes sweeping through their community. Broadway and Stull draw upon history, economics, social geography, and anthropology to offer a comprehensive portrait of this industry. They know the subject firsthand and write about it with great compassion.

The large meatpacking companies would like you to believe that America's current methods of raising livestock and processing meat are somehow inevitable, the result of irresistible economic forces and technological advance. They would like you to think that things cannot be done any other way. In fact no other industrialized nation produces beef the way that the United States does—except Canada, where the industry has lately fallen under American control. There's a good reason why our system is unique. It imposes enormous costs upon society that are not reflected in the price of meat. Much like industrial polluters in the days before environmental laws, today's meatpacking companies are now imposing their business costs on the rest of the nation. As Stull and Broadway demonstrate, the current system needlessly harms workers, consumers, and the environment. It mistreats animals. It brings poverty, drug abuse, and crime to rural communities. When all the social costs are tallied, our cheap meat is much more expensive than we can afford.

Slaughterhouse Blues traces the origins of these problems, describes their latest manifestations, and suggests how things might be otherwise. Far from being inevitable, this centralized, industrialized meat system cannot be sustained. From antibiotic resistance to outbreaks of food-borne disease, it is producing threats to the public health that won't be tolerated in the long term. Changes will not simply happen, however, because of some immutable law. Changes will occur when consumers realize what they've been eating, get angry, and demand something different. This book offers a comprehensive view of what has gone wrong. It remains our responsibility, with every vote and every dollar spent on food, to start making it right.

Eric Schlosser

Preface

Meat. In the King James Bible, *meat* refers to food of any kind, and as late as the medieval period, "white meat" meant milk and cheese, not chicken. Only in recent times has the word been used primarily to denote the edible flesh of mammals (and distinguished from fish and poultry). The term may have lost its inclusive Old English meaning, but meat remains the most esteemed of foods in Western society. A meal is not a proper meal without it.

Not everyone eats meat, of course. Adam and Eve were vegetarians, and not until after The Flood did God give humans permission to consume the flesh of animals (Genesis 9:2–4). Until recently, anthropological notions of the role meat eating played in human evolution weren't all that different from the biblical one. Although current thinking no longer attributes the technological and biological advances that characterize the appearance of *Homo sapiens* to hunting, and thus meat eating, there is no doubt that humans eat more meat than any other primate. And some anthropologists argue that cooking, specifically the cooking of the flesh of animals, is what distinguishes humans from other animals (Fiddes 1991:15).

Maybe cooking (and eating) meat is what made (and makes) us human, maybe not. In any event, meat eating is increasingly under attack, from those who say it is bad for our health to those who say it is bad for our planet to those who argue that humans do not have the right to slaughter and consume other animals. For these and other reasons, the number of persons in affluent Western countries who avoid some or all forms of meat is increasing. Yet, paradoxically, in the developing world rising per capita incomes are correlated with increasing meat consumption (Fiddes 1991:13).

Most of us come to know meat only through the grocery store or the restaurant. But meat must be made, and it can only be made by the slaughter of animals. Indeed, the Judeo-Christian tradition forbids the eating of animals that die by other than human hands (Leviticus 17). For Jews, tradition dictates that the slaughter of domesticated animals be accomplished by an officially authorized and supervised slaughterer, who ensures that the animal is conscious when its throat is severed by a single knife stroke (Davidson 1999).

Most of us have no compunctions about eating meat, but few relish the thought of where that meat comes from or how it was transformed from animal to edible (our apologies to Noelie Vialles [1994], whose excellent book gave us this phrase and some of the ideas presented here). Death and dismemberment are never pleasant to witness, and while they are essential in the making of animals into meat, most of us would just as soon know as little as possible about the whole process.

This seems like a good place for a confession. We are both enthusiastic eaters of animal flesh—beef, pork, mutton, lamb, poultry, fish—we love them all. In fact, we met over cheeseburgers, big juicy ones, if memory serves us. It was 1986, August, and it was a scorcher. Of course, every day in August is a scorcher in Wichita, Kansas (so is every day in June and July, for that matter). But weather aside, we knew little—

and cared even less—about the meat and poultry industry. We had been invited to lunch by a mutual friend—Ken Erickson, then refugee services coordinator for southwest Kansas—to consider a study of the Vietnamese refugees who were coming to Garden City—4 hours to the west—to work in its two beef plants.

Serendipity isn't given near enough credit in the shaping of human destiny. Not many folks would mistake Wichita for Paradise, but those cheeseburgers changed our professional lives. We have hungrily studied the people and places that produce our meat and poultry ever since.

We became perhaps the first social scientists to systematically study the modern meat and poultry industry and its impact on workers and the communities where its plants are located. Our research has taken us to rural communities across the United States and Canada, and our publications have informed scholars, journalists, industry insiders, community leaders, and general readers. Since we wrote our first article together in 1990, scholarly and journalistic writings on the meat and poultry industry have mushroomed. Still, our work remains the broadest in geographical coverage and the deepest in research experience on this subject.

While a literature on the meat and poultry industry has begun to emerge, it remains scattered and disjointed. Most of what has been written on today's meat and poultry industry has appeared in journals, edited collections, and popular periodicals. Books on meatpacking are generally narrow in scope and focus on a particular segment of the industry (Thu & Durrenberger 1998), a single community (Andreas 1994), workers in a particular plant (Fink 1998), or the history of unionization in meatpacking (Stromquist & Bergman 1997). Works on this subject are often partisan and may be biased either for (Limprecht 1989) or against (Rifkin 1993) the industry. On rare occasions it is the subject of popular fiction, as in Ruth Ozeki's (1998) *My Year of Meats.*

Slaughterhouse Blues is our attempt to pull together what we have learned about the meat and poultry industry and its consequences for growers and production workers, communities, and consumers. We discuss in depth each major sector of the meat industry—beef, pork, and poultry—and present the results of our research in several states and provinces in the United States and Canada. We combine macro- and microlevel analyses with geographic and anthropological perspectives. Drawing upon extensive ethnographic materials, we often quote directly from interviews and fieldnotes. We like to think our presentation is balanced, but after nearly two decades of research we have reached certain conclusions and taken definite positions. For research to be useful, we believe it must be put to use, and we have worked with local governments and community groups as well as union and industry representatives to apply our knowledge. In short, we have tried to tell readers what we know, how we learned it, and what we have done with that knowledge.

Slaughterhouse Blues is the first comprehensive treatment of the modern meat and poultry industry by social scientists. Written for a general audience, it is not a "theoretical work" or embedded in a single paradigm. It is, however, informed by and contributes to topics of considerable immediacy: globalization; immigration; economic and community development; cultural, ethnic, and linguistic diversity; sustainability; participatory research.

Canada and the United States are urban societies and, despite our collective dependence upon agriculture, most North Americans have lost any connection to their agrarian heritage. Yet, if we do not understand where our food comes from and how it gets to our table, who produces it and at what cost, we stand to jeopardize the very food supply that sustains us. Over the course of the last century, the meat and poultry industry has reshaped North American agriculture and its rural communities. In the process, it has significantly altered what we eat and how.

We may or may not be what we eat, but what we eat has real consequences for workers, communities, and the environment. And whether we eat meat or not, knowing more about the meat industry's impact on our diet and our lives behooves us all. This book is our attempt to identify some of the ramifications of North Americans' seemingly insatiable appetite for meat.

ACKNOWLEDGMENTS

Social science research is a collaborative enterprise, founded on trust and reciprocity, and dependent on the goodwill and generosity of those who share their knowledge and their lives with investigators. We have studied the meat and poultry industry and its impact on people and places for nigh on 20 years. After so long a time, and after working in so many communities, we have amassed professional and personal debts well beyond enumeration and repayment. We cannot begin to acknowledge all who are deserving of our recognition, and we herewith apologize to everyone who we should thank but simply can't because of the limitations of space and memory.

We are indebted to the following institutions and individuals for supporting our research and the writing of this book: The Ford Foundation's Changing Relations Project; the Aspen Institute; Wichita State University; the State University of New York at Geneseo; the Canadian Studies Program, Canadian Embassy, Washington D.C.; Terry Seethof, Dean of the College of Arts and Sciences of Northern Michigan University; the Kansas University Endowment Association; and the University of Kansas for grants from its General Research Fund and sabbatical leaves.

Chapter 7 is revised from "'We Come to the Garden' . . . Again: Garden City, Kansas, 1990–2000," which appeared in *Urban Anthropology and Studies of Cultural Systems and World Economic Development* (30[4]:269–300, Winter 2001). We are grateful for permission to reproduce it here in somewhat different form.

Of the many people who have been so hospitable and so patient with us during our research, we are especially grateful to Jim Andrews, Gary Bright, Marcial Cervantes, Keith Downer, Bobbie and the late R. L. Dunville, Jerry and Debbie Dunville, Roger Epp, Ed Fitzgerald, Jose and Hilda Flores, Bob Halloran, James Hawkins, Lorine Hewson, David Kattenburg, Paul and Joanne Kondy, Greg Lauby, Barry and Lana Love, Ian MacLachlan, Joyce and Laine McGaughey, Dennis Mesa, Karen Munro, Milt Pippinger, Bill Podraza, Marcus Qualls, Mary Regan, Lee Reeve, Amy and Jeff Richardson, Roberta Rogers, Levita Rohlman, Penney Schwab, Dwight and Blondell Simpson, Olivia, Bill, Jeannine, and Brian Stull, Roxy Thompson, and Dave Whitson.

To our mothers, Marjorie Stull and Phyllis Broadway, we owe debts beyond measure, but here we wish to thank them for sharing some of their memories. For sharing her home and her marvelous cooking with her wayward nephew, Frances Horner commands never-ending gratitude and devotion.

Several people kindly read and commented on portions of this book as we wrote it: Aloma Dew, Bill Hatley, Roger Horowitz, Paul Kondy, Michael Paolisso, Penney

Schwab, Marjorie and E. B. Stull, and John Young. But the one who labored longest and hardest with us in this vineyard was Laura Kriegstrom Stull, who read every word—many, many times—and offered valuable editorial commentary and advice.

Mary Clouse first introduced us to the concerns of poultry growers and her tireless efforts on their behalf continue to inspire us. Aloma Dew's labor and leadership on the Sierra Club's campaign to raise public awareness of the environmental costs of confined animal feeding inspired us to write Chapter 9. Steve Bjerklie, Rich Dunville, Roger Horowitz, Steve Striffler, and Michael Stumo provided valuable source material, as did Aloma Dew, Frances Horner, and Blondell Simpson. Bill Hatley and Paul Kondy kindly helped us get some of our facts straight.

Steve Bjerklie provided photos from *Meat&Poultry*'s files from the time when he was the magazine's editor. Mary Brohammer and Melissa Filippi-Franz transcribed the taped interviews.

We owe Eric Schlosser dinner and drinks for doing us the honor of writing this book's Foreword, and we are eager to settle that debt.

Laura Kriegstrom Stull drew the maps, designed the graphics, formatted the final manuscript, suggested photo layout, prepared the photographs, recommended the cover design, and otherwise helped us make this an attractive book.

To all these generous and talented people—and more—we offer our thanks, a thousand times over. And we absolve them of any errors or omissions in this work, for which we are solely to blame.

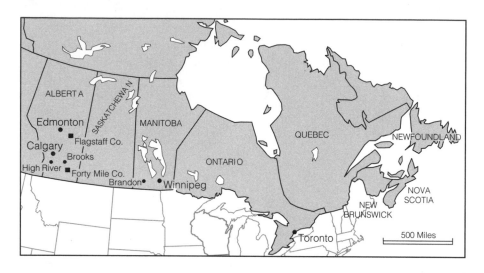

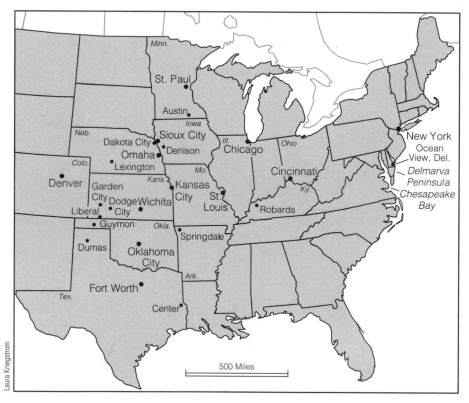

Laura Kriegstrom

F.1 Significant Canadian and U.S. locations in the text

Introduction

THE TOUR

The doors to the guard station were marked in Spanish and Vietnamese—but not in English. The uniformed guard behind the glass window said to sign in. Then we were let inside a high chain-link fence and led down a long walkway and into the plant. From there we were ushered through the cafeteria and into a training room where we were given brand-new white hardhats and smocks along with yellow foam rubber earplugs. As we clumsily adjusted the plastic headbands inside the hardhats, buttoned up our smocks, and removed the earplugs from their plastic envelopes, a middle-aged Anglo man dressed in a golf shirt, polyester Western dress jeans held up by a trophy buckle, and snakeskin boots began to speak:

> Welcome to IBP. IBP is the largest beefpacking company, and this is the largest and most sophisticated plant in the world. Please do not talk to the employees, for their safety and yours, since they are operating machinery and using knives. And please stay together for your safety. Because of the high noise level, and since you'll be wearing earplugs, we won't be able to answer your questions in the plant, but we will return here after the tour and you can ask questions then.

Our guide was Vietnamese, in his early thirties. We followed him through two heavy swinging metal doors and out onto the "killfloor," where we were met by a moving row of dead cows, suspended upside down on meat hooks, their tongues hanging out, their limbs jerking. As they passed by, quivering like monstrous red and black shirts being called up at the dry cleaner, an Anglo man clipped off their hooves with a tool resembling large pruning shears, while above us on a catwalk a Latina slapped plastic sheets onto their skinned rumps.

Forty-five minutes later, back in the training room, we removed our earplugs and took off our smocks and hardhats, still dazed by what we had just experienced. The man in the snakeskin boots, who turned out to be the personnel manager, asked if we had any questions. For almost an hour, he cheerfully answered our questions, taking great pleasure in his statistics, and in our wonder at "the Cadillac of all packing plants."

Here at the Finney County plant, we kill between 30,000 and 32,000 head of cattle a week. Since many feedyards in this area have a capacity of about 40,000 head, we empty the equivalent of about one feedyard per week. Every day we receive 101 trucks of live cattle and load out one truck of boxed beef every 22 minutes of every day, 7 days a week. From hoof to box, the longest a cow will stay in this plant is 6 days; the prime time is 2 to 3 days.

The number of head we can process depends on whether we're doing "bone-in" or "bone-out." Bone out is largely for institutional buyers, such as hospitals and restaurants, and requires more cuts, since most of the bones are removed. It's heavy work—and hard. We can do about 350 head an hour on bone-out. Bone-in is mainly what the housewife will buy at the local grocery store, and it moves a lot faster—400 head an hour or more. They do 240 cuts of meat here; nine of ground beef alone!

Right now, this plant has 2,650 employees and an annual payroll of $42 million. Each job is ranked, and paid, according to importance and difficulty. There are seven levels. Starting pay for someone just off the street with no experience on a level-1 job is $6.40 an hour in processing, $6.70 in slaughter. The base for level-7 employees is $9.40 in processing, $9.58 in slaughter. After 6 months you get an automatic 50 cents raise and another 72 cents at the end of one year. We have profit sharing and yearly bonuses. IBP is self-insured. We offer an excellent insurance package—health, dental, vision, retirement, disability, alcohol and drug abuse coverage. Line workers are eligible for coverage after 6 months.

Absenteeism normally averages 1.7 percent. We compensate for absenteeism by having more workers on a shift than we absolutely need. If too many show up, we assign the extra workers to different tasks, which helps them qualify for more than one job, or we experiment with new techniques.

The man in the snakeskin boots spewed his statistics with ease, and he neatly sidestepped a question about worker turnover. Instead, he informed us that

more than a thousand of our workers have been in this plant for 2 or more years. As plants get older their workforce becomes more stable. Most workers stay on the same job for about a year. By then they are getting bored and usually bid to another job.

We have an internal job posting system here at IBP. Current employees are given the opportunity to apply for and fill jobs before we hire from outside. New hires are placed wherever the need is greatest. After the initial 90-day probationary period, you can bid on other jobs and move around the floor. The more jobs you are qualified for, the more competitive you are for supervisory jobs. Each supervisor oversees 45 employees and has a trainer working under him. Although it helps, supervisors don't have to be qualified on the jobs they oversee. We look around the plant for workers who show real promise—leadership, potential, interpersonal communication skills. The supervisor runs his own business out there; he is responsible for his crew's production and is given daily reports on its output.

We stress safety here. We spend $1 million a year on training and employ 28 hourly trainers. Each new hire receives 3 days of orientation, then comes back each day for 30 minutes of stretching exercises until he gets into shape to do his job. Depending on their job, each worker may wear as much as $600 worth of safety equipment—hardhat, earplugs, cloth and steel-mesh gloves, mail aprons and leggings, weight-lifting belts, and shin guards. Knife users normally carry three knives. Each one is owned by IBP and has its own identification number. The workers use the same knives as long as they work here. They grow very attached to their knives; they know their feel, and this helps them do a better job. Knives are turned in at the end of the day for sharpening and are picked up at the beginning of the next shift. They also carry sharpening steels with them and sharpen their knives while they work.

"With all those knives, they must cut themselves a lot?" one of us asked.

"The most common injuries are punctures, not lacerations," he replied.

These wounds usually occur when a knife slips and pokes the other hand. Such injuries are usually caused by workers not wearing their safety equipment. But we've had very few such injuries so far this year. In fact, we won the President's Award for the best safety record of any IBP plant.

The list of products we produce at this plant is almost never ending. We separate the white and red blood cells right here in the plant, and each is used for different things. Blood is used to make perfume. Bone meal is used as a feed additive. Kodak is the biggest buyer of our bone gelatin, which is used in making film paper. Intestines are used to string tennis rackets. The hairs from inside the cow's ears are used for paintbrushes. Spleens are used in pharmaceuticals.

Processing begins at 6:05 a.m. Slaughter starts an hour later. Workers get a 15-minute break after about two-and-a-half hours and a 30-minute lunch break after about five-and-a-half hours. The day shift, we call it A shift, ends at 2:35. B shift begins at 3:05. In between shifts we do a quick, dry cleanup. From midnight to 6:00 a.m. we contract out for a wet cleanup which holds down bacteria.

Our heads were swimming. There was so much more we wanted to know, but we were exhausted from trying to absorb it all and remember even a fraction of the facts and figures he glibly tossed back in response to our questions. The man in the snake-skin boots made no attempt to hurry us, and he seemed a little disappointed when we could no longer think of anything more to ask. As we uneasily shuffled in tacit recognition that this adventure was about to end, someone asked, "Do you get any flak from the animal rights people?"

"Not really," he quipped. "Most people enjoy a good steak."[1]

* * *

And so began our research on meatpacking and meatpacking workers. What left us in awe on that June day in 1988, as we followed our guide through a confusing maze of men, machines, and meat, was remarkably similar to what Upton Sinclair had witnessed more than 80 years earlier in the packinghouses of Chicago.

It was all so very business-like that one watched it fascinated. It was pork-making by machinery, pork-making reduced to mathematics. And yet somehow the most matter-of-fact person could not help thinking of the pigs. . . . Then the party went across the street to where they did the killing of beef—where every hour they turned four or five hundred cattle into meat. . . . This made a scene of intense activity, a picture of human power wonderful to watch. . . . The way in which they did this was a sight to be seen and never forgotten; they worked with furious intensity, literally on the run. . . . It was all highly specialized labor, each man having his task to do; generally this would consist of only two or three specific cuts. (DeGruson 1988:28–32)

Upton Sinclair did his research for *The Jungle* in 1904, but were he to visit one of today's packinghouses he would be struck with how little the industry—its work or its workers—has really changed. Knockers still start the killing, but now they use a stun gun instead of a sledgehammer. Splitters are still the most expert and highly paid workers on the killfloor, deftly cutting carcasses in half with band saws from moving platforms, where once they used massive cleavers. And, just as they did a century ago, today's stickers and gutters, tail rippers and head droppers, chuckboners and short ribbers still wield razor-sharp knives as they turn 400 cattle an hour into meat.

Meatpacking plants remain massive factories, employing hundreds or even thousands of workers, but instead of the Lithuanian, Serbian, and Polish workers of Sinclair's day, today's packinghouses are crowded with immigrants from Mexico and Guatemala, refugees from Vietnam and Somalia. Immigrants are still attracted to packinghouse jobs because command of English is not required, and because the wages they can earn on their "disassembly" lines are better than they can earn elsewhere in North America—or in the jobs they left behind.

Companies still "make a great feature of showing strangers through the packing plants, for it is a good advertisement" (Sinclair 1985:43). And somewhere in between pointing out the "wonderful efficiency" of the plant, the unbelievable speed with which they kill and disassemble cattle, and the "many strange and unlikely products (that come from) such things as feet, knuckles, hide clippings, and sinews" (Sinclair 1985:50), the guide will chuckle and say, "They don't waste anything here. IBP markets every part of the cow but the moo. My father used to work at IBP before me, and he used to tell me that the little toy boxes that moo were made by IBP." The group will laugh, and the tour guide will smile to himself that we should take this ancient witticism as his own.

STUDYING THE MEAT
AND POULTRY INDUSTRY—AND WHY

When Upton Sinclair wrote *The Jungle* at the beginning of the twentieth century, cattle were raised on the plains and prairies of North America and shipped by railroad to be slaughtered in packinghouses in the stockyard districts of Chicago, St. Louis, Toronto, New York, and other major cities. But the United Nations now stands on the site of an old meatpacking plant, the Kansas City and Omaha stockyards have been razed, and the Fort Worth stockyards have been transformed into chic boutiques and upscale restaurants. The largest Home Depot in Canada now stands on the grounds of Toronto's meatpacking district.

Urban stockyards and packinghouses are no more, but demand for the meat they once provided is greater than ever. In their place, giant modern meat processing plants have sprung up throughout rural North America, from beef plants on the plains of Kansas and Alberta, to pork plants in Oklahoma and Manitoba, to chicken plants in Maryland and Kentucky.

This book tells the story of the modern meat and poultry industry in North America, of its impact on those who make animals into meat and on the communities where they live and work. It is also a story of discovery; of a cultural anthropologist and a social geographer as they seek to understand the social and economic forces at work in modern food production and how their research might be best put to use in the service of the communities and the people they have studied.

In the mid-1980s we began studying Garden City, Kansas, as part of a national research project on immigration funded by the Ford Foundation. Our team consisted of five anthropologists and a social geographer, and we lived and worked in Garden

City on and off for 2 years. Several of the original team members, including the authors of this volume, have returned over the years to conduct research, provide technical assistance, and visit friends.

It soon became clear that any understanding of the social processes at work in Garden City required an understanding of the beef industry itself. Michael Broadway's role as a geographer was to explain the presence of the new immigrants in the community and to document the social and economic changes that accompanied the arrival of the beef industry. Michael explored the evolution of the industry, collected data on its changing structure, and even interviewed the founder and chief executive officer (CEO) of a major beef company.

Don Stull was the team leader and, like Michael, his research focused on beef-packing and cattle feeding. He was to study ethnic relations in the workplace, but the packinghouses refused to cooperate. Participant observation is the hallmark of ethnography, and ethnographers actively participate in the lives of those they study. So how could he learn about how packers relate to their coworkers without ready access to the killfloor and the processing line?

Don subscribed to *Beef Today;* toured the plants every chance he got; attended workers' compensation hearings, which offered detailed job descriptions and graphically illustrated why meatpacking is among America's most dangerous industries. He enrolled in Meat and Carcass Evaluation at Garden City Community College to learn more about the industry, make contacts, and gain regular entry to the "cooler," where carcasses are graded. Don helped his instructor tag carcasses for Beef Empire Days as the dead animals snaked along the chain, being skinned and gutted before entering the cooler. He rode with friends on the Santa Fe work train to pick up tallow and hides at IBP. He interviewed packers, feedyard managers, meat inspectors, and others who work in the meat and cattle industries.

But Don did most of his research on work in Tom's Tavern. There he could meet a cross-section of Garden City—packinghouse line workers and supervisors, farmers and ranchers, feedyard pen riders, doctors and lawyers, railroad engineers and truck drivers—the unemployed and the well to do; whites, blacks, Hispanics, and an occasional Vietnamese; old-timers and newcomers alike. Lacking access to the packinghouses, Don found that Tom's offered the best opportunity to talk candidly with workers. In its relaxed atmosphere, people talked openly and often of their work. Don became one of the Tom's regulars, playing Trivial Pursuit and hearts with a circle of devotees, shuffleboard and pool with friends and acquaintances. On Thursdays—payday at the packinghouses—he helped tend bar from midnight till closing at 2:00 A.M., waiting on, talking with, and listening to thirsty line workers coming off B shift. On Sunday—"zoo day," so called because it was the only day off for many workers—he worked from 10:00 P.M. to 2:00 A.M.

But meatpacking and meatpacking workers were only part of the story. We were also interested in learning how Garden City had dealt with the unique challenges posed by an influx of new immigrants and the accompanying rapid population growth. This involved interviewing teachers, school principals and administrators, police officers, health care providers, clergy, city officials, business owners, and everyday citizens.

As our initial fieldwork came to a close in the fall of 1989, we wondered whether what we were discovering in Garden City was also occurring in other industry towns. Throughout the 1990s several of our team studied beef, pork, and poultry processing

Laura Kriegstrom

Figure I.1 Don Stull (center) talks with Joyce McGaughey, owner of Tom's Tavern, and her son Laine while doing fieldwork in Tom's.

plants and their impact on workers and communities throughout North America—from Oklahoma to Alberta, from Kentucky to Manitoba. Along the way, we have been joined by other social scientists seeking to understand the meat industry and influence its direction. In what has become an extended natural experiment, the ethnography of Garden City has evolved into an ethnology of the meat and poultry industry and its host communities.

This book integrates what we have learned about the meat and poultry industry in more than 15 years of study. It also traces our involvement in studies of how this industry alters the communities where its plants are located—and how we have used our research for the betterment of the people who are its subjects.

· · ·

Chapter 1 identifies the processes behind the emergence of industrialized agriculture in North America following World War II and pays particular attention to the changing structure and geographical location of beef, poultry, and pork production and processing since the 1960s.

Chapter 2 presents an overview of the beef cattle industry, beginning with the emergence of the "cattle kingdom" on the Great Plains after the Civil War. Until the 1960s, cattle feeding was centered in the Corn Belt of the Midwest, and cattle were slaughtered in cities such as Chicago and Kansas City. Subsequent restructuring has been accompanied by relocation to the High Plains of the United States and Canada.

Modern poultry production is the model for what has come to be called factory farming. Born on the Delmarva Peninsula in the 1920s, specialized production of "eating chickens"—commonly called *broilers*—spread to Georgia and Arkansas during World War II. In the 1990s, chicken processors started expanding into new territories. One of those was Kentucky. In the fall of 1998, Don Stull returned to his hometown of Sebree, Kentucky, to study the impact of a nearby Tyson Foods chicken processing plant. Chapter 3 presents the history of modern poultry production and its effects on an agricultural community from the perspective of a native ethnographer.

Modern pork production has emulated poultry. Until recently, commercial hog production was centered in the Upper Midwest, especially in Iowa. But like poultry in the 1990s and beef in the 1970s and 1980s, pork processing is relocating, even as its production processes are being restructured. Chapter 4 draws on our research in pork processing communities to explore the consequences of hog production and pork processing.

Packinghouses at the turn of the twenty-first century are a far cry from those at the turn of the twentieth. But for all their computerization and laser technology, their robotics and ergonomics, the knife, the meat hook, and the steel are still the basic tools of the trade. And today's plants remain, like the ones they replaced, rigidly organized, labor-intensive factories that turn animals into meat on disassembly lines. Chapter 5 begins with an overview of working conditions at the beginning of the twentieth century, known to many readers through Upton Sinclair's famous novel, *The Jungle*, and then briefly reviews union efforts to improve wages and working conditions in the meat and poultry industry. The chapter closes with a glimpse at what it is like to labor in the factories that produce the meat and poultry that grace our tables.

Chapter 6 takes the reader onto the plant floor as it explores labor relations in one of these modern meat factories from the vantage point of Don Stull's 1994 participant observation in a plant we call "Running Iron Beef."

The world's largest beef processing plant, which opened in 1980, is located a few miles west of Garden City, Kansas; another plant, which opened in 1983, is located on its eastern edge. The authors have studied Garden City since the mid-1980s, documenting its transformation from a predominantly Anglo American community to the first majority-minority city in the state. Combining data from our 1987–1990 study with follow-up research in 2000, Chapter 7 presents the social, economic, and cultural changes that have beset Garden City over the past two decades, along with the community response to these changes, and how we, as researchers, have influenced and assisted community efforts.

Chapter 8 discusses the authors' efforts to help communities throughout the United States and Canada plan for and mitigate the negative consequences of meat and poultry processing plants and the lessons we have learned about applying social science knowledge at the local level.

When we began studying the meat and poultry industry in the mid-1980s, few people knew of—or cared about—its environmental consequences. But community opposition to confinement animal feeding operations and meat processing plants has been mounting across North America. Chapter 9 examines the environmental issues surrounding hog production and processing in Canada and poultry production and processing in Kentucky.

Industrialized agriculture has changed the face of rural North America forever. The imperative of being the lowest cost producer means that farmers have adopted factory farming techniques and processors have moved to rural locations. But given the constant search for lower cost production sites, agribusiness will continue to confront rural communities with the Faustian bargain of economic development at the cost of social and environmental disruption. Most North Americans have willingly signed on to this agreement in exchange for low food prices.

Meat and poultry processors offer rural communities a similar bargain: the creation of jobs, not only in their plants, but in related industries and services. Some argue that the jobs and tax revenues these plants bring are essential if rural communities are to survive. But these plants also bring high population turnover, relatively low wages, and working conditions that remain among the most hazardous in manufacturing. And communities inevitably experience rising rates of crime, a shortage of affordable housing, increased enrollment and turnover in schools, and greater demand for health and social services. Companies do little, if any, to help communities meet the challenges presented by their workforces. But is this how it must be? In Chapter 10 we conclude by exploring alternatives to North America's model of industrialized meat production.

NOTE

1. The information presented in the question-and-answer period after the tour is from several sessions over more than a year (Stull fieldnotes June 17, 1988; July 10 and 22, 1988; and May 5, 1989). Although it did not come in a single session, or in such a flowing narrative, most is from the man in the snakeskin boots. Supervisors, line workers, and industry observers at times dispute some of these facts and the conclusions drawn from them. Wages, number of employees, and other "facts" are from 1988–1989 and have changed since then. "The Tour" is slightly modified from an earlier publication (Stull 1994:44–48).

1/Setting the Table

At the beginning of the twentieth century, land-hungry homesteaders flocked to the Canadian prairies, creating a vibrant rural landscape of farms and ranches, small towns and villages, just as homesteaders had settled the Midwest and the Plains of the United States in the nineteenth century. But even as family farming was blossoming on both sides of the border, it was sowing the seeds of its own demise.

In the early 1900s, farmers began increasing output and income by investing in machinery and fertilizer. These investments, coupled with improvements in seed quality and livestock, raised yields and ultimately lowered commodity prices, forcing farmers either to increase production by purchasing more inputs, such as seeds and fertilizer, or to quit farming. Since the 1930s, millions of families have abandoned farming. In their place today are highly specialized and capitalized farms that produce one or two commodities, often under contract to agribusiness giants such as ConAgra, Smithfield, Tyson, and Cargill. It is these transnational corporations, not family farmers, that determine how and where our food is produced.

This shift in power from producers to processors reflects a change in consumer demand for food, from fresh seasonally based produce at the beginning of the twentieth century to highly processed convenience foods at its end. Innovations in refrigeration, packaging, and transportation made this transition possible by allowing processors to gain year-round access to different sources of produce and enabling them to operate their plants more efficiently. At the same time, societal changes have reduced the time spent in the kitchen.

One hundred years ago, a typical woman in the United States spent an average of 44 hours a week preparing meals and cleaning up after them. By the 1950s, this figure had dropped to fewer than 20 hours a week (Bowers 2000). And with the rise of two-income families, single-parent households, and "soccer moms" in the 1980s and 1990s, Americans devote even less time to food preparation. Food companies have responded to these societal changes by further processing agricultural products and supplying consumers with ready-to-eat meals and restaurants with prepared portions. A visit to any supermarket or restaurant kitchen confirms these trends.

Michael Broadway

Figure 1.1 Tyson Foods trailers outside a warehouse in Chicago's stockyard district

MORE INPUTS, FEWER FARMS

Agriculture is presently in the midst of its third revolution (Troughton 1986). The first revolution originated in Southwest Asia about 10,000 years ago and was associated with the development of seed agriculture, the domestication of animals, and the invention of the plow. Agriculture offered a distinct advantage over hunting and gathering because it could support many more people on less land. Agriculture ultimately formed the economic basis for permanent settlements, and complex urban centers emerged in both the New and Old Worlds.

Industrialization emerged in western Europe in the late eighteenth century, and with it a second agricultural revolution that replaced subsistence agriculture with a system based upon creating surpluses and profit. Fast-growing urban populations created a commercial market for food, and farmers responded by boosting output. They began purchasing fertilizers, improving field drainage, and incorporating new horse-drawn machinery. The feudal system of communal land holdings had already been replaced with individual farms, and Europeans exported this model of small family farms throughout much of the world. This second agricultural revolution cemented agriculture's ties to industry. Farmers purchased machinery and other inputs, and in the process replaced labor, improved productivity, and created surpluses for trading (Bowler 1992).

Agricultural industrialization—the third agricultural revolution—originated in the United States at the beginning of the twentieth century. It is characterized by mechanization, chemical farming, and food manufacturing (Bowler 1992:11). It aims to sell crops and livestock at the lowest possible cost by creating scale economies,[1] purchasing inputs from other segments of the economy, and substituting capital for labor (Symes & Marsden 1985). Mechanization replaces labor and animals with tractors, combines, sprayers, and other machinery. These and other innovations boost productivity and reduce the demand for farm labor, leading to out-migration from rural areas as fewer farm workers are needed. In 1890, 65 percent of Americans were rural and 43 percent of workers were employed in agriculture. In 1990, only 25 percent were rural and fewer than 2 percent worked on farms and ranches (Mills 1995:105).

Chemical farming relies on inorganic fertilizers, fungicides, and pesticides to increase crop yields. Developed on a large scale in the 1950s, the use of such chemicals, combined with improvements in seed quality, dramatically improved crop yields. In 1950, the average yield for an acre of corn was 38 bushels; in 2000 it was 137 bushels (USDA National Agricultural Statistics Service n.d). The use of biotechnology to develop genetically modified organisms (GMOs), or transgenic plants, such as Monsanto's Roundup Ready™ soybeans, marks the latest phase in this development. Their long-term effect on improving yields remains controversial (Lappé & Bailey 1998).

Food manufacturing is the most recent stage of the third agricultural revolution. It involves adding economic value to agricultural products through processing and packaging, and as its importance has risen farmers have received a dwindling proportion of the final sale price. In 1980, farmers received $82 billion out of the $264 billion Americans spent on food—31 percent of the total. By 1999, their share had dropped to only 19 percent of the $618 billion spent on food. The remainder is absorbed by processors, wholesalers, distributors, and retailers (Elitzak 2000). This means that increases in consumer food prices rarely benefit farmers, who are at the beginning of the production process. And because farmers generally have limited options for marketing their crops and livestock, they are often forced to accept lower prices, making it even harder for them to profit from their labor.

The farm is no longer at the center of the production process; instead, it is one component in a complex agribusiness system that consists of five separate but connected sections: agricultural inputs, farm production, processing, distribution, and consumption. Each section is, in turn, affected to varying degrees by the physical environment, government policies, trade agreements, and the availability of credit and finance. In the beef industry, for example, cattle feeding is just one part of a complex food network in which agribusiness supplies producers with seeds, fertilizers, and pesticides to grow feed grains, as well as antibiotics and hormones to keep animals healthy and accelerate maturation, while specialized facilities, often owned by these same companies, slaughter and process the animals. The more control a company can gain over this network, the greater its ability to control costs and profits. This strategy, known as *vertical integration,* is most evident in the poultry industry, where companies like Tyson control each step of the production process, from when the egg is hatched to when it appears as a boneless chicken breast in a restaurant kitchen or supermarket.

EAT IN OR EAT OUT?

Processing and adding value to raw commodities is, in part, a response to changes in the demand for food. During the 1980s and 1990s more women entered the labor force, and Americans spent more of their time at work. By 1998, 3 out of 4 married couples no longer conformed to the "traditional family"—a working husband, a wife who stays at home, and their children. Increases in divorce and children born out of wedlock have produced an upsurge in single-parent households, while persons living alone now account for 1 in 4 households. As a result, Americans eat fewer meals at home and spend less time preparing them. Found in over 90 percent of American homes, the microwave oven has provided a technological "fix" for those without the time—or inclination—to cook (Bowers 2000). Meanwhile, supermarkets offer an array of processed foods such as Armour Perfectly Seasoned Pork®, which consists of:

> several different cuts that are perfectly seasoned in a variety of succulent flavors. They are sealed in convenient packages that can be used for future use. When you are ready for a perfect meal just empty the contents into a baking pan, place in the oven and your meal is ready in minutes . . . and you don't even get your hands dirty! (Armour Pork Products 2002)

In promoting its Healthy Choice® line of dinners, ConAgra offers more than 20 different ready-to-eat meals "that are convenient and flavorful, leaving you *time* to do the things that you want to do" (Healthy Choice 2002, authors' emphasis). Tyson (2002a) has introduced seven different "Meal Kits," such as Beef Fajitas, Chicken Stir Fry, and Chicken Fried Rice, with the promise that in "only 8–12 minutes you're sitting down to a full spread of fulfilling entrees." It also offers Tyson Time Trimmers®—beef and chicken ingredients ready to add to your "favorite recipes."

Supermarkets have adapted to these changes. Late-afternoon shoppers at Wegmans' in suburban Rochester, New York, cruise the aisles amidst aromas of freshly prepared meals ready to take home to the oven, microwave, or dinner plate. As demand for easy-to-prepare meals has risen, so, too, has the proportion of the food dollar spent eating out—from 30 percent in 1965 to 48 percent in 1999 (Elitzak 2000). This trend translates into demand for more processed and prepared meals in restaurants. McDonald's relies on Tyson to supply it with prepared portions of Chicken McNuggets and on ConAgra, through its Lamb Weston subsidiary, to supply it with french fries. Tyson supplies chicken to 90 of the top 100 U.S. restaurant chains, mostly in the form of nuggets or cutlets (Schlosser 2001:140).

AGRICULTURAL INDUSTRIALIZATION

Bowler (1985) identifies three structural forces behind agricultural industrialization: intensification, concentration, and specialization. *Intensification* occurs when farmers increase their purchases of nonfarm inputs (fertilizers, machinery, agrichemicals) to improve yields. For livestock producers, advances in selective breeding have meant a reduction in the time it takes an animal to reach its slaughter weight, which, in turn, allows farmers to increase their output. One of the unintended consequences of intensification, however, is that production costs increase faster than the prices farmers receive for animals and crops. This situation is exacerbated by declining commodity prices, which put pressure on farmers to increase output levels even more, and the cycle repeats itself.

Critics charge that intensification is promoted by government price support programs that guarantee commodity prices. The 2002 Farm Security and Rural Investment Act, commonly called the farm bill, provides farmers with price supports costing an estimated $190 billion over 10 years (Allen 2002). In signing the bill, President Bush (2002) noted that "Americans cannot eat all that America's farmers and ranchers produce. And therefore it makes sense to sell more food abroad."

But guaranteeing commodity prices and selling subsidized surpluses abroad leads to similar demands from farmers in other countries and the production of more food, which eventually depresses prices. Soon after President Bush signed the 2002 farm bill, Canadian farmers demanded that their government provide them with $1.3 billion (Canadian) a year to deal with the impact of the new legislation (Edmonds 2002). Subsidies also disrupt agriculture in the developing world, since poor countries often import subsidized commodities and in the process put their own farmers out of business.

Concentration means fewer but larger units use economies of scale to produce a greater share of the output of a particular product or commodity. Producing calves on a ranch with 500 cows costs nearly 50 percent less than on a ranch with fewer than 50 cows (Lamb & Beshear 1998). Similarly, production costs on farms with more than 3,000 hogs are estimated to be nearly a third less than on farms with fewer than 500 hogs (Drabenstott 1998). Between 1970 and 2000, these economies of scale resulted in the loss of more than 900,000 cow-calf operators and 800,000 hog operators (Table 1.1). The largest producers control the vast majority of production (see Tables 1.2 and 1.3). In North Carolina, for example, 98 percent of the 9.6 million hogs grown in the state in 1997 came from farms with 1,000 or more hogs, and more than a third of the state's hog production comes from just two counties (USDA National Agricultural Statistics Service 1999a; Sullivan, Vasavada, & Smith 2000).

Processing firms increasingly contract with producers to provide them with livestock. In the early 1980s, less than 5 percent of all U.S. hogs went to market under some type of contract; in 2001 more than 75 percent were committed to packers through direct ownership or contract arrangements (Lawrence et al. 1998; USDA Grain Inspection, Packers and Stockyards Administration 2001). Large producers want the certainty that comes from a guaranteed market, while processors want the certainty of a guaranteed supply to run their operations efficiently. This system favors large producers, sometimes referred to as *factory farmers*, since processors do not want the added costs of dealing with many small suppliers.

Some family farmers have tried to survive by banding together in cooperative arrangements (Grey 2000b). Many others have elected to sell out. Fewer farms mean fewer links to the local rural economy, since large factory farms tend to purchase inputs from outside the local area, which fuels further loss of capital from rural areas (Ikerd 1998). Thus, when family farms fail, local businesses, schools, and grain elevators soon follow.

Specialization is the natural outgrowth of intensification and concentration, as farmers elect to focus their expertise, land, and labor on a narrow range of commodities (Bowler 1992). This means fewer farm products are grown on each farm and in each region. U.S. cattle feeding has gravitated to the High Plains of Texas, Kansas, and Nebraska. The abundance of feed grains in these states helped increase their share of U.S.-fed cattle from 40 percent in 1980 to 54 percent in 2002 (USDA National Agricultural Statistics n.d). A ready supply of corn, the primary feed for hogs, centered pork production in the Corn Belt, from western Ohio to eastern Nebraska, until the mid-1980s. Iowa is still first in hog production, but changes in how hogs are raised and resulting environmental concerns have been behind industry expansion to North Carolina, Oklahoma, and Utah. U.S. poultry production doubled between 1980 and 2000, with most of the growth in an arc from East Texas to North Carolina. The region's mild climate provides year-round growing conditions and low

TABLE 1.1   NUMBER OF U.S. LIVESTOCK
PRODUCERS, 1970–2000 (SELECTED YEARS)

Year	Cattle and Calves	Hogs and Pigs
1970	1,935,380	871,200
1980	1,619,750	666,550
1990	1,283,980	268,140
2000	1,077,560	86,360

Source: USDA National Agricultural Statistics Service;
URL:<http://www.nass.usda.gov:81/ipedb/> (May 17, 2002)

TABLE 1.2   STRUCTURE OF U.S. HOG OPERATIONS, 1993 AND 2000

Year	Number of Head					
	1–99	100–499	500–999	1,000–1,999	2,000–4,999	5,000+
1993	131,160	56,295	18,270	7,955	3,390	990
2000	48,210	17,755	7,630	5,850	4,825	2,090
Difference	−82,950	−38,540	−10,640	−2,105	+1,435	+1,100

Source: USDA National Agricultural Statistics Service;
URL:<http://www.nass.usda.gov:81/ipedb/> (May 17, 2002)

TABLE 1.3   STRUCTURE OF U.S. CATTLE
AND CALVES OPERATIONS, 1993 AND 2000

Year	Number of Head				
	1–49	50–99	100–499	500–999	1,000+
1993	774,600	204,180	209,140	17,125	8,735
2000	653,150	179,560	189,700	18,720	9,780
Difference	−121,450	−24,620	−19,440	+1,595	+1,045

Source: USDA National Agricultural Statistics Service;
URL:<http://www.nass.usda.gov:81/ipedb/> (May 17, 2002)

heating and cooling costs for the houses where chickens are raised. The preponderance of small marginal farms is a key factor in the location of the poultry industry in this region (Broadway 1995).

The structural forces of agricultural industrialization are also at work in Canada. Cattle feeding converged in Alberta because of its surplus feed grains, and the province increased its share of Canadian-fed cattle from 47 percent in 1984 to 73 percent in 2000 (Canfax 2001). Quebec and Ontario have historically been at the focal point of Canada's hog production. But in the mid-1990s, the province of Manitoba tried to emulate North Carolina by allowing pork processors to contract with individual producers. As a result, Manitoba's share of Canadian pork production rose from 17 percent in 1996 to 22 percent in 2001 (Canadian Pork Council 2002). A system of supply management restricts imports and establishes provincial production quotas and prices in Canada's poultry industry. This system ensures industry stability by linking the distribution of poultry production to population. In 2001, Ontario and Quebec accounted for 62 percent of Canada's population and 60 percent of its poultry output (Statistics Canada n.d).

CONSEQUENCES OF AGRICULTURAL INDUSTRIALIZATION FOR THE MEAT AND POULTRY INDUSTRY

All three components of agricultural industrialization are manifest in the North American meat and poultry industry. *Growers*, as farmers are increasingly called, specialize in a single species, using custom-built cattle feedlots, hog barns, or chicken houses, and incorporating off-farm inputs. Each specialized facility confines animals to restrict their movements and maximize weight gain. Hormones and antibiotics are added to the animal's feed to promote growth and prevent disease. In the poultry and pork industries, large processors, called *integrators,* own the animals and contract with growers to raise them until they reach their slaughter weight, when the company picks them up and transports them to its processing plants. This system has serious consequences for farmers, rural communities, the environment, and consumers.

Contracting versus Farming

The U.S. poultry industry pioneered vertical integration in agribusiness, and its "success" has become a model for the pork and beef industries. Tyson Foods, the largest poultry company in the United States, contracts with 7,600 "farms" in 16 states to grow its chickens. Growers are judged primarily on "feed-conversion ratio," and the goal is to grow birds to slaughter weight with as little feed as possible. If Tyson is not satisfied, it may cancel its contracts with growers, leaving them with no way to pay off their loans on chicken houses and equipment (Yeoman 1989).

Smithfield, the largest U.S. pork processor, is also its biggest producer of hogs. It owns 700,000 sows in 10 states, which gave birth to more than 12 million hogs in 2001—roughly three-and-a-half times more than its nearest competitor (Smithfield Foods 2002).

Four companies—IBP, ConAgra, Excel, and Farmland—controlled more than 81 percent of U.S. beef slaughter in 2000 (USDA Grain Inspection, Packers and Stockyards Administration 2001). And the beef companies are poised to emulate those in poultry and pork by owning their own cattle and contracting with feeders to raise them. Efforts to prevent such practices failed when a U.S. Senate ban on packer ownership or control of cattle, hogs, or sheep within 2 weeks of slaughter was struck from the final version of the 2002 farm bill. Supporters of the proposed ban cited studies linking lower cattle prices to increases in the number of animals committed to the dominant packing companies through ownership or contract (Connor et al. 2002). The only impediments to the beef industry's vertical integration appear to be lawsuits alleging price collusion filed by producers and feedlot owners against major packing companies (Looker 2002; Hord 2002).

Contracting has put many small, independent livestock producers out of business and has led to calls for a system of sustainable agriculture that considers the ecological and social impacts of production. Such a system would rely "more on people, including the quality and quantity of labor and management, and less on land and capital" (Ikerd 1998:158).

Michael Broadway

Figure 1.2 The Kansas City Stockyards stand empty the day after they closed in 1991. These stockyards have since been razed.

Packers Say Good-bye to the City

The processing companies that now dominate the beef and pork industries replaced older urban-based companies by constructing large slaughter and processing plants close to livestock supplies in rural areas. IBP, Inc., now owned by Tyson Foods, began this process in 1960, when it opened a plant about 80 miles northwest of Des Moines in the small town of Denison, Iowa. At the time, most hogs and cattle were shipped to stockyards in large urban centers, such as Chicago, St. Paul, Omaha, Kansas City, and Toronto, then slaughtered in adjacent multispecies plants.

Locating packing plants near supplies of fed cattle lowered procurement and transportation costs. Worker productivity rose with the construction of single-species slaughter facilities and a disassembly line that made each worker responsible for a single task.

IBP introduced boxed beef at its new Dakota City, Nebraska, plant in 1967. Instead of shipping sides of beef, the carcass is "fabricated" into smaller cuts, vacuum packed, and shipped out in boxes. Demand for this boxed beef was strong, and IBP built new plants in small towns on the High Plains. Old-line urban-based companies had diffi-culty competing with this lower-cost competitor and declared bankruptcy or sold out. ConAgra bought Armour, and Cargill purchased Missouri Beef Packers Excel Corporation and renamed it Excel. These new companies followed IBP's example by cutting wages and building plants in small towns near their source of animals.

But the communities that hosted these plants lacked the workers to run them, and companies recruited new immigrants and refugees in large numbers. As a result, packinghouse towns have been subject to rapid growth as well as ethnic, cultural, and linguistic transformation.

Figure 1.3 El Primo, which caters to Mexican workers at the nearby Tyson Foods chicken plant, stands alongside of Dave's Pizza in Sebree, Kentucky.

Hog processing was concentrated in the Midwest until the 1980s, when the industry moved into North Carolina and then Oklahoma. The major processors—IBP, ConAgra, Cargill, and Smithfield—adopted beefpacking's rural industrialization strategy, with similar consequences for host communities (Grey 1995).

Poultry plants share many characteristics with their counterparts in the red meat industry: they are located in small towns, the work is tedious and dangerous, the pay is low. African American women provided most of the labor in its plants until recent years, when companies started recruiting Latinos and other immigrants to replace them, and in the process transformed many small southern towns (see Griffith 1995; Horowitz & Miller 1999).

Competitive pressures also forced the restructuring of Canada's red meat industry (MacLachlan 2001). During the 1970s and 1980s old urban plants closed, from Vancouver in the West to Charlottetown in the East, and a new generation of single-species plants with large slaughter capacities sprang up in small towns on the Canadian Prairies. Cargill opened a beef plant in High River, Alberta, in 1988; 6 years later IBP bought Lakeside Packers of Brooks, Alberta, doubled its slaughter capacity, and added a boxed-beef plant. At the close of the 1990s, Maple Leaf Foods opened a large pork plant in Brandon, Manitoba.

What's That Smell?

Concentrated animal feeding operations (CAFOs) —feedlots, hog barns, and chicken houses—produce massive amounts of manure that pose a threat to the environment. Nitrogen and phosphorous are the principal components of manure, and they cause problems when they enter water systems in large quantities. Typically, farmers apply manure to fields before planting, but if applied at levels above the nutrient absorption

Michael Broadway

Figure 1.4 Canada Packers Meatpacking Plant, St.-Boniface, Manitoba, Canada, closed in 1987

rates of soil and crops, the potential for runoff and subsequent ground and surface water pollution increases.

The number of CAFOs in the United States dropped from 435,000 to 213,000 between 1982 and 1997, but it was smaller operators who accounted for this decline. Livestock and poultry farm acreage also declined, but because large operations were expanding the amount of nutrients produced by CAFOs actually increased by 20 percent. This means that many confined livestock operations have to look off site to dispose of their manure. Among the largest producers, 72 percent have an inadequate land base to utilize all the nitrogen produced on site; the comparable figure for very small farms is just 15 percent. The disposal issue is particularly acute in the southeastern United States, the locus of poultry and swine production. The Southeast accounts for more than 27 percent—200,000 tons—of the national total of excess nitrogen (Gollehon & Caswell 2000:15).

Feed People, Not Cows!

Inefficiency of feed conversion in the livestock industry and the export of the North American model of meat production to the developing world have been widely criticized. Advocates for the world's poor argue that feeding grain to animals instead of humans makes little sense (Lappé 1982; Lappé, Collins, & Rosset 1998; George 1986). As developing countries become richer, their citizens eat more animal protein, and local farmers are changing from *food* production to *feed* production. The poor and small landowners feel the consequences of this changeover most severely. In Brazil the cost of black beans, a staple of the poor, has risen sharply as farmers have started growing soybeans for domestic and European cattle feeders. These large modern farms have displaced thousands of small farmers, many of whom have migrated to the Amazonian state of Rondonia, where they cut down the rainforest, planted crops, then moved on after the soil was exhausted (Lappé, Collins, & Rosset

Figure 1.5 In 1999, Maple Leaf Foods opened a plant in Brandon, Manitoba, that has the capacity to slaughter 108,000 hogs per 6-day week.

1998). India diverts grain to support a domestic poultry industry that has targeted the country's rising middle class, but the poor cannot afford the grain used to feed the poultry, let alone its meat (Gold 1999).

What's for Dinner?

Rising affluence during the twentieth century increased North Americans' meat consumption, even as their meat preferences were also changing. Per capita consumption of beef peaked in the United States in the late 1970s at about 126 pounds per year and fell to 95–100 pounds by the end of the 1990s (Table 1.4).[2] The same thing was occurring in Canada (MacLachlan 2001). These reductions are due, in part, to medical reports that a diet rich in animal fat and cholesterol increases risk of heart disease and strokes, government recommendations that consumers choose a diet low in saturated fats, and popular diatribes against the beef industry, such as Jeremy Rifkin's (1992) *Beyond Beef* and Howard Lyman's (1998) *Mad Cowboy*. Interestingly, pork has not been subjected to the same medical and public scrutiny as beef, and consumption has remained largely unchanged throughout most of the twentieth century (Table 1.4). The biggest change in American meat-eating habits has been the explosive growth in consumption of chicken, from about 10 pounds per person at the beginning of the twentieth century to more than 90 pounds at its close. These trends have been repeated in Canada (MacLachlan 2001).

Americans and Canadians continue their love affair with meat despite growing public concerns about its negative health and environmental consequences, and overall consumption continues to rise. Low costs have contributed to this increase, and meat prices, when adjusted for inflation, were at 50-year lows in the 1990s (Putnam 1999).

Meeting changes in demand has meant expanding and quickening the pace of meat production and processing. Critics charge that faster line speeds translate

TABLE 1.4   U.S. PER CAPITA CONSUMPTION
OF MEAT, 1930–2000 (SELECTED YEARS)

Year	Beef[1]	Pork[1]	Chicken[2]
1930	48.6	66.6	21.5
1950	62.6	68.2	20.3
1970	113.7	66.4	41.4
1990	96.1	67.0	72.2
2000	99.3	67.6	91.0

[1]Carcass weight equivalent or dressed weight in pounds
[2]Pounds per capita

Source: USDA Agricultural Statistics, various years, Washington, DC:
U.S. Government Printing Office.

into a greater likelihood that meat will be contaminated by manure and by the contents of animals' stomachs. According to the U.S. Centers for Disease Control (2000), food poisoning in the United States annually results in 76 million illnesses, 325,000 hospitalizations, and 5,200 deaths. The most common meat-borne pathogens are *Campylobacter, Salmonella,* and *Escherichia coli* O157:H7. *Campylobacter* is a bacterium found in the intestines of healthy birds, and it is present in most raw poultry. The intestines of most animals contain *Salmonella* bacterium, while *E. coli* O157:H7 is a bacterial pathogen found in cattle (Centers for Disease Control 2000). Public awareness of *E. coli* O157:H7 stems from an incident in 1993, when four children died and 700 people were hospitalized after eating contaminated Jack-in-the-Box hamburgers (Schlosser 2001). Since then a number of highly publicized meat recalls in the United States and Canada have led government regulators to require that safe cooking and handling instructions accompany the purchase of fresh meat.

Other critics note the growing scientific evidence that the use of antimicrobials and antibiotics[3] to promote growth and prevent disease in livestock threatens human health, either by resistant animal pathogens infecting humans or by resistant animal pathogens transferring their resistance to human pathogens (Tauxe 1997). Agricultural uses account for 40–70 percent of all antibiotics sold in the United States. The World Health Organization and the U.S. Centers for Disease Control agree that the use of antimicrobials is an important cause of antibiotic resistance in food-borne illness and a substantial contributor to the emergence of antibiotic-resistant diseases. But U.S. congressional efforts to restrict the use of antibiotics in animal feed have been unsuccessful (Union of Concerned Scientists n.d.). Companies are beginning to respond to these concerns, and Tyson Foods recently announced it would cease using the fluoroquinilone class of antibiotics in its broilers (Burros 2002; Tyson Foods 2002b).

CONCLUSIONS

Industrialization has transformed agriculture. Its goal has become the production of large quantities of uniform products at the cheapest possible price. Under this regime producers purchase more inputs to increase output, which ultimately lowers commodity prices and forces "inefficient" producers out of business. Under this "survival of the fittest" model, the spoils have gone to the biggest producers. In 1997, fewer than 4 percent of U.S. farms accounted for nearly 57 percent of agricultural sales, and the only category of farm that gained in numbers during the decade was those with sales of more than $500,000 (USDA National Agricultural Statistics Service 1999b). Small independent producers are an endangered species.

In the meat and poultry industry, large transnational corporations determine how and where cattle, hogs, and poultry are produced by owning the animals themselves, contracting with large producers, slaughtering and processing the animals, and adding value. This system has proved highly profitable for processing companies. Smithfield Foods (2002) has seen its pork sales soar from $570 million in 1983 to more than $6 billion in 2000; during the same period its *annual* earnings per share averaged 27 percent—outperforming such well-known companies as General Electric and Colgate Palmolive. It achieved these successes while the number of independent hog producers declined by nearly 600,000. Tyson (2002c) saw its sales increase from $3.9 billion in 1991 to more than $10.7 billion in 2001. And like Smithfield, Tyson has bought out competitors in an effort to gain a greater share of the meat market. In 2001, it purchased IBP, the world's largest red meat processor, to enhance its "value-added protein portfolio" and become the world's largest meat and poultry company.

The next three chapters provide historical analysis of the evolution of the beef, pork, and poultry production systems in North America and how Smithfield, Tyson, and other companies have attained their dominant position in the industry. The remaining chapters consider the consequences of this production system for workers, producers, communities, and consumers.

NOTES

1. Economies of scale are evident in meat-packing. Unit costs are 20 percent lower in a plant that slaughters 300 head of cattle per hour than in one that slaughters 47 head an hour. Large-capacity plants also average lower fixed costs (electricity, water) and can spread them over two shifts (Duewer & Nelson 1991).

2. Data on meat consumption can be misleading, depending on how it is measured. For example, according to the 2001 Statistical Abstract of the United States (U.S. Census Bureau 2001), beef consumption in 1999 amounted to 65.8 pounds per capita (boneless trimmed weight), and the equivalent figure for chicken was 54.2. By contrast, the 2001 Agricultural Statistics (United States Department of Agriculture) lists beef consumption at 98.7 pounds per capita (carcass weight equivalent or dressed weight), and chicken is listed at 90 pounds per capita (ready-to-cook basis). Despite these discrepancies, trends are clear. Overall meat consumption continues to rise in the United States, fueled by increased chicken consumption. Americans' taste for beef peaked in the late 1970s and has since declined and stabilized. Pork consumption has remained relatively stable throughout most of the twentieth century.

3. "Antibiotic growth promoters stimulate an animal's growth by improving weight gain and feed conversion efficiency as a result of their effect on the microflora of the gut. Antimicrobials are used to kill or inhibit the growth of micro-organisms (bacteria, fungi, protozoa and viruses). They include antibiotics, disinfectants, preservatives, and other substances such as zinc and copper" (Report of the Policy Commission on the Future of Farming and Food 2002:102).

2/From Roundups to Restructuring:
The Beef Industry

A BRANDING ON THE FLYING V

I arose at 5:00 A.M., well before sunup. Chet had already rounded up the horses, and, with his wife Kris, was putting homemade cinnamon rolls in the oven. It was Kris's first branding, and she was nervous about whether she had made enough food and whether it would be the right kind—not a repeat of what had been served earlier that week at a neighbor's. Reed, Chet's 15-year-old son, and the hired man came in from the bunkhouse, and we ate rolls and drank coffee while the hired man talked of earlier brandings when the fog was so thick riders passed each other—and the cattle— unseen. It was only the first of many stories of brandings, ranch work and life, local characters and hilarious antics that would be told and retold throughout the day.

After we finished eating we went to the barn, where Chet's brother, Scott, was brushing down and saddling up his horse. Scott, 43, balding with a short gray beard and not more than 5'5", is as round as he is tall. Never married, he is everyone's favorite uncle—fun loving, full of stories.

Neighbors began arriving shortly after 6:00, their pickups hauling horse trailers with mounts already saddled. As the men got out of their trucks, often with sleepy-eyed but eager children in tow, they checked with Chet to see what they would be doing and what equipment was needed. All in all, about 20 men showed up—the women would come later to help Kris get dinner ready for the men when branding was done.

Some looked the part in well-worn black Stetsons; pearl-buttoned Western shirts; faded Wranglers held up by trophy buckles and tucked into underslung, high-heeled boots; chaps and spurs, often decorated with their brands or initials. Others wore "gimme" caps, Lees, buttoned-down sport shirts, and ropers—"cowboy tennis shoes." Several had yellow slickers tied behind the cantles of their saddles in case of rain. All wore jackets against the early morning chill.

When everyone was there—horses unloaded, saddles adjusted, instructions given—15 riders, including two preteen girls complete with braces, loped off into the early morning light, up a draw and over a sandhill. Five men, and two old cow dogs, followed out shortly in two pickups. In the lead was Chet—"It isn't couth to rope at your own branding." He would stay afoot, manage things, and do some of the dirtier work. In the cab with him was Pat—tall, thin, young, his dusty black hat settled down on his ears. They carried the branding irons and other necessaries. In the second pickup came Chet's uncle Norm, another elderly gentleman, and me.

The Flying V is a cow-calf operation, located in the breathtaking, treeless expanse of the Sandhills of western Nebraska. The ranch covers 52 or 53 sections, Norm wasn't sure exactly. (A section is one square mile, 640 acres.) It is owned by a family that lives in town, about an hour south of the ranch, but Norm's family has managed it since his father's time. The ranch is divided into two operations—Chet manages one operation, encompassing about 16,000 acres, his brother the other. Half the cattle—about 900 head—belong to the ranch owners; the other half to Norm and his sons. Chet's hired hand runs a few head. Most are Black Angus, with a few Black Baldies, or Black Whiteface, as they are called up here.

After 15 minutes, we drove down into a pasture surrounded by low rising hills, where a portable corral had been set up the afternoon before. While we waited for the riders to drive the "mama cows" and their calves into the corral, Chet opened up bags of yellow ear tags, black plastic ear hormone implants that get put on with the ear tags, and loads of vaccine guns. Before long the first riders appeared, stretched in a straight line behind the herd. Occasionally, a stray would break loose and one of the riders would chase it back in the bunch. When all the calves were in the pen, and the gates closed, the men dismounted and stood in a line in front of the herd, by now mooing and bawling in a strangely melodic cacophony, which continued until each bunch was completely branded and let loose, mamas and calves free to graze together once again.

Chet and Pat drove a few mama cows out of the corral with buggy whips, while the truck bearing the branding irons and the stove to heat them was backed into the corral and the butane tank and heating stove were unloaded and heated up.

By now more pickups had arrived, bringing kids and adults. Everyone pitched in—the only people who didn't do anything to speak of were me, a 3-year-old who stood in the truck bed by me, a man in a weathered cowboy hat, boots, and overalls, and his granddaughter. (I volunteered, but they must have figured I would be more trouble than I was worth.) For the young ones, it was a time to learn, and to show what they were made of. During the branding and at dinner afterward, men talked about how "stout" certain youngsters were and how well they "rastled" the calves. Norm's son Todd, in his late thirties and wearing a beat-up straw hat, good-naturedly made sure the kids stuck to the rastling, no matter what. They got right into it, and the consensus was that they did a right good job of it. There is a pride that goes with getting in there and getting dirty, and at one point an old-timer turned to a 12- or 13-year-old girl and said, "You know, you've gotta have shit on you to get any dinner." She had nothing to worry about, and she proudly threw dirt on her jeans to "wash" the dung off.

This branding was little different from those of a century earlier (cf. Ward 1989:59–62), except for basic changes in technology—a butane-fueled fire, rather than one of wood; plastic ear tags instead of markings made with a knife; hormone implants. Some outfits try to recreate the old days, and one farther north takes out a chuckwagon for two or three days, brings in cowboy poets (and cowboy wannabes), and uses a wood fire to heat the branding irons.

Don Stull

Figure 2.1 Driving cattle into branding pens on the Flying V, May 1992

Four teams worked systematically and efficiently. Riders rode into the herd, picked a calf, and let their catchrope sail. Calves were usually "heeled"—roped around their hind feet and dragged out to two rastlers, who worked in tandem—it might take three, if kids made up part of the rastling team. Thus immobilized, the calf was branded, tagged, vaccinated, and, if a male, castrated.

The butane stove was set up behind the pickup in the middle of the corral: Pat worked one side; Norm the other. A half-dozen branding irons, each about 4 feet long and bearing the "flying V" (~V~), were lined up on the stove's grate. When the irons were hot, the branding began. It takes an experienced hand to put a brand on right, and Norm and Pat were very careful. The calves were always branded in the middle of the ribs, for both the brand and its placement are necessary to establish ownership. As the iron was applied to the calf, white smoke rose from its side—and occasionally a bright red flame. The smell of burning hair floated on the still morning air.

Neither the iron men nor the rastlers were in any way cruel, and they always tried to be gentle and soothing to the calf. Never did I hear anyone curse in anger. Yes, the calves experienced pain, but only minimally and briefly. As much as anything, the calves were frightened by all the strange activity and because they were separated from their mothers. After their release, they ran out of the corral gate to rejoin their mothers, soon to recover.

Chet and Red castrated the bull calves; one to each side of the truck. Scott applied yellow ear tags to each animal, while other men stood on each side of the truck vaccinating them—one shot in the hind leg, another in the neck, while two pills were put down the throats of some animals with a long plastic applicator. Virgil, a freckled old hand in his sixties, and Becky, a pretty short-haired woman in her thirties, sat on folding chairs in front of me cleaning calf testicles, slicing them out of their sacks and putting them in a bucket of water. Though slightly bloody, this is a coveted job, since

Don Stull

Figure 2.2 Paul Kondy heeling a calf at the Flying V branding

it is done sitting down. Decky was clearly enjoying herself and joked easily with the men about her job.

Chet and Red did all the castrating, but generally others traded off—rastling sometimes, roping sometimes. Done from atop a horse, roping is the most prestigious job at a branding, less strenuous than rastling and much more romantic.

By 9:00 A.M., the first bunch was branded, and pairs of riders headed out over the surrounding hills and through draws to gather the next bunch of cattle to be branded. As soon as they left, it was up to those of us in the trucks to load up the corral panels and haul them to the next site, set up the corral, and wait for the riders to bring in the cattle. I finally got to earn my keep, helping dismantle, load, unload, and reassemble the metal panels of the corral. This is not a popular job, and the riders headed out soon after the last calf was branded, leaving those behind to joke about their hasty departure.

We branded two more bunches, both in the second corral, and finished up a little before noon. I never heard how many head they branded—I was told later it was about 600. As Chet would say afterward, "It doesn't seem to matter how many head you do, we always seem to finish up around noon." This has something to do, I'm sure, with the fact that a big dinner, and the women, are waiting back at the house. Anyway, they had run out of ear tags and drinking water. By now it was probably 80 degrees or better, and everyone was down to their shirtsleeves and some to T-shirts. The day had proved to be warmer than expected, and still. With all the dust swirling, it had been thirsty work, and most of the men were parched.

The riders loped off, and the rest of us rode back in the trucks. Chet wasn't going to bother loading up the corral panels—they would do that tomorrow, or whenever they felt the urge. Right now a cold beer and dinner were on their minds.

Don Stull

Figure 2.3 Branding a calf on the Flying V

Cars were lined up in front of the house by the time we got there, and it was filled with wives and mothers and daughters—from Norm's 94-year-old mother on down—who had come to help prepare and share in the meal. Card tables were set up in the living room and food filled every available surface in the kitchen. Most of the men were nowhere in sight. Paul, who had invited me to the branding, and Kim—a tall, bearded, quiet man in a beat-up black hat and a T-shirt extolling Angus cattle—and I were the first through the line. We loaded our plates with green salad, pot roast, baked ham, lasagna, and dinner rolls, leaving the chicken and dumplings and several other dishes to others. I followed them out to a large prefab metal building, where most of the men were congregated on metal folding chairs at several long tables borrowed from the Baptist church. Entering the side door, we passed large pots of coffee and iced tea and three coolers—one filled with beer, one with soft drinks, and one with ice.

At the first table sat Chet, Scott, Pat, and one or two others. A frosty, half-empty quart bottle of Old Grandad sat in front of Scott, and several of the men occasionally came over to take swigs. The men clustered in groups of three or four, drinking beers, talking over the morning's work, telling stories of past brandings.

By ones and twos the men went in the house and returned with heaping plates of food. Dinner stretched on into the afternoon—the men talking a little, drinking a little, eating a little, going back for seconds and dessert. Talk was leisurely and comfortable, revolving around a shared past—a men's group trip to Mexico to repair a church; rounding up cattle in blinding snow with a wind chill of 70 degrees below zero. They laughed at retellings of a local legend already in the making—a branding a few days ago got a bit rowdy and afterward someone pulled out electric shears and cut off another's hair. Before long every man there looked like a skinhead. Then they drove into town and went through the pool hall, shearing everyone in sight till somebody finally cut the electrical cord. Pat's ill-fitting hat attested to his involvement.

Gradually the men took their leave. Virgil had a yard to mow; others had chores too. Besides, there was a branding at a neighbor's tomorrow, and more to follow in the days ahead. The cycle of early days and big noon dinners with too many leftovers was beginning to take its toll on some.

After everyone but Scott left, we cleaned up the tables and folded the chairs, to be returned to the church tomorrow. Scott, Paul, and I lingered, swapping tales in the shade of the barn. Scott talked of how much this country suited him. He'd almost bought some land in Alberta, but it had too many trees and he didn't want to work cattle in trees. Chet fed the chickens, Reed and the hired man drove off in a pickup, Kris napped. Chet joined us about 4:30 and we talked on till 6:00. They tried to talk Paul into going to the branding tomorrow, but his aching muscles said "No." Chet invited me to stay on—and I would have loved to—but I didn't want to wear out my welcome. They should have saddled me up a horse, they reckoned, but just didn't think of it. I guess they had decided I wasn't a total rube after all.

A little after 6:00 P.M. Scott decided it was time to go home, and I followed him back out to the highway. As I started the long drive back to Kansas, I remembered how Becky had remarked to me as she sat in the corral, her long fingernails bloody from cutting calf testicles, which would soon become prairie oysters, out of their sacks: "This is really a social event." It is, in fact, a ritual of both renewal and passage, one that brings neighbors together each spring, after a long winter of cold and isolation, to help one another; to share tools and labor; to visit and retell tales over good food and drink; to demonstrate their common bond and community—to reaffirm a living heritage.

As the Busch beer commercial says, "It doesn't get any better than this," and for them it probably doesn't. They remain practitioners of the most romantic and most American of all occupations—it is not a job, but a way of life. Much is drudgery and hard and dangerous, but, at this time at least, it is a joyous celebration of a treasured way of life. And I felt incredibly lucky to have taken part in it (Stull fieldnotes, May 13–14, 1992).

THE CATTLE KINGDOM

Today's beef cattle industry got its start in antebellum South Texas. After the close of the Civil War in 1865, what Walter Prescott Webb (1981) calls the cattle kingdom spread rapidly out of the brush country, or *brasada,* of South Texas onto the Great Plains. From 1866 to 1880, more than 4 million head of Longhorn cattle were driven up out of Texas along the Chisholm and Western Trails to Kansas towns such as Abilene, Ellsworth, Hays, and Dodge City, then shipped east by rail to be slaughtered in Chicago and cities farther east (ibid.:223). Many more were driven to the emerging cattle ranges of New Mexico, Colorado, Oregon, and the Northern Plains of the United States and Canada along the Western and the Goodnight-Loving Trails. (See Figure 2.4.)

The spread of the beef cattle industry throughout the Great Plains and intermountain West is one of the great stories in American history. In little more than a decade, men, horses, and cattle became the undisputed masters of what had once been called the Great American Desert. In reality it was a vast empire of grass (Dale 1965).

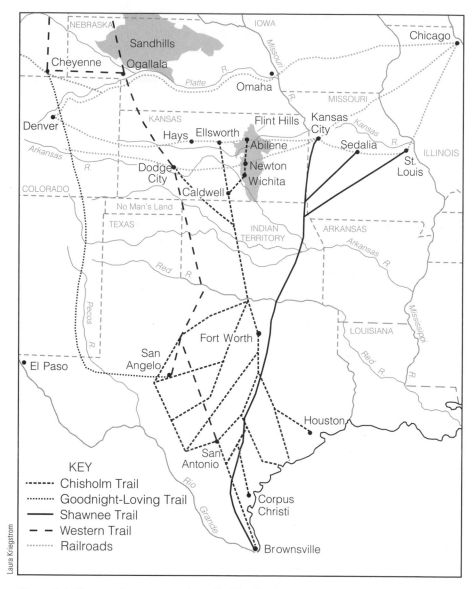

Figure 2.4 Nineteenth-century cattle trails (The Cowboys, *Time-Life Books, 1973*)

Laura Kriegstrom

The era from the close of the Civil War until the late 1880s has been immortalized as the age of the open range. In those days, land and grass were free, water
belonged to first-comers, and all a man needed to set himself up in the business was
a bunch of cattle, enough common sense to handle them, and the courage to protect
them. Such a man was Doc Barton. In February 1872, Doc, his brother Al, and 14
drovers left South Texas driving 3,000 head of Longhorns up the Pecos Trail. In July,
they set up camp under a cottonwood tree along the old Santa Fe Trail, where Garden
City, Kansas, now stands. That fall they established ranch headquarters in a sod
"dugout" built into the bank of the Arkansas River. From there Doc Barton's cattle,

Michael Broadway

Figure 2.5 Ingalls Feedyard near Garden City, Kansas

marked with his OS brand on the left side and a crop off the right ear, ranged south through No Man's Land (the Oklahoma Panhandle) and the Texas Panhandle to the Red River, a distance of about 250 miles (Blanchard 1989:45–52).

In the early 1880s, yearlings could be bought for $4 or $5 a head, fattened on free grass for another dollar, and sold for $60 or $70 profit. But the open-range cattle empire soon ended. The Homestead Act passed in 1862, and cheap land, tales of bountiful harvests, and incentives offered by the railroads attracted settlers. The first piece of barbed wire was sold in the United States in 1874, and the open range gave way to fenced range.

Doc Barton lost 1,200 cattle in the blizzard of 1886, which decimated cattle herds throughout the Plains. In the following year, the best grass-fed Texas steers brought only $2.40 a hundredweight (cwt)—a mere $28.80 for a 1,200-pound steer, which after expenses would bring the owner $5–$9, depending on where it was marketed.

The open range and the golden age of the cowboy had disappeared by the turn of the twentieth century. But cattle still generate more revenue than any other agricultural commodity, and cattle ranching remains vital to the economies and cultures of western North America (American Farm Bureau Federation n.d.).

HOME ON THE RANGE:
THE SHORT, HAPPY LIFE OF A BEEF COW

Today, fewer than 2 of every 100 Americans work on farms and ranches, but agriculture remains the largest component of the U.S. economy, and beef production is its largest segment (Katz, Maddox, & Boland 1998:11). More than 900,000 farms and ranches raised some cattle in 1998, but big spreads like the Flying V account for

only 1 in 7 cattle raised in the United States and only 1 out of 100 cow-calf operations. In fact, farmers and ranchers with fewer than 100 head produce half of all cattle raised in the United States—almost a third have fewer than 50 head (Lamb &
Beshear 1998:56).[1]

Calves are weaned at 300 pounds or so. Until they reach "feeder" weight,
600–800 pounds, when they go to feedyards, they may graze on corn stubble in the
fall or wheat before it ripens in the spring. Farmers or ranchers may "background"
their animals, placing them in pens where they are "broken to the bunk" (feed
trough), as their diet is slowly shifted to feed grains in preparation for their feedyard
diet (see Pollan 2002:47). Backgrounded cattle gain about 2 pounds a day, but yearlings grazing on good pasture will gain just as much or more—and cost a lot less
(Hoy 1997:7).

The Flint Hills run through the eastern third of Kansas, from the Nebraska border
down to the Osage Hills of Oklahoma. They are all that is left of the tallgrass prairie,
which once stretched as far east as Indiana and from the plains of Texas to those of
Canada. In the summer, the region's bluestem grasses offer some of the best pasture-
lands in North America, but in winter the grass is dormant and of little food value. As
a result, the region is home to thousands of "transient" cattle each summer (Hoy 1997).
Each spring, "stockers," weighing 300–600 pounds, are trucked in from cow-calf
operations across the country to fatten on the region's lush pastures for a few months
before being shipped to feedyards around nearby Emporia or in the southwest part of
the state, where they are "finished" in final preparation for slaughter.

Cattle may come to the feedyard from anywhere and at any time. Weighing
from 400 pounds (light feeders) to 800 pounds (heavy feeders), they are hauled to
feedyards in "bull wagons"—18-wheeled stock tractor-trailers. "Bullhaulers" stop
only for gas and meals from the time they pick up a load of cattle in some Flint
Hills pasture—or on a farm or ranch someplace in Texas, or Kentucky, or Florida—
until they reach the feedyard, many hours later. Shipping is hard on cattle. They
lose 5–6 percent of their body weight ("shrink") when they are transported over
long distances, even 2–3 percent on short hauls. And when cattle lose pounds their
owner loses dollars (Raab 1997:18).

Upon arrival at the feedyard, cattle are unloaded into metal-fenced pens holding
as many as 500 head. Commercial feedyards buy cattle, but most feedyards are what
is known as "custom feeders"—they finish someone else's cattle. Feedyards are
really "bovine hotels": they house the cattle, feed and water them, doctor them when
they are sick, and market them to packing plants when they are "finished." Like hotel
guests everywhere, cattle pay room and board. Their owners are charged by the day,
due once the cattle are sold. The cost is passed on through a markup on the price of
feed and medicine, or through a "yardage fee"—a flat fee per day—or both.
Currently it costs about $1.60 a day to feed a steer in a southwest Kansas feedyard
(Pollan 2002:44).

It takes one human to care for 1,000 head of cattle in a feedyard. A 30,000-head
yard typically employs three or four cowboys, or "pen riders," four or five maintenance men, four or five workers in the feed mill, a secretary, a manager, a couple of
people to scrub and maintain the water tanks in each cattle pen, and feed-truck drivers. And there are plenty of odd jobs that always need doing.

Cattle are fed twice in the morning and once in the afternoon. The daily ration—
mainly corn, with alfalfa and corn silage for roughage—is carefully calibrated to

Don Stull

Figure 2.6 Cattle feeding at the bunk, Lexington, Nebraska

maximize "rate of gain." Trucks drive in alleys between the pens, automatically dispensing a measured ration into concrete feed bunks. Feedyard cattle eat somewhere between 24 and 32 pounds of feed a day, depending on the amount of moisture in the ration and the weather, and they gain about 3 pounds a day—more for steers, less for heifers.

If a steer eats 30 pounds or so, and gains only 3, he produces 27 pounds of waste each day. Liquid manure may be mixed with water and pumped onto fields during irrigation; solid manure is spread on fields. Not only is manure an effective fertilizer, it is free. Some feedyards stockpile their manure and give it away or pay someone to take it. Others do not generate enough manure to fertilize all their fields and must pay to have it hauled in from another yard.

Cattle remain in feedyards until they reach slaughter weight at 1,100–1,300 pounds. Buyers from the packing plants bid on "show" pens of "fat cattle," offering so much per hundredweight for all the animals in the pen. Owners often work through "cattle curators" who specialize in buying and selling cattle. Once a price is agreed upon, the buyer sets a date and time for delivery to the packinghouse. Cattle are usually picked up at the feedyard early in the morning. They are driven out of their pens, down the alleys that divide them, and into a bull wagon like the one that brought them there four or five months ago. The loaded trucks are weighed before leaving the feedyard, and the price is based on that figure. When the packinghouse pays the feedyard for its cattle shipment, it deducts its costs and fees, then writes a check for the balance to the owner.

The lives of beef cattle are measured in months, and today's steers are only 14–18 months old when they "go to town," as the trip to the slaughterhouse is sometimes euphemistically called. A century ago steers were 4 or 5 years old before they made the trip to town.

GO WEST, YOUNG STEER, GO WEST

Cattle feeding in the manner and on the scale described here is of recent origin. But cattle feeding is not. Cattle are fed to increase their weight as rapidly as possible and to improve the quality of their meat. Cattle were also fed in the eighteenth and nineteenth centuries to convert surplus crops into a marketable commodity and to fertilize fields. Until railroads came west and refrigerated boxcars were invented in the 1870s, livestock and whiskey were about the only ways farmers on the frontier could turn their surplus grain into cash. Cattle could walk to market, and a few barrels of good corn whiskey brought a handsome return in the city.

The perceived wisdom in the cattle business was that young cattle—3 years and under—lacked flavor, so cattle usually did not go to market until they were 4 or 5. But in the early 1900s, the Swensons of the famous SMS ranch in Texas began pushing their cattle to maturity in under 2 years. Soon other cattlemen decided it was more efficient to feed young animals than older and bigger ones. But not until chain grocery stores emerged as a major meat market in the 1940s, and began demanding top quality, corn-fed beef, did "baby beef" become the standard of the industry.

The Plains of North America are not blessed with an abundance of rivers, lakes, and streams. Not until the windmill became readily available in the 1870s could farmers and ranchers be assured a steady supply of well water for their stock and themselves. Nearly a century later another innovation—center pivot irrigation—turned the Texas and Oklahoma Panhandles, southwest Kansas, and much of central and western Nebraska into one of the most productive agricultural areas in the nation—a new corn belt. This new technology allowed farmers to tap the Ogallala Aquifer, a huge underground reservoir, and enabled them to bring marginal land under cultivation. Soon they were producing mountains of grain, and before long Western cattlemen realized it would be far more profitable to keep their grain and the animals it fed at home.

In 1960, half the cattle on feed in the United States were in the Corn Belt—Ohio, Indiana, Illinois, Wisconsin, Michigan, Minnesota, Missouri, and Iowa. Less than one-fourth (23 percent) were in the Plains—the Dakotas, Oklahoma, Nebraska, Texas, and Kansas. Thirty years later, those numbers were reversed—55 percent of the cattle on feed were in the Plains and only 21 percent were in the Corn Belt. By 1980, Texas, Nebraska, and Kansas had become the top three cattle-feeding states (Krause 1991:5).

FROM HOGSHEADS TO DISASSEMBLY LINES: THE RISE OF THE MEATPACKING INDUSTRY

Grazing their cattle, hogs, and sheep on open range, stockmen were at the forefront of the American frontier as it advanced in the eighteenth and nineteenth centuries. But the slaughter, butchering, and processing of livestock—meatpacking—was an urban enterprise.

Commercial meatpacking began in the American colonies in 1660, when William Pynchon of Springfield, Massachusetts, bought hogs, then slaughtered and packed them for the West Indies trade. Before mechanical refrigeration appeared after the Civil War, most meatpacking took place in the winter and the means to preserve meat from spoilage were primitive. Beef did not preserve well, even as jerky, so cattle were slaughtered year-round as needed for fresh meat. Pork was "packed"—cured, salted, and stuffed into large barrels known as *hogsheads.*

In the colonial period every city had its own slaughterhouses. Then, as now, large concentrations of livestock—and their slaughter—offended the sensibilities of city dwellers, and commercial meatpacking moved ever westward. The first commercial pork packing plant was built in Cincinnati, Ohio, in 1818. Thirty years later, Cincinnati's 40 plants were sending pork and lard to the eastern seaboard and beyond (Skaggs 1986:33–44).

Chicago's first slaughterhouse was built in 1827. Located in the midst of what was becoming the nation's primary cattle feeding area, and linked to the eastern seaboard by the Great Lakes, the Erie Canal, and later the railroads, Chicago quickly became "the most important packing center in the country" (*Prairie Farmer,* as quoted in Ball 1992:11). Livestock pens and slaughterhouses were consolidated on the city's southern boundary as the Union Stock Yards in 1865. The Yards, as they were known, held 200 horses, 21,000 cattle, 22,000 sheep, and 75,000 hogs, as well as hotels, saloons, restaurants, and offices. Workers lived nearby in an area called Back of the Yards (Skaggs 1986:45–48).

In the latter half of the nineteenth century, technology transformed meatpacking from a small-scale, localized, and seasonal activity into a national industry dominated by a handful of giant companies. First came the expansion of the railroads, which tied the nation together by the beginning of the twentieth century. Then came the invention of an efficient refrigerated rail car in 1879, which enabled meatpackers to ship beef carcasses instead of cattle. Three beef carcasses could be shipped in a refrigerated car for what it cost to ship one live steer by rail. Even better, meatpackers could ship three carcasses from Kansas City to New York for what it cost to send one live steer to Chicago. Lured by the promise of cheap western cattle, tax abatements, and the promise of greater profits, Chicago's meatpacking giants began building slaughterhouses in cities throughout the Midwest and the Plains (Skaggs 1986:97).

By World War I, New York City was the only major meatpacking center left in the East. Chicago remained the largest producer of red meat in the United States, followed in order of volume by Kansas City, Omaha, St. Louis, New York, St. Joseph, Fort Worth, St. Paul, Sioux City, Oklahoma City, Denver, and Wichita (ibid.:98). And five companies—Swift, Armour, Morris, Cudahy, and Wilson—had become the "beef trust." In 1916, the Big Five, as these companies were known, killed 9 out of every 10 cattle and 8 of 10 hogs in the 12 major meatpacking cities (Horowitz 1997:13).

Railways and refrigeration transformed meatpacking from a local and seasonal small business enterprise into an industry that distributed its product year-round and nationwide. But meeting the demands of a growing and urbanizing nation required a steady supply of workers to make meat cheaply and efficiently. In 1870, there were only 8,366 packinghouse workers in the United States, including 202 women and 258 children under age 16. They earned an average of $305 for the 3 months or so they worked each winter. By the turn of the century, meatpacking employed 68,500

Figure 2.7 Postcard from the early twentieth century of the beef dressing department, Swift & Company, Chicago.

workers, of whom 3,000 were women and 1,700 children. Their earnings had risen to an average of $488, but they worked all year long (Skaggs 1986:108–109).

Butchering is a skill, requiring precision to kill, eviscerate, skin, and bone an animal without damaging its hide or its meat. Into the 1880s, "all-round" butchers killed and cut up animals. They were paid by the head and worked at their own pace. But if the tasks required to slaughter and butcher an animal could be divided, the pace of work could be increased, more animals could be processed, and more profit could be made.

"Disassembly" lines appeared in Cincinnati's pork packinghouses in the 1830s and were refined in Chicago. Animals were driven up a runway to the top floor of the slaughterhouse, several stories above ground. As the animal was killed and disassembled, gravity brought hides, intestines, and other parts of the animal to lower floors through chutes. Trolleys, hooks attached to rollers on overhead rails, moved the carcass down the line, where crews of workers performed their assigned tasks. In 1908, the introduction of a conveyor system, using an "endless chain," allowed supervisors, rather than workers, to control production speed. Animals were brought directly to the workers, and the pace of their work was determined by the speed of the chain, which the floor supervisor controlled with a lever (Barrett 1987:23-26).

With division of labor came "deskilling." Each task in the complicated process of slaughtering and butchering an animal could be separated and assigned to a single worker. While tasks at critical junctures in the process still demanded considerable skill, these workers no longer dictated their own pace, and jobs became ever simpler. Splitters, who used giant cleavers and later saws to split the carcass down the middle of the backbone, were the most skilled workers—and the best paid—on the killfloor. But their skill was restricted to a single task, and it paled in comparison to the butchers of an earlier day. And if you could stand the stench and keep up with the chain, you could learn most any job in a packinghouse—and learn it quickly.

BEEFPACKING MOVES TO THE COUNTRY: RELOCATING AND RESTRUCTURING THE INDUSTRY

The companies that created the meatpacking industry at the turn of the twentieth century are gone. IBP, Excel, ConAgra, and Smithfield have replaced the industry's original Big Five by dramatically cutting costs and increasing productivity. Meatpacking has always been a marginally profitable industry. Profits run between 1 and 2 percent of sales, while more than 90 percent of sales are eaten up in direct production costs. Minimizing operating costs and maximizing productivity are essential to survival, let alone prosperity.

Plant capacity is key to cutting costs: the cost of slaughter is reduced by nearly one-half at a plant that operates at 325 head an hour versus one that processes only 25 head an hour. But reducing costs through economies of scale is not enough. Live animals lose value through shrinkage, bruising, and crippling during shipping. Since ownership is transferred from the producer to the packer at point of purchase, packers do not want finished animals to travel any farther than necessary, so fat cattle are rarely trucked more than 150 miles to slaughter.

Shipping costs have also been reduced at the other end. No longer are carcasses shipped to wholesalers or retailers as hanging sides of beef. Fat and bone are removed at the plant and subprimal cuts of meat are trucked in boxes directly to retail outlets. Aside from the animal, the single largest expense in meatpacking is labor. Meatpacking companies have succeeded in driving down wages and crippling once-powerful unions.

These changes, which rocked meatpacking, and ultimately led to the demise of its original Big Five, began in 1960, when Iowa Beef Packers, Inc., opened a one-story beefpacking plant in the small town of Denison, Iowa. Twenty years later, the company's name had been changed to IBP, and it had become the leading producer of red meat in the world and the pacesetter for the entire industry.

NOTE

1. Nevertheless, the number of small cattle producers is falling rapidly, while the number of large operations is rising. Table 1.3 (see p. 14) shows this trend quite dramatically.

3/Chicken Little, Chicken Big:
The Poultry Industry

DOWN ON THE FARM

Mother and Frances shared a laugh about Birdie, a "Banty" (Bantam) hen they used to haul around in their little red wagon when they were girls. They pulled the wagon up and down the front walk, and sometimes Birdie would lay an egg for them. Mother also remembered a mean old rooster that used to harass her when she was a girl. She had to pass through the chicken yard—and by Old Red—on the way to the outhouse. She was afraid of him, and once when Old Red attacked her, she picked up a tobacco stick that stood by the gate and hit him with it. As luck would have it, she "hit him right between the eyes—like David killed Goliath—and Old Red fell over dead with one flop!"

Grandmother didn't scold her, but Mother knew she was not happy since Grandmother then had to scald the rooster to get his feathers off and cook him. "I used to hate to go to the outhouse because of that rooster. Maybe he's why I'm still always constipated," Mother laughed.

POULTRY PRODUCTION AND CONSUMPTION IN THE EARLY TWENTIETH CENTURY

Chickens were part of daily life for every farm kid who, like my mother and aunt, grew up in the 1920s. Their mothers raised the birds for their eggs and meat. There was a chicken house and a large fenced chicken yard behind my grandparents' house, and Grandmother sold eggs to the egg man who came by every week or so. For Grandmother, and farm wives all across America, "egg money" was about their only independent source of cash. Grandmother used it to buy an occasional luxury item for herself, and in lean times egg money might have to pay for clothing or groceries, such as coffee or sugar. But more often it went to treats for her children when they went to town on Saturdays—and later for her grandchildren.

I spent summers on my grandparents' farm, and I always looked forward to helping my grandmother shell corn to feed the chickens in the morning. I also liked gath-

Michael Broadway

Figure 3.1 Hens in a farmer's chicken house

ering eggs, though I must confess to being a little afraid of the roosters and the hens when they were sitting in their nests in the chicken house. A fried chicken dinner was a treat, even into my teenage years in the early 1960s. After all, it was a lot of work—the chicken had to be killed; the feathers, head, and feet removed, and then the carcass eviscerated before cooking—and few things smell worse than scalded chicken feathers (Stull fieldnotes, September 17, 1998).

Chickens, like cattle, came to the Americas with the first European colonists. The birds are small and easy to transport, and they require little, if any, care. They eat virtually anything, reproduce quickly, and offer a ready source of fresh meat and eggs (Gordon 1996:56). Until well into the twentieth century, every American farm had a small flock of chickens. Surplus eggs were bartered or sold, and once a hen grew too old to lay, she was either eaten or sold in town. Tender meat came from cockerels, young roosters culled from the flock each spring and sold to brokers, who sent them off to big-city hotels and restaurants. What passed for eating chickens in those days—tough old hens and cockerels—were a byproduct of egg production and were not readily available to most people (Williams 1998:7–9).

Its scarcity made chicken a delicacy. Had you gone shopping in Chicago in 1914, then stopped off for lunch at the exclusive Blackstone Hotel, you might have dined from a menu that offered:

Crabmeat Supreme	$0.60
Prime Rib	$1.25
Imported Venison Steak	$1.50
Broiled Lobster	$1.60

But if you really wanted to impress your dinner companion, or just indulge yourself, you could have ordered:

| Chicken | $2.00! (Snow 1996:5) |

All that was about to change.

MRS. STEELE'S CHICKS:
THE BIRTH OF THE MODERN POULTRY INDUSTRY

America's beef cattle industry was born in the brush country of South Texas; its broiler industry began on the Delmarva Peninsula, a 200-mile finger of flat farm country extending from the northern border of Delaware through the Eastern Shore of Maryland to Cape Charles, Virginia. Bounded on one side by the Atlantic Ocean and on the other by Chesapeake Bay, Delmarva has remained rural and agricultural despite its proximity to some of the largest urban centers on the eastern seaboard.

In the spring of 1923, Mrs. Cecile Steele of Ocean View, Delaware, ordered 50 chicks from a hatchery a few miles down the road to replenish losses to her small flock of laying hens. The hatchery misread her order and sent her 500 chicks. Instead of sending them back, she had a small shed built to house them and raised them as broilers—young chickens grown to be eaten. Eighteen weeks later, the 387 survivors weighed more than 2 pounds each, and she sold them for 62 cents a pound to a local buyer, who shipped them to northern cities for the restaurant and hotel market. Today, that 62 cents would be worth more than $5 a pound (Williams 1998:11–12).

The next year Mrs. Steele ordered 1,000 chicks, and her husband left his job with the Coast Guard to raise chickens. By 1926 they were growing 10,000 birds at a time. It didn't take long for word to spread. In less than a decade, the peninsula was producing 7 million broilers a year. But along with this dramatic increase in production came a sharp decline in the price growers received for their birds. In 1934, chicken farmers were paid 19 cents a pound, live weight—less than one-third the price Mrs. Steele received in 1923. As prices—and profits—fell, growers searched for ways to reduce production costs and the time it took to "grow out" their birds, while simultaneously increasing the size of the birds they marketed (Gordon 1996:60; Williams 1998:20).

Chickens mature quickly, and experiments in chicken genetics and nutrition offered rapid results. By the mid-1930s, breeders were developing chickens that would grow bigger and faster, and nutritionists were experimenting with improving feed efficiency. These innovations paid off handsomely. In 1927, Delmarva broilers went to market at 2.5 pounds in 16 weeks; in 1941, they averaged 2.9 pounds after only 12 weeks. Over that same period, the amount of feed it took to produce a pound of chicken meat fell by half a pound (Williams 1996:26–28).

Corn is the main ingredient in chicken feed, and as more and more farmers began growing broilers, demand for chicken feed rose rapidly. Companies like Pillsbury and Ralston Purina opened feed mills and began selling premixed feed. They also funded research on poultry nutrition.

Humans are not the only animals that like the taste of chicken—so do foxes, raccoons, rats, and chicken hawks. To protect them on the farm, chickens are usually kept in a fenced yard and brought into a shed, called a chicken house, at night. But as broiler flocks climbed into the thousands, and as farmers began growing them throughout the year, something had to change.

Chickens, like humans, need vitamin D to prevent rickets and ensure proper bone growth, and they need sunlight to synthesize vitamin D on their own. But as long as chickens had to spend at least part of their time outside, death loss from predators, weather, and disease presented a serious problem. And the more chickens move around, the longer it takes them to reach market weight. The first major breakthrough in chicken nutrition came with the discovery that by adding cod liver oil (and later purified vitamin D) to their feed, growers could raise chickens entirely indoors (Gordon 1996:60). Chicken yards and wooden sheds gave way to long, low, metal buildings in which thousands of birds could be grown completely indoors.

Chickens mature in a fraction of the time it takes for cattle and hogs, and, as the saying goes, armies march on their stomachs. In 1941, the year the United States entered World War II, the Delmarva Peninsula produced two-thirds of the nation's broilers—77 million. This fact, coupled with the peninsula's proximity to seaports, placed a premium on its broilers. But the armed forces' insatiable appetite for chicken created opportunities for other areas to expand their broiler production (Williams 1998:37).

Responding to increased wartime demand, Delmarva farmers raised 90 million broilers in 1942; far ahead of Arkansas's 11 million and Georgia's 10 million (Williams 1998:38). In that same year, the War Food Administration placed price controls on chickens and commandeered the peninsula's broilers for the armed forces. As a result, the center of broiler production shifted to Georgia and Arkansas, as urban markets looked elsewhere for chickens, which, unlike beef and pork, were never rationed (Gordon 1996:66). Soon chickens from Georgia, Arkansas, and North Carolina were replacing Delmarva broilers in New York and Philadelphia.

Broiler production expanded rapidly after World War II, and the "broiler belt" stretched from the Delmarva Peninsula through North Carolina, Georgia, Alabama, Mississippi to Arkansas and East Texas. As the broiler belt was wrapping itself around much of the Deep South, the industry was pioneering what some say is "the most advanced form of food production in the entire world" (Williams 1998:ix) and others decry as "industrial agriculture" (Heffernan 1984).

INDUSTRIALIZING, INTEGRATING, AND MARKETING THE CHICKEN

By the late 1950s, the structure of the modern poultry industry was in place, and the stage was set for the appearance of the giants of today's industry. In 1935, John Tyson began buying surplus chickens from Arkansas farmers and hauling them to Kansas City and St. Louis. Soon he bought a hatchery so he could sell baby chicks to farmers. By the late 1940s he was supplying chicken feed to farmers from his own mill, and in 1958 he built his first processing plant in Springdale, Arkansas. In the 1920s, Arthur Perdue began raising laying hens and selling eggs on his farm near Salisbury, Maryland. In the 1940s he started hatching and raising broilers. His son, Frank, took over the business in 1950 and signed contracts with farmers to grow broilers. He built a feed mill and, in 1968, purchased a chicken processing plant, making Perdue Farms, Inc., a fully integrated firm (Long 1991:D-30; Williams 1998:98–99). Men like John Tyson and Frank Perdue

> started in their backyards and built regional and national operations that contributed to the industrialization of the nation's poultry industry. Each managed the production of fertile eggs, hatching of chicks, milling of feeds, raising, slaughtering, processing, and marketing of the product within a single company. (Morrison 1998:146)

By combining production, processing, and distribution in the same firms, the poultry industry achieved complete vertical integration (Heffernan 1984:238). It also developed close working relationships with poultry specialists and university agriculture extension agents, whose job it is to provide farmers with the latest research findings. Poultry companies funded university research on avian genetics and nutrition, while extension agents worked directly with company servicemen to increase grower efficiency and expand markets. The interests of poultry companies, university researchers and extension agents, and retailers converged in a national campaign to create "the chicken of tomorrow."

The poultry research director for A&P Food Stores, then the leading retail poultry distributor in the United States, told a Canadian poultry convention in 1944 that "what the poultry industry needs is a better meat-type chicken similar to the broad-breasted turkey." He was widely quoted, and in 1946 A&P joined with the U.S. Department of Agriculture (USDA), poultry companies, and university extension services to form the National Chicken of Tomorrow Committee. Its task was to find the ideal broiler.

State and regional contests in 1946 and 1947 winnowed the competition to 40 breeders, who submitted their eggs for the national contest in the spring of 1948. The chicks from these eggs were raised under controlled conditions at the University of Delaware Extension Station. The winner of the National Chicken of Tomorrow contest was announced on June 23, 1948. It was a red-feathered Cornish-New Hampshire crossbreed developed by the Vantress Hatchery & Poultry Farm in Marysville, California. The runner-up was a White Plymouth Rock from Arbor Acres Farms near Hartford, Connecticut. The press proclaimed "the chicken of tomorrow" a "breakthrough for American agriculture" (Bjerklie 1993:24; cf. Horowitz 2002).

The University of Arkansas hosted a second contest in 1951. It even built a new facility to grow out the birds. Climaxing a week of festivities, Vice President Alben Barkley announced the results of the competition to a crowd assembled in the university's football stadium. Vantress won again, and Arbor Acres Farms was again the runner-up. Ironically, the runner-up, not the winner, ultimately became the chicken of tomorrow. Arbor Acres' White Plymouth Rock became the industry's standard in part because of its white plumage, which processors preferred over the dark-plumed birds of Vantress, because stray white feathers were not as easily seen on plucked birds. Ann Arbor Farms went on to become the largest broiler breeder in the world, accounting for nearly 40 percent of the U.S. supply and a third of the world's supply. Continued modification of its genetic stock has produced a bird that maximizes rate of growth, feed conversion, and "liveability" (Bjerklie 1993).

In 1968, Perdue Farms became the first poultry company to label, or "brand," its product. Beginning with radio commercials and expanding to television in 1971, the company embarked on a major campaign to convince American shoppers its chicken was worth paying more for. With its president, Frank Perdue, telling television viewers that "it takes a tough man to raise a tender chicken," Perdue Farms quickly rose from twelfth to fourth among poultry companies (Williams 1998:103–105; Durand 1999:20).

Rapid and dramatic changes in poultry production and processing after World War II, combined with aggressive marketing, transformed chicken from an expensive delicacy, reserved for Sunday dinner or special occasions, into an everyday, inexpensive meat. At market in 1923, Mrs. Steele's chickens cost more than $10 a pound in today's dollars—no wonder the average American ate only 14 pounds of chicken a year. Today, the descendent of one of those birds weighs twice as much, is raised in less than half the time, and sells for less than a dollar a pound. And "chicken" has replaced "beef" as the most likely answer when Americans ask, "What's for dinner?" According to industry data, annual per capita consumption of chicken in the United States now stands at 77 pounds, compared to 68 pounds for beef and 53 pounds for pork, "the other white meat" (Crews 2001b:22; WATT Poultry USA 2000:18C.)

Consumer surveys indicated that chicken's reputation as healthier and leaner than beef and pork and its cheaper price were behind its meteoric rise in market share. Chicken's short "generation interval" from conception to consumption, as well as vertical integration, enabled poultry companies to rapidly respond to changes in the market and gave the poultry industry a clear advantage over beef and pork. The introduction of "further-processed," "prepackaged," and "pre-prepared" products added convenience to the equation, and 70 percent of Tyson Foods' overall sales were "value-added" products (Richards 1992:58; Katz, Maddox, & Boland 1998:11).

CONTRACT GROWING AND FACTORY FARMING

By the late 1950s, a contract system was taking shape that promised to reduce risk for growers and maximize profits for companies. The poultry company provided the farmer with day-old chicks from the hatchery, as well as feed, medications, and technical assistance. The farmer in turn provided fully equipped chicken houses, utilities, and labor. He also was expected to dispose of dead birds and manure. In return, the farmer received a guaranteed payment, which was often tied to the feed-conversion ratio—the less feed it took to grow the bird to market weight, the better (Morrison 1998:146; Williams 1998:50–51). By the early 1960s, the independent chicken farmer, who raised his own birds and made his own decisions about how best to do it, had been transformed into a chicken grower who signed a contract to raise the poultry company's birds according to its specifications.

As poultry companies achieved vertical integration, farmers' ability to market their eggs and birds vanished. These firms, now called integrators, owned not only the broilers they supplied to contract growers, but the eggs that hatched the birds, the feed that went into them, and the plants that processed and then sold them to grocery stores. By the early 1980s, 95 percent of the broilers sold in the United States were grown under production contracts with fewer than 40 companies (Heffernan 1984:238). For growers, contracts offered a guaranteed income from their flocks and took the risks out of raising chickens, save one—the company did not have to renew the grower's contract.

BIG CHICKEN COMES TO ROOST IN KENTUCKY

Fueled by growing domestic demand and escalating exports, broiler production increased by 5 percent a year throughout the 1970s and 1980s (Stentz 1995:22). But the old broiler belt—Arkansas, Georgia, Alabama, and the Delmarva Peninsula—was becoming saturated with chicken houses, and concerns were mounting about the industry's treatment of its growers and processing workers, as well as environmental problems associated with disposal of manure and dead birds. Poultry integrators started expanding into new territories. One of those was Kentucky.

Kentucky is within a day's drive of 70 percent of the U.S. population and is criss-crossed by interstate highways (Ulack, Raitz, & Pauer 1998:3). Its low educational and income levels, coupled with declines in its major industries—coal and agriculture—held promise for a readily available supply of workers for processing plants and growers to supply them. Adding to its appeal were an abundance of corn and water, generous tax incentives, a besieged tobacco industry, minimal environmental regulations, and an absence of rural zoning. As if those factors weren't enough, there was the $165 million in state and local tax credits and incentives for the poultry companies (Associated Press 2000).

If Kentucky had much to offer poultry, poultry was also attractive to many Kentucky farmers. Tobacco—the state's primary cash crop—was under attack on every front, and tobacco farmers were being encouraged to find alternative crops (Stull 2000). The state's farms are small—151 acres on average, of which only a third is in harvested cropland (Ulack, Raitz, & Pauer 1998:159)—making them ideal for poultry production. Take Shawn (not his real name), for example. Together he and his semi-retired father have about 750 acres, scattered over several farms. They erected six broiler houses on about 30 acres of a hilly 130-acre farm. They decided to grow broilers because 750 acres is not enough ground to support their two families on what they can make from corn and soybeans, cattle, and tobacco, and they were unable to rent enough additional acreage.

Chickens also appealed to Kentucky's farmers because the chickens are raised inside massive houses, which eliminate weather as a factor in production, and growers are guaranteed a minimum price per pound for each bird they grow out. Poultry companies also promised easy financing for minimal investment, coupled with attractive incomes in exchange for a modest amount of labor (University of Kentucky College of Agriculture 1994).

These factors led to a staggering 154-fold increase in Kentucky's production of chickens in little more than a decade. From 1.5 million in 1990, Kentucky's production of broilers soared to 178 million in 1998 and then to 231 million in 2001 (Kentucky Agricultural Statistics Service n.d.). Absent at the beginning of 1990, by the end of 1998 Kentucky boasted four large processing plants and 2,000 breeder, pullet, and broiler houses to supply them—all in the western half of the state (Stinnett 1994, 1996a; Kentucky Poultry Federation, personal communication, April 2, 1999). Kentucky now ranks tenth among the states in chicken production. Poultry and eggs are second only to horses in the state's agricultural commodities, bringing in $603 million in 2001 (Associated Press 2002; Hefling 2002).

Tyson's Robards, Kentucky, plant, originally built by Hudson Foods, opened on July 9, 1996. Today, it employs more than 1,500 workers to process 2 million chick-

Figure 3.2 A complex of 16 broiler houses, each home to more than 25,000 birds, in McLean County, Kentucky. The buildings with the open doors store chicken litter until it is spread on fields.

cns a week (Stinnett 1996b). At this rate, 80 broiler houses, each home to some 25,000 birds, must be emptied every week.

The first houses to serve the Tyson plant were completed in September 1995. Four years later Tyson's plant was supplied by 124 growers who operated 667 chicken houses in 10 counties: 32 pullet houses, 68 breeder houses, and 567 broiler houses. Of those houses, 572 (86 percent) are found in three adjacent counties immediately to the south of the processing plant. The greatest number, 227, are in Webster County (Tyson Foods n.d.:6).[1] (See Figure 3.3.)

OLD MACDONALD TAKES A FACTORY JOB: HOW CHICKENS ARE GROWN

Bill's (not his real name) two breeder houses sit long, low, and shiny at the edge of a cornfield. The door opens into an anteroom where stacked trays of eggs are stored at a constant 62 degrees, awaiting pick up for delivery to the hatchery.

Laying hens and roosters come to Bill at 20 weeks of age—10,700 hens and 980 roosters for each of his two houses. They are trucked from pullet houses in the next county where they have been raised from day-old chicks driven up from Alabama. The "working life" of a breeder hen is only 45 weeks; after that Bill says she is "destined for the soup can." Roosters fight and kill one another over "their hens" and must be periodically replaced. They also attack humans. When entering the laying area, you always knock on the door so the chickens won't be startled, and you walk

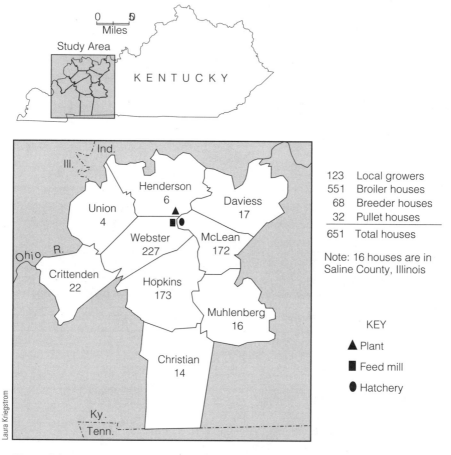

Figure 3.3 Tyson Foods chicken houses in western Kentucky, 1998 (Tyson Foods n.d.:6)

slowly to avoid being attacked. Even so, roosters sometimes fly up on Bill's back and attack him. Hens are aggressive, too, and peck at your legs as you stand in the house. But more than the frequent pecking, the thing a first-time visitor notices most is the sound—a constant cacophony of clucking hens and crowing roosters.

On each side of the floor, where the chickens move freely about, is a row of metal laying cubicles running the full length of the house. They are positioned on both sides of a conveyor belt, which is covered with a removable roof. To lay their eggs, hens enter the small compartments, where they rest on nothing but the bare metal. The laying compartments are slanted slightly inward, ensuring that eggs will roll through a rubbery fabric flap down onto the conveyor belt.

Twice a day, Bill's daughters stand in the anteroom, turn on the conveyor belt, and collect the eggs as they come out of the laying area onto a metal-frame work station. Good eggs are placed in the racks and stored for later pickup. Dirty, small, misshapen, and double-yoked eggs are culled. Bill receives 32 cents per dozen for regular eggs, 10 cents a dozen for culls.

On average, a hen lays an egg every 23 hours for five or six days, then doesn't lay for one or two days. As hens get older, they lay less often, and by 45 weeks their

Don Stull

Figure 3.4 Hens lay eggs inside metal cubicles that run along both sides of the breeding house. From these "nests," eggs roll through a rubbery flap down onto a conveyer belt and into an anteroom where they are sorted.

productivity is below acceptable levels. Bill's two houses combined generate about 18,000 eggs per day when the hens are at their laying peak, but toward the end of their 45-week laying period they will produce only 10,000–11,000 eggs.

Bill and his daughters each take a third of the income from their operation. The daughters gather eggs twice daily, which takes them 4–5 hours, although Bill says they really should gather them three times a day. Bill takes care of the houses and the flocks, which he figures requires 3 hours a day for each house.

Bill's eggs spend 3 weeks at the hatchery. Eggs are carefully monitored in the climate-controlled concrete and glass building on a two-lane road a few miles from the processing plant, where as 7 week old broilers they will meet their end. On the day they hatch, the chicks are placed in cardboard trays and driven in a white school bus to a broiler house.

Broiler houses are 43 feet wide and come in two lengths: 510 feet and 460 feet. The longer ones house about 27,000 birds, the shorter 24,000. Screened windows, which can be opened for light and ventilation, run down both sides of the houses, but they are usually covered with dark curtains, at Tyson's instructions, to keep the birds calmer. Large exhaust fans at one end of the house kick on periodically for ventilation and to suck out the smell of ammonia that can become stifling as the flock matures. Next to each house are two large metal bins from which feed is dispensed automatically into round red plastic trays, divided into compartments, much like a school cafeteria tray. Two rows of brooders (heat lamps), feed trays, and plastic water lines, which dispense water through metal nipples, run the full length of the house.

Attached to each house is a small control room containing all the switches, knobs, and electrical breakers needed to run it. Temperature regulation is key to flock

Laura Kriegstrom

Figure 3.5 Don Stull stands between feeding trays and a water line inside a broiler house

survival, and house temperature is set and monitored from a control panel—85–88 degrees for days 1–3; 85 degrees for days 4–7; 65–70 degrees by the time the flock reaches 42 days of age.

As the birds age, the feed ration is changed in both consistency and content. Initially, feed has the consistency of a fine powder, but as the birds grow it is pelletized. By the end of the grow-out cycle the ration is almost entirely corn, and the birds are emptying one 6-ton feed bin each day. Birds should put on a pound of weight for every 1.9 pounds of feed. Broilers should weigh about 5.4 pounds at 7 weeks, when they are caught and trucked to slaughter.

Feed conversion and death loss are the yardsticks of performance, and growers are measured against all others whose birds are slaughtered in the same week. Tyson sets the base price at 4 cents a pound. Of the 10 growers whose birds Tyson slaughtered the week ending January 31, 1998, three received the base of 4 cents and three received more than 5 cents.

A broiler house costs between $125,000 and $140,000 and must be built to company specifications. Breeder and pullet houses can cost even more. Approved growers can borrow up to 110 percent of the cost of their houses on a 10-year loan.

Breeder and pullet growers usually erect only two houses, but broiler growers usually build at least four, and some build as many as 16 houses in the same complex. Sam (not his real name) has 16 broiler houses. "I'm not really a farmer," he confided, and he never intended "to get into the chicken business." But he jumped at the chance when MetLife and John Hancock offered to loan him $2.4 million for $1,000 down, and their financing arrangement even included his $1,000.

Sam and his daughter, who attends night classes at a nearby community college, run the operation. It takes four full-time workers to run the 16 houses, and at peak times—the week before the flock goes out and the week after when they are cleaning the houses—it takes eight workers. Sam's operation needs every bit of the 14–18 days between flocks to get everything done.

Integrators claim that each broiler house will provide gross annual revenues of $27,000–$31,000 and generate profits of $3,000-$7,000. Of more immediate concern to growers, annual net cash inflow over the 10-year life of the initial loan averages only $1,070 per house (Gibson 1998:9). But none of these figures take into account the cost of the grower's labor or any help he may hire.

Shawn "walks" his six houses first thing each morning and works in them till he knocks off for dinner about 11:00 A.M. He may walk the houses again in the afternoon. Jack (not his real name), the hired man, is paid $6.00 an hour and lives rent-free in a small trailer a hundred yards or so down the gravel road that leads to the houses. Shawn figures it takes two workers about 4 hours each day to take care of six broiler houses. Shawn's father, wife, and two young children pitch in when extra hands are needed.

For the first few days, the chicks need special attention. As Shawn walks the house, chicks bunch up and run, almost in waves, from one side of the house to the other, or seek darker areas in the corners where they feel more secure. Bucket in hand, he picks up dead birds and culls diseased ones, which he dispatches with a blow from a tobacco stick or smashes underfoot. Once a bucket is filled, Shawn empties it into a large blue freezer that sits outside one of the houses. Periodically, Tyson picks up his dead birds and takes them to its "protein plant" for rendering.

Hanging on the door inside each house is Tyson's broiler mortality sheet, which lists the grower's name, house number, number of birds placed in the house, and the date delivered. Rows for each week allow the grower to record the number of culls and the number of dead birds by day. The Tyson field representative, or flock manager, comes by once a week and records the weekly total, as well as the mortality percentage for that week: 25,980 chickens delivered on August 11; 1.1 percent death loss for Week 1; 1.8 percent for Week 2; 2.1 percent for Week 3; 2.3 percent for Week 4.

His flock manager told Shawn his flock would be picked up at 51 days. The catching crew consists of seven men, six Mexican immigrants to catch and an Anglo American supervisor who drives a forklift. Catchers work at night when the birds are calmer. Using knee-high plastic barriers and folding plastic fences for catch-pens, wearing white cotton stockings and gloves to protect their arms and hands, they scoop up five birds in one hand, four in the other, then sling them into cages. Catchers move with remarkable ease, joking among themselves when they take a moment to rest once the cage is full and the forklift driver whisks it outside to be loaded on a waiting semi. Each semi holds 22 coops, each divided into 50 cages that hold 9 birds each—it takes three semi-loads to empty a house. The crew can catch a house in about 3 hours, and it catches three houses a night.[2]

In ten days or so, Tyson will mail Shawn a settlement ranking report, which determines how large the accompanying check will be. The report lists the number of chicks started, birds produced, birds dead on arrival at the processing plant, birds condemned because of disease, average weight of birds, feed-conversion and calorie-conversion ratios. The most important number on the report, however, is the

Don Stull

Figure 3.6 Chicken catchers at work

grower's rank in relation to all others whose birds were caught in the same week. It is this ranking that determines how much the grower is paid per pound, and that amount is the difference between making money on a flock, breaking even, or losing money. Growers are guaranteed 4 cents a pound, but most say they need at least 5 cents to do better than break even.

THE SKY IS FALLING

In the fall of 1998, Tyson's Kentucky plant was only 2 years old, and most of the growers had been in operation no more than a year or so. Most agreed with the pullet grower who said:

> I think it has been great. It's contributed to the decline of the unemployment rate. It's brought a lot of dollars in here. . . . Our grain farmers are getting prime money for their grain. . . . The wages paid out and the spinoff dollars . . . have tremendous effect on the country around here. It's a heck of an improvement. (Stull interview, November 24, 1998)

A few years later, many weren't so sure. Sam had quit the broiler business. He wasn't the only one—a number of broiler houses were standing empty, including Shawn's.

Growers get to keep all the money from the first flock—minus costs for electricity and water—so, as one local skeptic put it, " they get dollar signs in their eyes." Shawn made $36,000 on his first flock, more than most people in the county make in a year. But beginning with the second flock, loans start coming due, as well as payment for what wasn't taken out on the first flock—the reality of income, expenses, and cash flow becomes increasingly apparent.

Energy prices soared in 2001. Shawn spent $2,800 on electricity per flock for his six houses that summer and $25,000 to heat his flock that winter. Many of the chicks he received in his next flock were blind. Shawn and other growers complained that Tyson was extending the time between flocks to 20 days, the maximum allowed without paying a penalty. Such delays could cost a whole flock per year and mean the difference between making and losing money.

In the summer of 2002, Tyson picked up Shawn's last flock and terminated his contract. The company had told him to make $10,000 in improvements on his houses at his own expense. When he said he could not afford the expense, the company representative told him to borrow the money. When Shawn said he was so in debt he could not borrow any more, Tyson refused to send him more chickens. After expenses were deducted from the payment for his last flock, Shawn received a check from Tyson for $33.22.

The poultry industry hasn't been such "an improvement" for grain farmers either. The Tyson feed mill quit paying a premium for corn in the fall of 1998, and in spring of 2002 it quit purchasing grain from local farmers unless they had a contract with the company. Farmers now have to call corporate headquarters in Springdale, Arkansas, to negotiate a grain contract with Tyson's grain buyers, who can have it shipped in by rail if they find a cheaper price elsewhere.

To see their future more clearly, Kentucky poultry growers need only look to how their counterparts in the broiler belt have fared. Ever since the poultry industry achieved vertical integration in the 1960s, growers have complained of their powerlessness under such a system. Ironically, it was the general manager of a major poultry firm who summed up the growers' plight in a 1994 speech to the National Contract Poultry Growers Association, a growers' rights organization: "The trouble is that the way the contracts are written, if your whole income depends on raising birds for the integrator, you have to be just about the absolute best grower that integrator contracts with . . . to make a living, and on top of that you've got to be very frugal, prudent and conservative in your investments" (Bjerklie 1994:33).

There is no doubt that some among the nation's 30,000 poultry growers are glad to be growing chickens and are pleased with their relationship with their integrator (Shatzkin & Fesperman 1999a). But an 8-month investigation of poultry growers in 13 states conducted by the *Baltimore Sun* found that a new grower can expect an annual net income of $8,160 from his poultry operation—half the federal poverty level for a family of four—until the initial loan is paid off in 10–15 years. Fewer than half the poultry growers surveyed on the Delmarva Peninsula said they were making enough to cover expenses (Fesperman & Shatzkin 1999a:3). In fact, 13 Alabama broiler growers compared costs and income for 77 of their houses for one year (five flocks each). They found that those whose flocks averaged 22,500 birds (500-foot houses) cleared $866 per flock per house, but those whose flocks averaged 18,000 birds (400-foot houses) actually *lost* $148 per house per flock (*Poultry Grower News* 2001b:12).

Company spokespersons argue that it was never their intention for growers to derive their primary income from their birds—chickens were supposed to be but one aspect of a diversified operation. But one of the selling points integrators use to entice potential growers is to describe growing chickens as "part-time work for full-time pay." For example, notices distributed to farmers when the Robards plant was being built touted net income of $7,000–$10,000 per house per year for one-and-a-half to two hours of labor a day. And company representatives promise that "with a little effort, you can do better than that." But even happy growers say it is a full-time job if you want to succeed, and two-thirds of Delmarva growers now call poultry their full-time occupation (Fesperman & Shatzkin 1999a:7).

Companies and their growers are financial partners in the poultry industry. In fact, each side puts up about half the capital necessary to support the industry—but there the equality ends. While the industry depends on its 30,000 growers, the growers are at the mercy of only 50 or so companies, and of these four own more than half of all the broilers grown in America. According to industry critics, America's chicken growers have become serfs in a postmodern feudal system (Fesperman & Shatzkin 1999b:2; Guebert 1999)

There is, after all, no "market" for live chickens in the United States. Virtually everyone who grows chickens commercially grows them under contract to one of 50 companies, the integrators. Contracts are written by the integrator to favor the integrator. Growers are paid by the pound, live weight, at the plant, but they are not present when the birds are weighed and cannot challenge head counts, weights, death loss, or the peer rankings that determine the amount of payment per pound. Growers have little recourse in disputes with integrators, and stories of abuse and intimidation are commonplace. As one Louisiana grower put it, "If the company has a vendetta against you, you're out of business" (Johnson 1994:AC-1). The integrator can send you sick birds or "short" flocks; it can "short" you on feed or "short weigh" your birds when they are delivered for slaughter; it can keep your birds waiting at the processing-plant scales so they lose weight and you lose money; it can require you to make costly upgrades to your houses; it can require growers to sign away their rights to sue and mandate resolution of disputes through arbitration (Shatzkin & Fesperman 1999b:2). And if you challenge the company, it will cancel your contract.

It is a sad state of affairs, said Jean Bunting, who, with her husband William, has grown broilers in Bishopville, Maryland, for half a century. "We haven't made a bit more money [growing chickens] than we did 10 or 15 years ago. I wish my mother could see what they've done to the chicken industry. They've put the farmer all the way to the bottom" (Fesperman & Shatzkin 1999a:9–11).

It is indeed too bad Mrs. Bunting's mother cannot see what has happened to the chicken farmer. Her mother was Mrs. Cecile Steele!

NOTES

1. Don Stull was born to a family of farmers whose roots in Webster County reach back to the early nineteenth century. Although his parents no longer live there, most of his extended family does. In the fall of 1998, he returned to Webster County to study the impact of the poultry industry. It should be noted that 12 broiler houses border his family farm. For a more detailed discussion of his role as a native anthropologist and the research upon which this chapter is based, see Stull 2000.

2. April 20, 2001, the day the current union contract expired, was the last day on the job for these chicken catchers. They have been replaced by an automatic chicken-catching machine. According to Shawn, the machine, which looks somewhat like a combine, "sucks the birds up" and onto a conveyor by means of rotary blades, and then "shoots" them out of a "gun" directly into the coops on the truck. It still takes seven operators to run the machine and handle the coops, and the machine stresses the birds and causes wing damage and other injuries. The machine cannot empty a house any quicker than the human catchers, it requires the same number of personnel, and there is more injury, so what is the benefit? The only one Shawn could see was that it eliminates the catchers, who he says are illegal immigrants. Machine operators will be employees, not

contractors as the catchers had been, but, according to Shawn, it takes a long time to train them, and they don't stay long.

Tyson's move to automatic chicken-catching machines came a month before Perdue Farms agreed to settle a lawsuit brought by its chicken catchers in the Delmarva Peninsula for $2.4 million. The suit, filed in U.S. District Court in 1998, awarded about 100 catchers double the over-time pay owed them from 1995 through 2000, the maximum penalty under the law. Since filing the suit, catchers have formed a union and gained employee status, making them eligible to receive benefits and over-time pay (*Poultry Grower News* 2001a:7). But theirs is a hollow victory, since Perdue, Tyson, and other integrators have perfected the machinery to replace them.

4/Hog Heaven:
The Pork Industry

Undeterred, I opened the door and led my students into a small anteroom. In front was a glass door and visitors' instructions: "To enter 'Midwest State University's' Swine Facility, press bell and wait to be escorted into the building." I rang the bell, and a minute or so later, a short, rumpled, middle-aged man in blue overalls and safety glasses appeared. Frank, our guide for the day, cheerfully greeted us and led the way to the changing rooms, then instructed us to take a thorough shower before crossing over to the "clean side."

"You'll find overalls, socks, and underwear on the other side. We'll get your rubber boots when you are dressed."

After showering and donning our new clothes, we reassembled and were fitted with boots at the entrance to the "clean side." The pungent odor of ammonia immediately overwhelmed us as we entered the "clean" portion of the building. It appeared to come from beneath the metal-grated floor, and we later learned that hog feces and urine fall through openings in the floor and from there are either pumped out into a huge holding tank or collected for composting. Parts of the building were ventilated, but on this particular day, with an outside temperature in the mid-80s, there was little fresh air to be had. "Ordinarily it doesn't smell like this," Frank apologized. "You would choose the one day in the year that they came to empty the tank."

Fully assured that "pigs don't stink," we proceeded down a long corridor and entered a room filled with at least 100 hogs, each in its own metal stall. The exhaust fans were going full blast, and the hogs were squealing and grunting at us, making conversation impossible. Passing a second smaller room containing more hogs in stalls, we entered a small office, closed the door, and savored its tranquillity.

Frank reached inside a small refrigerator and grabbed a small plastic container. "This here is pig semen," he announced. "We collect our own. We inseminate the sows and expect each one to produce two litters of 10 to 12 piglets a year. We had one kid who had worked on a pig farm his whole life. He was able to get 300 milliliters of semen out of one of our boars. You just get better with practice." None of us knew whether we should be impressed—and nobody asked for further details. "Everybody wants their pork chops to look the same. If they don't look the same you can't get as much money for them. Actually you can't sell them at all. That's why when we breed our animals we try and control for leanness."

"Why the stalls?" one of us asked.

"When females are bred over and over again they become timid and are the last ones to feed. The crates allow equal-opportunity feeding. If we put you [pointing to a male student] in a room with the rest of these folks [pointing to three women] with some pizza in it, none of you guys [pointing to the women again] would get anything to eat because he would eat it all." To ensure "equal-opportunity feeding," all the animals are fed at once by an operator, who lowers a lever that releases feed into each animal's trough from a tube suspended from the ceiling that runs outside to a large grain bin.

After we left the office, we retraced our steps to another door that opened into the nursery. Inside were 10 sows, each confined to a metal crate by bars that kept it from turning around. They could only lie down on their sides to allow their piglets to suckle. Still, sows occasionally smother their offspring. Frank picked up a dead piglet, which was "striped" from a sow crushing it against the grated floor "This happens quite often. Mama just rolled over and squashed this little guy this morning." Glancing over at the record sheet at the end of the crate, like a doctor checking a patient's medical record, Frank added, "Oh, this was the second she squashed today." (Crates are outlawed in parts of Europe because of concerns over humane treatment of animals.)

Frank carried the piglet outside, tossed it onto a compost pile, and covered it, explaining that the piglet would decompose in about 48 hours. As if to prove his point, he picked out a small bone from the pile and easily snapped it in half. "Last week we had a 400-pound sow die that we threw on the compost pile. It should be gone within a week or two."

As Frank lectured us on how "the two best things to happen to a pig in my lifetime are grates and crates," a worker entered the nursery and picked up the latest litter, notched their ears (for identification), clipped their tales, filed their teeth, and castrated the males. Unwanted bits of pig anatomy fell through the grated floor.

"The tails are clipped because the other pigs would bite at them. This can cause infection, and if that happens you have to use antibiotics." Picking up a piglet and prying open its mouth, Frank pointed to a couple of long sharp teeth. "Do you see these little guys? Can you imagine what that feels like when he is biting down on a nipple? And [pointing to a group of piglets fighting over a nipple] do you see what they are doing? If we didn't blunt those teeth the piglets would injure each other and mama. Have you ever had bacon from a boar? You'd sure know it if you had, castrating them gives the meat a better flavor."

Our next stop was a small room off the central corridor, where Frank explained that hogs are highly vulnerable to diseases. In many operations they are fed antibiotics as part of their diet. But growing concerns over the reduction in human immunity to antibiotics have led the pork industry to reduce their usage. We were told that humans can transmit diseases to pigs, which explains the need for anyone entering hog-raising facilities to shower and change clothes. To further assure us they only

Figure 4.1 Hogs in a modern confinement facility

used a few antibiotics, Frank opened a refrigerator door and pointed to a couple of bottles. "These are all we use."

As we proceeded down the corridor, and looked in at each room, the pigs and pens got larger. As the animals grow they are transferred to the next room down the hall, until they reach slaughter weight of about 250 pounds. From the final room at the end of the corridor, a truck picks them up and takes them to a slaughterhouse.

This marked the end of our tour, and we returned to the changing rooms, showered, put our own clothes back on, and returned to the "unclean side." As Frank cheerfully waived good-bye, he called out, "I've been around pigs for more than 50 years, and from a human perspective this is by far the best place I've ever been. Go out and have some pepperoni pizza—its got pig on it." No one had pepperoni that night, but one of us did have a ham sandwich for supper (Broadway fieldnotes, April 18, 2002).

THE ESSENCE OF PIG

Despite Frank's enthusiasm, pigs are not easily raised, and in confined quarters they can easily infect one another with everything from influenza to roundworms (Skaggs 1986:148). Humans may "sweat like pigs," but pigs don't—they lack sweat glands and can die of heat prostration. When temperatures rise above 86 degrees F (30 degrees C), and pigs are deprived of clean mud holes or shelter, they will wallow in their own feces and urine to avoid heat stroke. As they grow, pigs become less tolerant of heat. Despite

Figure 4.2 Hogs being raised "the old-fashioned way." Note the shelters in the background.

such fragilities, hogs were the major source of meat for Americans from colonial times until the 1950s, when beef overtook pork (Harris 1985).

There is no such thing as a hogboy, and no wistful ballads about rounding up piggies on the open range, but hogs have always been a more valuable source of meat than cattle. A piglet gains one pound for every 3–5 pounds of feed; a calf needs 10 pounds. Four months after insemination, a sow will give birth to a litter of 10 or more piglets, and within 6 months each can be ready for market. Beef cattle, by contrast, have a 9-month gestation period and produce a single calf, which will not reach slaughter weight for well over a year. "The whole essence of pig," according to Marvin Harris (1985:67), "is the production of meat for human nourishment and delectation."

THE ROAD TO PORKOPOLIS

As pioneers settled the Midwest after the American Revolution, the center of live-stock production moved westward. Every farmer kept hogs, which usually ran free and scavenged for their own food. During the summer, hogs foraged on wild roots, vegetables, berries, and native grasses, and in the fall they survived on acorns and other nuts. Corn-fed hogs put on weight more rapidly, tasted better, and brought a better price at market than those fattened on nuts and roots, so farmers usually rounded up their surplus hogs in the autumn and fed them on corn for several weeks before driving them to market (Clemen 1923). Market price was based on the weight of the animal—the larger the hog the higher the price. Heavier hogs were believed to yield the highest quality pork, and the bigger and fatter the hog, the more lard it pro-duced. Pig fat was rendered into lard, which was a major source of oil for lamps until it was replaced by kerosene in the 1870s.

Elisha Mills opened Cincinnati's first meatpacking plant in 1818, and the "Queen City of the West" dominated pork packing until the Civil War. Writing in 1845, a local journalist pontificated:

> The putting up of pork has been so important a branch of business in our city for five and twenty years, as to have constituted its largest item of manufacture and acquired for it the soubriquet of Porkopolis. . . . Our pork business is the largest in the world. (cited in Clemen 1923:95)

Cincinnati's location on the Ohio River gave it access to rich farming country and provided a ready means to ship pork to New Orleans and beyond. By 1844 Porkopolis boasted 26 packinghouses; a decade later it counted 42.

Late fall and early winter is still known in the rural South as "hog-killing time." Winter was the farmer's ice box, and meatpacking remained a seasonal activity until the development of refrigeration after the Civil War. Pork packing usually began in November and ended when the supply of hogs ran out or it warmed up, whichever came first. Warm weather halted slaughter at the packinghouses because the meat would soon spoil. Frigid temperatures also shut down operations, since the buildings were unheated.

Hogs were driven into a pen next to the slaughterhouse. When the pen was full, workers killed the animals with a blow to the head. Dead or stunned animals were pulled by a drag line into a "sticking room," where their throats were slit. Carcasses were hung by their hind legs to drain, then dipped in boiling water and laid out on a table. A crew of workers, each with his own task, then set about cleaning the animal. Some furiously pulled out handfuls of hair and bristles, while others scraped the skin with knives. An experienced crew of six could clean a carcass in 20 seconds!

Three luggers then carried the carcass to the next station and hung it on a hook for the gutter, who removed its entrails and let them drop to the floor, which was covered in sawdust to absorb the blood and other body fluids.

> Once cleaned and gutted, the carcass was hauled to the cooling room, which was often little more than a well-ventilated section of the warehouse into which the freezing-cold winter wind penetrated. It remained there for twenty-four hours. When it was thoroughly chilled, a cutter severed the head with a cleaver; chopped off the feet, legs, and knee joints; split the carcass; and cut up the balance into hams, shoulders and "middles." . . . A four-hundred-pound hog usually was reduced to two hundred pounds of pork and forty pounds of lard. Blood-soaked sawdust, entrails, and other unwanted body parts were swept up at the end of the day and dumped into the Ohio River. (Skaggs 1986:39)

Cuts of pork were rubbed with salt and soaked in vats of brine or vinegar over the course of several days. Meat had to be carefully cooled before it was placed in the pickling mixture, otherwise the vinegar fermented and the meat could develop botulism. Meat inspection was purely voluntary and conducted by company workers.

A visitor to Cincinnati in December 1851 wrote with admiration that the city was

> crowded almost to suffocation, with droves of hogs, and draymen employed in delivering the barreled pork on board of steamers. Some 1,500 laborers are employed in the business from six to eight weeks, and in many cases it is kept in full operation both day and night, including Sundays, from the beginning to the completion of the season. (cited in Clemen 1923:97)

Pork was shipped to the Caribbean and Europe, accounting for 10 percent of America's foreign trade by the late 1870s. This market collapsed in 1880, when several European countries banned U.S. pork imports for fear American pork contained the parasitic nematode that causes trichinosis. Exports only resumed when the federal government introduced meat inspection in 1890 for meat intended for export. It would be another decade before federal inspection was required for meat sold to Americans.

Chicago replaced Cincinnati as America's meatpacking capital during the Civil War. Railroads radiating from the city linked it to the emerging Corn Belt, where more and more hogs were raised, and allowed their speedy shipment to the city's stockyards and slaughterhouses (Clemen 1923; Skaggs 1986). For nearly a century thereafter, Chicago remained, in Carl Sandburg's (1916) words:

> Hog Butcher for the World,
> Tool Maker, Stasher of Wheat,
> Player with Railroads and the Nation's Freight Handler,
> Stormy, husky, brawling,
> City of the Big Shoulders.

HOG HEAVEN OR HELL?

The Corn Belt extends from Ohio to eastern Nebraska. Its highly productive soils, reliable rainfall, and bountiful supplies of corn made it the center of hog production in the United States from the second half of the nineteenth century until the latter part of the twentieth. Raising hogs was until recently viewed as a relatively easy way for farmers to obtain cash with minimal investment, and hogs earned the nickname of "mortgage burner" (Strange & Hassebrook 1981).

The typical Corn Belt hog farm in 1976 averaged 320 acres, met 75 percent of its feed requirements, and produced 650 slaughter hogs. The operator and family members provided most of the labor. Animal waste was collected on site and spread as a fertilizer on crops and pasture (Van Arsdall & Gilliam 1979) Twenty-five years later, most of these farms have disappeared, to be replaced by large confinement operations producing hogs under contract to transnational processing firms. And hog production has dispersed from Corn Belt states to North Carolina, Oklahoma, and Utah (Drabenstott 1998).

Antibiotics have reduced hog vulnerability to disease and allowed them to be raised in climate-controlled buildings with automated feeding and manure systems. Confinement facilities require substantial capital investments on the part of growers, but mechanization allows many more animals to be raised with fewer workers. Proponents of this method of pork production argue that the system is driven by consumer preference for a uniform low-cost product. Factory farms meet this demand with their low labor costs and by supplying hogs from the same genetic stock using uniform feeding practices.

Critics charge that the supposed superior feed conversion made possible by antibiotics, nutritional supplements, and climate-controlled facilities have, in fact, been offset by the "stress" hogs experience in confinement, which, in turn, leads to lower feed conversion and weight gain. Newborn piglets suffer higher mortality in large operations than on traditional farms, a difference that has been attributed to the lack of individual attention provided in hog "factories" (Strange & Hassebrook 1981). Moreover, the displacement of family hog farms by confinement operations has a disastrous impact on rural economies. Studies conducted in Missouri indicate that a $5 million investment in contract production would generate 40–50 new jobs but displace nearly three times that number of independent hog producers (Ikerd 1998). With fewer farmers, there are fewer persons to support local businesses—and large-scale hog contract operators purchase inputs from outside the local region.

This transition from family farming to corporate hog raising is most evident in North Carolina, which pioneered the industrial model of hog growing. Its fivefold increase in hog production between 1982 and 1997 catapulted North Carolina into second place behind Iowa (see Table 4.1). But as the number of hogs in North Carolina leapt from 2 million to 9.6 million, its number of hog farms plummeted.

The state's rapid assent in hog production has been attributed to a combination of "governmental, entrepreneurial and local market factors" (Foruseth 1997:395). As early as 1960, the North Carolina Department of Agriculture and North Carolina State University identified swine production as a desirable replacement for tobacco as a cash crop. To that end, state government provided funds for swine research while the extension service touted the benefits of hog raising and helped farmers become established in the industry. The state legislature enacted tax incentives for the pork industry and provided a friendly regulatory environment. Hog farms were exempt from local zoning and minimum-wage regulations, while workers were banned from organizing unions. Wendell Murphy followed the lead of the poultry industry and used the contract method of raising hogs to become the largest hog producer in the United States (he has since been bought out by Smithfield Farms). North Carolina farmers were already familiar with contract poultry production, and financial and technical support from state agencies provided further incentive. Finally, the mild winter climate of southeastern North Carolina provides an advantage in terms of feed conversion: 8–16 ounces *less* feed is required to produce a pound of gain in North Carolina than in the Midwest (Foruseth 1997).

The average hog produces about 1.5 tons of solid manure and 5,270 gallons of liquid manure each year—2.5 times that of the average human (Grey 2000b:170; Alberta Agriculture 2000). The industry's solution to this dilemma has been to pump manure slurry from underneath confinement facilities and store it in waste lagoons, which use plastic liners to prevent seepage. Water in the manure evaporates and bacterial action breaks down the remaining material to make it safe for land disposal. Typically, manure is applied to fields prior to the growing season. If it is applied above the nutrient absorption rates of soils and crops, runoff into waterways and groundwater pollution occurs. Surplus manure in hundreds of U.S. counties has led to public efforts to curtail livestock expansion (Haley, Jones, & Southard 1998).

Lagoons threaten groundwater, and the odor they produce also affects the health of those who work and live around them. Airborne emissions from hog lagoons include ammonia, hydrogen sulfide, hundreds of volatile organic compounds, dust, and endotoxins that cause respiratory dysfunction in workers in hog-confinement facilities (Donham 1990, 1998). Neighbors of large swine facilities suffer elevated rates of tension, anger, fatigue, headaches, respiratory problems, eye irritation, nausea, sore throat, runny nose, and diarrhea (Schiffman et al. 1995; Thu et al. 1997; Wing & Wolf 2000).

TABLE 4.1 STRUCTURE OF NORTH CAROLINA
HOG FARMING, 1982 AND 1997

Inventory	1982		1997	
	Number of Farms	Percent of Hogs	Number of Farms	Percent of Hogs
1–24	6,548	2.5	944	0.1
25–49	1,513	2.5	170	0.1
50–99	1,088	3.6	125	0.1
100–199	716	4.6	72	0.1
200–499	701	10.3	77	0.2
500–999	366	11.9	132	1.0
1,000 or more	458	64.6	1,466	98.4
Total	11,390	100.0	2,986	100.0

Sources: U.S. Bureau of the Census, 1984, *1982 Census of Agriculture, North Carolina,* Washington, DC:
U.S. Government Printing Office. U.S. Department of Agriculture, National Agricultural Statistics Service, 1999, *1997
Census of Agriculture, North Carolina,* Washington, DC: U.S. Government Printing Office.

Lana and Barry Love, Alberta farmers who live about a mile from a proposed 24,000-feeder hog operation, speak for many who live near hog barns:

> We raised pigs a few years ago. We drive by barns currently in production in this County and let me tell you pigs stink. . . . Don't tell us we won't smell those barns where we live. I don't want to have to spend the rest of my life in the house because I can't stand the smell of our own backyard. This stench will be with us 24 hours a day, seven days a week all year long. (Subdivision and Development Board Appeal Hearing, Flagstaff County, Alberta, October 19, 2000. See Chapter 9 for a detailed discussion of this hearing.)

A detailed analysis of 2,514 swine-confinement facilities in North Carolina found they were disproportionately located in poor, nonwhite communities that are dependent on local wells for their household water supply. These areas also had the highest disease rates and least access to health care in the state, which raised concerns that the poor and people of color bear a disproportionate burden of pollution (Wing et al. 2000).

In response to widespread concern about the industry's threats to groundwater and public health, North Carolina imposed a statewide moratorium on new or expanding hog operations in 1997. Exempted from this moratorium, however, were those operations that did not use lagoons for waste storage.

Two years later Hurricane Floyd struck North Carolina—and the shit literally hit the fan! Flood waters overran hundreds of hog farms, inundated at least 46 waste lagoons, causing some to break and threaten drinking water and aquatic ecosystems. Subsequent water quality tests of wells in affected areas found fecal coliform bacteria levels significantly above average. Ammonia levels in the Neuse River were two orders of magnitude higher than the year before.

This latest assault on the environment led to an agreement between state government and Smithfield Farms, North Carolina's largest pork producer, that requires the company to fund research into "environmentally superior technologies" for manure disposal. Smithfield must contribute $15 million for research and $50 million for cleanup of abandoned waste lagoons. Growers producing hogs under contract to Smithfield are also required to convert their facilities to the new technology within 3 years of its availability (Taylor 2001). Two years after the agreement was signed, the various alternative technologies to be evaluated are in different stages of development, which suggests that it will be some time before the lagoon system is replaced.

Confronted by higher operational costs and growing opposition from local residents in densely settled areas of North America, the pork industry has gone in search of greener pastures.

MISS PIGGY'S NEW FRONTIERS

O, Canada

A 1998 study of the cost of hog production in North America and selected European and South American countries found that the lowest costs per 100 kilograms of pork produced were in Canada's eastern prairie provinces of Manitoba and Saskatchewan (Martin, Kruja, & Alexiou 1998). Part of the region's comparative advantage stems from a 1995 decision to eliminate a federal transportation subsidy for grain farmers. The so-called Crow rate was established in 1897 to underwrite the cost to farmers for shipping their grain to Canadian ports. But in the early 1990s, a large federal budget deficit, concerns that the subsidy discouraged the establishment of regional processing facilities, and fears that it contravened some of the terms of the North American Free Trade Agreement, led the Canadian government to remove it. Farmers must now pay the full cost of shipping grain by rail, so they have looked to sell their grain to local livestock producers (Ramsey & Everitt 2001).

Manitoba was the first prairie province to see the economic potential of a livestock industry based on local feed grains. In late 1995, the province's agriculture minister proposed doubling Manitoba's pork production in five years, hoping to replace Ontario and Quebec as the capital of Canada's hog industry. He proposed eliminating the province's "single desk" system of selling and replacing it with an "open market" system that would allow processors to contract with individual producers to supply them with hogs. Under the old single desk system, there was only one buyer of live hogs in the province, Manitoba Pork, which set the price for hogs and allocated them to slaughterhouses. Farmers were guaranteed the same price for the same quality of animal, regardless of how many they sold. But with processors able to negotiate individual contracts, producers who can supply large numbers of hogs have a much greater advantage than smaller producers in negotiating price (Boyens 2001).

Opponents of open markets cited North Carolina to illustrate the negative impact of contract growing on small producers. Between 1982 and 1997, the number of North Carolina farms with fewer than 100 hogs declined from 9,149 to 1,239, while farms with over 1,000 animals more than tripled (see Table 4.1 on p. 59). Despite this concern, Manitoba Pork's monopoly was eliminated in 1996, and processors have found it easier and cheaper to contract with large producers. Not surprisingly, the number of small producers has declined: in 1991 there were 1,348 farms with 77 hogs or less; by 2000 this number had dropped to 381. Over the same period the number of operations with 4,685 or more hogs almost doubled (Table 4.2).

TABLE 4.2 NUMBER OF MANITOBA HOG FARMS
BY SIZE OF HERD, 1991, 1996, AND 2000

Size of Herd	1991	1996	2000*
1–77	1,348	665	381
78–272	661	437	250
273–527	433	360	180
528–1,127	324	294	251
1,128–2,652	101	166	188
2,653–4,684	52	77	91
4,685 & Over	50	96	99
Total	2,969	2,095	1,440

*Estimate based upon July 1 livestock survey

Source: Statistics Canada, *Census of Agriculture*, various years, Ottawa.

The increase in large producers combined to boost Manitoba's share of Canadian hog production from 17 to 22 percent in only 5 years. This expansion, combined with the removal of single desk selling, enabled the province to attract a state-of-the-art pork processing plant to Brandon (1996 pop. 39,175), 120 miles west of Winnipeg. Maple Leaf Foods, a Canadian transnational food processing company, paid $1.00 for the 12-acre site and received $12 million (Canadian) from the city and province to construct a wastewater treatment facility for its new plant, which opened in the fall of 1999. Fully operational at the end of 2002, the plant employs over 2,000 people and has the capacity to slaughter 15,000 hogs a day.

The provincial government was so anxious to get the Maple Leaf plant up and running that it waived Clean Environment Commission hearings on the impact of its effluent on the Assiniboine River—a violation of provincial law. Concerned citizens were left to organize their own hearings on the "environmental, economic, social and public health aspects surrounding industrial scale hog production and processing" before an independent chair and six commissioners (Ramsey & Everitt 2001). For two-and-a-half days the authors of this volume and numerous others testified on the social and economic changes that accompany large meat processing facilities and the environmental impact of industrial hog raising. Our testimony was based upon the recent experience of Guymon, Oklahoma.

Oh, Oklahoma!

In 1992, Seaboard Corporation, a transnational agribusiness and transportation company and the third largest hog producer in the United States, selected the Oklahoma Panhandle town of Guymon as the site of a pork processing plant that would eventually slaughter 16,000 hogs a day. Guymon lured Seaboard much as Brandon had Maple Leaf, with land, tax incentives and abatements, and a sales tax to help pay for the plant. The state of Oklahoma also paid for highway improvements.

In return Seaboard promised to pay $175,000 a year to the school system for 25 years. It also promised to create jobs—and it has. According to company figures, 2,800 workers were employed by September 1998, when the plant was fully operational.

Don Stull

Figure 4.3 Hog barns in Meade County, Kansas, where animals are "grown out" for Seaboard's pork processing plant in Guymon, Oklahoma.

Salaries ranged from $15,000 to more than $70,000. But 91 percent of workers made $25,000 or less, while only 1 percent made $50,000 or more.

At the time of the company's announcement, the region proclaimed itself the "cattle feeding capital of the World," and the five counties that make up the Oklahoma Panhandle were home to a mere 8,000 hogs. There weren't many hogs, but there weren't many people, either. In 1990, just over 16,000 souls were scattered across the 2,000 square miles of Texas County, which would soon become home to Seaboard's Guymon plant. Only 3,500 occupied the 1,800 square miles of neighboring Cimarron County. Such a low population density promised to reduce the number of potential complaints from neighbors of the confinement facilities that would be needed to supply the plant. The Oklahoma Panhandle, once known as No Man's Land, also offered a "mild" climate for good feed conversion, the ready availability of feed grains, sandy soils, and plenty of land for manure disposal.

When Seaboard announced its plans in 1992, there were 39 farms raising a few thousand hogs in Texas County. And within weeks of the announcement company officials were dispatched to the region to preach the gospel of contract hog raising. A farmer or rancher would be expected to construct three confinement buildings at a cost of about $500,000 and sign a 10-year production contract. Hitch Enterprises, a major cattle feeder in the region, contracted to raise hogs for Seaboard, but there were few other converts, and Seaboard was forced to buy land and raise its own hogs for the plant. Vall, Inc., a Spanish-owned agribusiness company, also invested in the region. By 1997, these three firms were producing the bulk of the 900,000 hogs raised in Texas County (Constance & Bonanno 1999). Big Pig had invaded "the cattle feeding capital of the World."

TABLE 4.3 GUYMON'S DECADE OF CHANGE, 1990–2000

Indicator	1990	2000
Population	7,803	10,472
Percent Latino	12.0	38.0
Median age	33.7	30.0
Percent foreign born	1.4	22.2
Percent of persons 5 years and over who speak a language other than English	8.6	32.8
Percent of families below poverty level	8.3	10.1
Percent of population 25 years and over with high school education or higher	75.0	67.6

Sources: U.S. Bureau of the Census, 1993, *1990 Census of Population, Oklahoma,* Washington, DC: U.S. Government Printing Office. U.S. Bureau of the Census, 2002, *2000 Census of Population, Oklahoma,* Washington, DC: U.S. Government Printing Office.

Most of the 2,800 jobs Seaboard promised—and delivered—to Guymon and the surrounding area did not go to Oklahomans. Nine of 10 workers at the Seaboard plant are Hispanics, most from Mexico and elsewhere in Latin America. One in 3 are women.

Guymon's population grew by more than one-third from 1990 to 2000, up from 7,803 to 10,472. Even more striking, the Hispanic share of the town's population tripled—from 12 percent to 38 percent (Table 4.3).

High employee turnover is endemic to meatpacking, and three years after the plant opened, yearly turnover stood at 98 percent. That turnover was also felt in the community: 1997 witnessed 2,021 new residential utility connections in Guymon, but by April 1998, only one-third were still active. Guymon's public schools were experiencing a "mobility rate" well in excess of 25 percent (Stull 1999). With 9 out of every 10 jobs it created paying less than $25,000 a year, after the plant opened the number of families living in poverty actually increased. Guymon followed the lead of Garden City and established a homeless shelter—the Oaks of Mamre—that offers temporary housing and two meals a day for low-income persons seeking work in the Guymon area. The Oaks, as it is called, is in an old downtown hotel and was purchased with the assistance of grants from Seaboard and the federal government. Its operating budget is dependent upon grants and donations from individuals, churches, and local businesses.

Guymon has had a much harder time providing permanent housing for Seaboard's workers. Several mobile home parks have opened, and apartment complexes and single-family homes have been constructed. But according to a housing survey completed in October 1997, the increase in new housing units in Guymon—9.3 percent from 1990 through 1997—was "well below the population growth rate during the same period," and occupancy rates for rental units approached 100 percent. New homes averaged around $140,000, while the average resale for a home in Guymon was around $55,000. Nine of 10 Seaboard employees and 1 of 2 households in Texas County earned less than $25,000 annually, placing home ownership effectively out of their reach. Compounding this problem, rents increased $20–$50 per unit per year from 1994 to 1997 (Ard 1998).

As a result, many of those who have come to Guymon seeking work simply cannot afford to live there, given prevailing wages, rents, damage deposits, and down payments. Although vacancies do exist, demand for modestly priced rental units exceeds supply, forcing a substantial number of workers either to commute or live in overcrowded conditions in Guymon.

Seaboard offers health insurance after 90 days, but given its high turnover, many employees never qualify for insurance, and others do not insure family members because they cannot afford the monthly payments. Working conditions, combined with a workforce that is impoverished, poorly educated, and transient, strains the health care system. By the late 1990s, Guymon's hospital was experiencing increased demand for obstetrics and emergency room treatment, an increase in uncollected bills, and a drop in net income. Effective service provision was also hampered by a shortage of Spanish-speaking service providers (Stull 1999).

Before Seaboard came to town, Guymon's schools suffered from declining enrollment. Since the plant opened, enrollment has increased by 12 percent. At the same time, the number of students eligible for the federal government's free or reduced-price lunch program jumped from 41 to 51 percent. Students requiring instruction in English as a second language (ESL) soared from 7 in 1991 to more than 220 in 1999, and by the 2000–2001 academic year Hispanics accounted for 45 percent of the student body, up from 29 percent 5 years earlier. During this time, the district's graduation rate dropped from 83 to 72 percent (Education Oversight Board, Office of Accountability, various years).

Crime has also increased in Guymon, which is to be expected in any rapidly growing community. Calls for service rose 30 percent from 1994 to 1999, accidents increased 34 percent, and total arrests went up by 38 percent. In response the police force added five additional officers. The police chief acknowledges that many crimes go unreported (Stull 1999).

With Seaboard's arrival, Guymon joined a growing number of similar communities—Dodge City, Garden City, and Liberal in Kansas; Lexington and Grand Island in Nebraska; Storm Lake and Columbus Junction in Iowa; Mayfield and Sebree in Kentucky; Brooks in Alberta; and Brandon in Manitoba. Despite the great distance and divergent historical and cultural traditions that separate them, these communities face similar challenges: growth, often rapid and explosive; population mobility; dramatic increases in cultural and linguistic diversity; escalating crime, health, and social problems; strains on infrastructure and social services. These challenges stem from a common source: the meat and poultry processing industry's hunger for workers.

5/The Human Price
of Our Meat

THE JUNGLE

Most people think little about where the meat on their dinner table comes from, and even less about the industry that puts it there. For those who do, awareness of meatpacking usually begins—and ends—with *The Jungle,* Upton Sinclair's landmark novel about the squalid conditions in which immigrants lived and worked in Chicago's packinghouses at the beginning of the twentieth century. Thanks to countless high school literature teachers, *The Jungle* has become, and no doubt will remain, the icon for every writer who wants to evoke the ills of this bloodiest of businesses.

Labor historians are fond of pointing out that the February 1906 publication of *The Jungle,* with its revelations of wretched working conditions, filthy packinghouses, and tainted meat, prompted enactment of the Meat Inspection Act and the Pure Food and Drug Act, both signed into law by President Theodore Roosevelt on the same day, June 30, 1906 (Barrett 1987:1; DeGruson 1988:xvi; Skaggs 1986). They are equally fond of quoting Sinclair's (1962:126) famous lament: "I aimed at the public's heart and by accident I hit it in the stomach."

In the summer of 1980, a young man pulled his truck up to the library at Pittsburg State University in southeast Kansas. He went inside and fetched Gene DeGruson, the university's curator of rare books, to come take a look at the rotting, mildewed papers in the bed of his pickup. The young man had been hired to clean out the cellar of a farmhouse in nearby Girard. When he noticed Upton Sinclair's name on several letters, he decided to see if the library wanted the papers before he took them to the dump.

> Too fragile to handle, the papers were covered with brightly colored mold, dyed purple by typewriter ribbon and red and green by inks used to write and print the documents. The fetid mass eventually proved to be over a thousand business records, inner office memos, and correspondence of the *Appeal to Reason,* once the nation's leading Socialist newspaper. (DeGruson 1988:xiii)

Figure 5.1 Don Stull and Michael Broadway stand under the arch that once served as the entrance to Chicago's Union Stock Yards. The authors journeyed to see what remained of the Yards in August 2002, as they were completing this book. The photo was taken by a friendly passerby.

In September 1904, *Appeal to Reason* editors selected 26-year-old Upton Sinclair to investigate the working conditions in Chicago's packinghouses. With $500 and a plot outline from the paper's editors, Sinclair traveled to Chicago in October (ibid.:xiv–xv). For 7 weeks, he conducted what anthropologists would today call participant observation among packinghouse workers and their families: "Dressed in overalls and carrying a metal lunch pail, Sinclair haunted the killing floors and canning rooms, the saloons and tenements of Packingtown" (Barrett 1987:1).

Appeal to Reason financed Sinclair's research in exchange for the rights to publish his work as a serial. The first installment appeared in February 1905, and by October of that year 28 installments had been published, but the final chapters were discontinued because of disagreements with Sinclair and a disappointing response from subscribers. However, in January 1906, Sinclair signed a contract with Doubleday, Page & Company, which published *The Jungle* the following month.

Despite his protestations that he wished the novel published as he had written it, revision was drastic. It reduced the work from thirty-six chapters and a conclusion to thirty-one chapters and a conclusion. The greatest number of deletions was passages pertaining to Socialism, followed closely by paragraphs dealing with what Sinclair termed the Press Trust, prostitution, and derogatory comments about "big business," especially those concerning the self-made man or "captain of industry." Paragraphs were added to emphasize the malpractices of the meatpacking industry. . . . Carefully eliminated were . . . statements containing Socialist sentiment. . . . The most curious deletions are those of passages which made the immigrant workers more empathetic or less alien to the reader. (DeGruson 1988:xxiv–xxv)

For all its sanitizing, *The Jungle* was an instant best-seller and remains today a powerful indictment of the evils of capitalism, industrialization, corporate greed, and exploitation of working men and women.[1] While his novel failed to inspire labor reforms, as Sinclair had hoped it would, it did reveal in stark detail the dire circumstances under which working men and women toiled and lived at the turn of the twentieth century. It remains the benchmark against which the meat and poultry industry is measured.

Despite the intervening century, with its dizzying array of technological advances and dramatic social reforms, meat and poultry processing at the beginning of the twenty-first century is regrettably reminiscent of what Sinclair described at the beginning of the twentieth. The Big Five of the beef trust are gone, only to be replaced by a new Big Four—Tyson, ConAgra, Excel, and Smithfield. Swift and Armour vertically integrated meatpacking, from ownership of animals and other raw materials through production to distribution of meat products, in the 1890s; three-quarters of a century later Tyson and Perdue accomplished this feat in the poultry industry (Barrett 1987:15).

Profit margins were no higher in the nineteenth century than in the twenty-first, and the packers still make much of their profit from the sale of byproducts. Hoof, horn, blood, bone, gland, and hair are still turned into glue and soap, tallow and leather goods, but to that list we can now add deodorants and detergents, marshmallows and mayonnaise, asphalt and brake fluid, shampoo and shaving cream, cigarette papers and matches, Sheetrock and wallpaper, and a host of pharmaceuticals, including insulin, amino acids, blood plasma, cortisone, estrogen, surgical sutures, and vitamin B-12 (Moore 1984; Kansas Beef Council, n.d.; Zane 1996).

The industry's processing plants abandoned Chicago and other major cities, which in Sinclair's day teamed with immigrants desperate for work, for small towns in the Midwest and South. But immigrants still flock to packinghouse gates, only now they speak Spanish, Vietnamese, Marshallese, or K'iche Mayan instead of German, Polish, Czech, or Lithuanian.

Multistoried plants that slaughtered cattle, sheep, and hogs have been torn down, along with the stockyards that once supplied them, to be replaced by single-story plants that kill and process one species only. No matter, they are still factories that mass produce meat. This should come as no surprise. It was, after all, from the Chicago packinghouses that Henry Ford got the idea for the automotive assembly line. They were the first American workplaces to fragment tasks, deskill work, and mechanically regulate output with a continuous-flow production process (Horowitz 1997:17).

Although Sinclair would certainly recognize much of what goes on in a modern beefpacking plant, he would also marvel at the dramatic modernization of the disassembly line. Steers still enter the killfloor through the knock box, where they are rendered unconscious before slaughter. But in the 1950s, the knocking hammer gave

Figure 5.2 An abandoned packinghouse in Chicago's stockyard district, 2002

way to the cylindrical captive-bolt stun gun, which propels a steel bolt into the skull upon impact with the animal's forehead.

No longer is the animal laid out on the floor as workers scurry around the carcass performing their assigned jobs, then hoist it onto an overhead trolley and move it down the line for another work crew to lower, do its duties, raise, and send on its way. The Can-Pak system, invented in Canada in the early 1950s, allowed "on-the-rail dressing." Standing underneath the knocker, the shackler wraps a hook and chain around the animal's left hind pastern (ankle), and as the animal is stunned it falls forward and down, to hang upside down by one leg. It then moves continuously along an overhead rail past stationary workers who stick, bleed, skin, saw, gut, and split the steer into a carcass, from stations positioned to maximize their specific task (MacLachlan 2001:172; Stull 1994).

Moving platforms, mechanical hide pullers, hydraulic skinners and hock cutters, electric band saws and skinning knives have combined with on-the-rail dressing to produce a higher quality carcass and make work on the killfloor less difficult and dangerous. They have also decreased by almost half "carcass throughput," the elapsed time from when the steer is knocked until its carcass, now gutted, skinned, and split into "swinging sides" enters the "hot box," where it cools for about 24 hours before entering the "cooler," there to be assigned a yield and quality grade by USDA meat inspectors.[2]

From the cooler, the carcass goes to fabrication, or processing, where workers wielding razor-sharp knives break it down into ribs, loins, and rounds; shrink-wrap these "subprimal cuts"; then box them for shipment to supermarkets. At the world's largest beef plant outside Garden City, Kansas, the trip from the knock box to the hot box takes a mere 42 minutes. And only 2 or 3 days pass from the time a steer is wheeled up to the plant's holding pens in a bull wagon until it leaves in a box in the back of a refrigerated semi (MacLachlan 2001:172; Stull 1994:62). (See Figure 5.3, p. 70–71.)

By mechanically moving the carcass along a "chain" where stationary workers disassemble it, the time lost and the dangers associated with walking around carcasses on bloody floors are diminished. In mechanizing and modernizing the process, the work was also simplified—or deskilled—and worker productivity has substantially increased. In 1952, one man-hour of labor produced 51 pounds of meat; 25 years later that same hour accounted for 155 pounds (Horowitz 1997:253).

As worker productivity rose, so did company profits. On-the-rail dressing reduced labor costs and boxed beef saved on transportation costs, since unusable bones and scraps were eliminated at the plant and could be converted into salable byproducts. Along with reorganization of work on the kill and fabrication floors came relocation of the plants where this work is done. As the old Big Five closed their plants in the stockyard districts of Chicago, Kansas City, and Omaha, a new Big Four were building plants and giving birth to new Packingtowns in remote places like Garden City, Kansas; Guymon, Oklahoma; and Brooks, Alberta, Canada. While the packers were abandoning the cities they had called home for a century, they were also crushing the unions and driving down the wages and benefits for which workers had struggled so long.

"ON TO ORGANIZE"

Horrendous working conditions and low wages made meatpacking workers ripe for union organizing. Chicago cattle butchers organized the first meatpacking union in 1878. For the remainder of the nineteenth century and into the early twentieth, meatpacking was the most strike-prone of all American industries (Barrett 1987:119). Campaigning for the 8-hour day, the Knights of Labor, which represented the majority of organized workers in the United States in the 1880s, focused its organizing campaign on meatpacking. It won the 8-hour day in 1886, then promptly lost it in the public backlash against organized labor in the aftermath of the Haymarket Riot in Chicago that same spring (Skaggs 1986:111; Barrett 1987:121–125).

The beginning of effective unionization in meatpacking can be traced to the founding of the Amalgamated Meat Cutters and Butcher Workmen of North America in 1897. By 1904, it was able to mobilize 50,000 workers in a nationwide strike for higher wages. With an ample supply of meat in their coolers and an economic recession fueling unemployment, the packers broke the strike, and union membership plummeted. It was Upton Sinclair's account of this strike in *The Jungle* that immortalized the struggle of working men and women for fair wages and decent working conditions. Striking workers were forced back to work on company terms and at lower wages than before the strike, but working conditions and wages did begin to improve, and the ranks of the union rose once again (Skaggs 1986:113–118).

Extreme division of labor on the disassembly lines and deskilling provided employment opportunities for women, who occupied the bottom of the pay scale in meatpacking. Their share of the workforce rose from 1.6 percent of those employed in Chicago's packinghouses in 1890 to 12.6 percent in 1920 (Barrett 1987:52). Despite the growing presence of women in the packinghouses, it was nationality, race, and language that marked plant floors. Bohemians and Slovaks, Germans, Lithuanians, Poles, and native-born whites each made up at least 10 percent of Chicago's packinghouse employees in 1909 (ibid.:39).

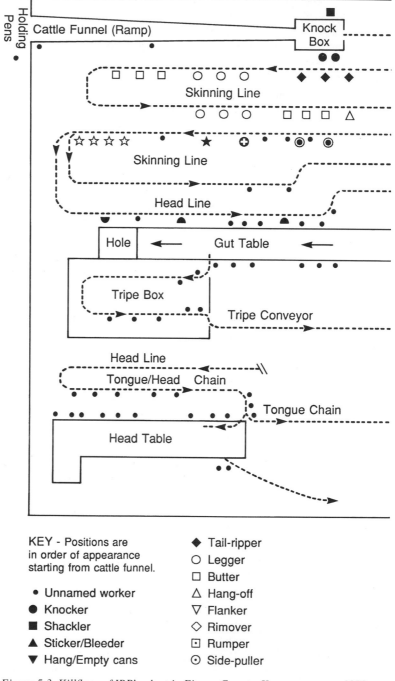

Figure 5.3 Killfloor of IBP's plant in Finney County, Kansas, summer 1989

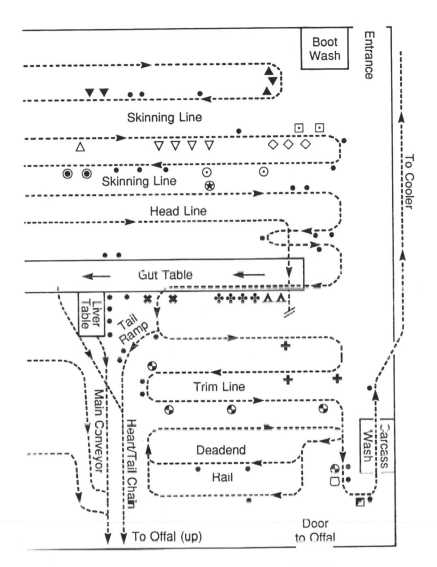

Boot Wash

Entrance

To Cooler

Skinning Line

Skinning Line

Head Line

Gut Table

Liver Table

Tail Ramp

Main Conveyor

Heart/Tail Chain

Trim Line

Deadend

Rail

Carcass Wash

To Offal (up)

Door to Offal

◉ Tie-down
⊕ Down-puller
★ Number carcass/head
☆ Head-dropper
▼ Horn-sawer
▲ Tongue-dropper
⊛ Brisket-sawer
▲ Pregutter

♣ Gutter
✖ USDA inspector
✚ Back-splitter
⊙ Trimmer
� USDA stamp
▨ Scale operator

The structure of the meatpacking industry and its production methods, the diverse composition of its workforce, and the militancy of union stalwarts made packinghouses ripe for unionizing—and for periodic and often bitter strikes (Horowitz 1997:3–5). Southern blacks and other "new" groups entered meatpacking as strikebreakers. Management and unions competed for the newcomers' loyalty, but common grievances and ethnically mixed work crews helped organizers transcend gender, ethnic, and national divides to build strong unions (Barrett 1987:273–278).[3]

The Packers and Stockyards Act of 1921 forestalled vertical integration by forbidding packer ownership of stockyards and apportionment of supplies of livestock between companies. The National Labor Relations (Wagner) Act of 1935 established the National Labor Relations Board (NLRB), guaranteed workers the legal right to organize and bargain collectively, and outlawed unfair labor practices, such as blacklisting. Divided between the Amalgamated Meat Cutters and Butcher Workmen of North America, who favored negotiating with the packers, and the Packing House Workers Organizing Council (PWOC), who would rather strike, meatpacking workers struggled for the 8-hour day, the 40-hour work week, and time-and-a-half overtime pay. By the close of World War II in 1945, collective bargaining had been accepted in the industry, and some companies had signed "master contracts" that covered workers in all their plants (Skaggs 1986:159–165). But the Labor Management Relations (Taft-Hartley) Act of 1947 greatly restricted union ability to challenge management. Under its provisions, the president was empowered to suspend strikes for 80 days in the interest of national health and safety; unions were required to bargain with management; closed shops, sympathy strikes, and secondary boycotts were outlawed; states were permitted to ban union shops; and, to gain access to the NLRB, union officials were required to sign affidavits that they were not members of the Communist Party (Skaggs 1986:199–200; Horowitz 1997:181).

Union power peaked in the decade following World War II, as successful strikes and joint efforts by United Packinghouse Workers of America (UPWA) and Amalgamated Meat Cutters led to master contracts with Armour and Swift that granted wage increases and better working conditions. As it gained concessions from management, the UPWA also fought for civil rights, opposing discrimination in hiring, as well as in housing, retail businesses, entertainment, and public facilities (Horowitz 1997: Chap. 9).

Organizing efforts in the poultry industry lagged behind those in meatpacking: it is a newer industry; its plants were located in the rural South, long known for antiunion sentiment; and it drew heavily on African American women to work its lines. In June 1953, poultry workers in the East Texas town of Center asked the Amalgamated Meat Cutters to help them organize. At the time, poultry workers were paid the minimum wage of 75 cents an hour, worked 10–11 hours a day in filthy conditions without overtime pay, and were denied grievance procedures, seniority, and paid holidays. Center's two poultry plants—one staffed by black workers, the other by whites—both voted to join the union. When the companies refused to negotiate in good faith, the Amalgamated Meat Cutters organized a national boycott of plant products, and the workers staged wildcat strikes.

At the time, less than a quarter of the poultry sold in the United States was federally inspected, and neither of the Center plants employed inspectors. With the support of its 500 locals and the endorsement of the AFL-CIO, the Amalgamated Meat Cutters organized a national campaign to mandate federal inspection of poultry.

Subsequent congressional hearings revealed that one-third of known cases of food poisoning could be traced to poultry. Despite opposition from the poultry industry and the U.S. Department of Agriculture, which oversees meat inspection, a poultry inspection bill eventually passed Congress. In August 1957, President Dwight Eisenhower signed the Poultry Products Inspection Act, which requires compulsory inspection of all poultry that crosses state lines or is sold overseas.

And what of the striking workers? Eastex, the plant that employed only black workers, settled after 11 months, agreeing to wage increases, time-and-a-half overtime pay, three paid holidays and vacations, a grievance procedure, and reinstatement of strikers. Eastex was subsequently sold to Holly Farms, which was later bought by Tyson. In 1958, three years after the Eastex strike ended, Amalgamated called off the strike against Denison, the all-white plant. By then Amalgamated's boycott had cost the company most of its markets, and it eventually went bankrupt (Green & McClellan 1985).

Union efforts won significant benefits for meatpacking workers. In 1960, for example, meatpacking wages were 15 percent *above* the average wage for manufacturing workers in the United States (Broadway 1995:25). But union victories were elusive and short lived. In that same year, financed by a loan of $300,000 from the Small Business Administration, Iowa Beef Packers opened its first plant. It was the opening shot in what came to be called the IBP Revolution, which would rapidly restructure meatpacking—and, as many have argued, make jungles once again of its killfloors and fabrication lines (Nunes 1999; Horowitz 1997; Stull 1994).

The transformation was sudden and complete. In the wake of mechanization and plant closings, 46,000 meatpacking workers lost their jobs between 1960 and 1990, even as jobs in poultry processing more than doubled. The United Packinghouse Workers of America and the Amalgamated Meat Cutters and Butcher Workmen merged in 1968, then merged with the Retail Clerks International Union in 1979 to form the United Food and Commercial Workers (UFCW), which represents meat, poultry, and grocery workers today. By the mid-1980s, master contracts were a thing of the past, and by 1990 wages in meatpacking had fallen to 20 percent *below* the average wage in manufacturing (Broadway 1995:24; Horowitz 1997:246).

Meatpacking unions did not give up without a fight. Strikes closed IBP's beef plant in Dakota City, Nebraska, four times between 1969 and 1984 (Skaggs 1986:204). In August 1985, UFCW Local P-9 went out on strike against Hormel's pork plant in Austin, Minnesota, over company demands for wage and benefit concessions. By the time it ended in defeat the following June, the Hormel strike had captured national attention (Hage & Klauda 1989; Green 1990). In December of that same year, IBP locked workers out of its Dakota City plant after they rejected demands for pay cuts and concessions. Giving in to IBP's demands the following July, the UFCW accepted a two-tiered wage scale that paid new workers 60 cents less per hour than continuing workers and assured substantial savings—and a significant competitive edge—for IBP (Horowitz 1997:273–274).

"IT DON'T PAY GREAT"

Industry critics say the meat and poultry industry has returned to the days of *The Jungle*. Industry spokespersons scoff at what they say are simplistic comparisons and point to "remarkable progress" in ergonomics and injury reduction, food quality and safety (Nunes 1999). And no one can deny many of its transformations—most evident in poultry processing, which has led the way in mechanization and further processing of its basic product. The shorter interval time between generations and the controlled environment in which chickens are raised enable the poultry industry to select for specific genetic traits and improve upon them (Nunes 1995:38). These factors, and chickens' small and uniform size, have allowed poultry processors to replace many workers with machines. But, as Horowitz and Miller (1999:3) observe, chickens are not pretzels, and "despite the best efforts of the companies, the chicken remains an irregular natural product."

> In the "modern" processing plant, mechanical devices are extensively applied in a wide variety of cutting operations once performed by workers with knives. Separating a carcass into quarters, for example, is accomplished by machines which perform the necessary cutting operations. . . . But the chicken still needs to be inserted into the machines and positioned properly for the cuts to be applied in the right place. . . . Labor may have been deskilled, and the number of knife workers reduced, but the need for labor remains in the many positioning and transitional stages of the dismembering and cutting operations, as well as hand and eye tasks such as inspecting and separating kidneys and hearts. The increasingly important deboning operations remain the province of relatively skilled workers equipped with sharp shears and knives, rather than machines. (ibid.)

Machines may now work alongside people on meat and poultry lines, but jobs on the line remain tedious, monotonous, and risky. And workers who fill them rarely earn a "living wage," one sufficient to feed, clothe, and shelter themselves and their families. Table 5.1 presents recent hourly wage rates for line workers in leading beef, pork, and poultry plants.

In 2000, base wages for line workers at the IBP and ConAgra beef plants in southwest Kansas started at $9.00 an hour. Gross annual pay for someone working a full 52 weeks at 40 hours a week comes to $18,720. IBP's maximum hourly wage was not available, but the company said its line workers averaged $11.20 an hour at its Finney County plant, which comes to $23,296 per year (Cultural Relations Board, Garden City, Kansas 2001:14). For line workers at IBP's Lakeside Packers plant in Brooks, Alberta, hourly wages started at $9.25 (Canadian) and topped out after 18 months at $13.50 in processing and $14.40 in slaughter. Workers were also eligible for "skill premiums" ranging from $0.45 an hour for level-1 jobs to $1.85 for level-4 jobs (Lakeside Packers 2000:4). (Note: The Canadian dollar is worth only about two-thirds of its U.S. counterpart.)

In 1998, hourly wages at the Seaboard pork plant in Guymon, Oklahoma, ranged from $7.00 to $10.25—someone making the maximum hourly wage of $10.25 would realize $21,320 in gross annual wages (Stull 1999:2). The minimum base rate for Tyson production workers at the Robards, Kentucky, plant under the UFCW contract that expired on April 20, 2001, was $6.80, rising to $7.15 after 60 days and up to $7.75 after 12 months. This comes to a gross annual wage of $16,120 for a full-time worker after one year with the company (United Food and Commercial Workers 1997). Still, as one Tyson worker put it, "It don't pay great, but it's, well, down here it's one of the better paying jobs for a family."

Work on a meat or poultry line does indeed offer "some of the better paying jobs" in the surrounding areas, but such wages mean that the income of line workers in these plants, which pride themselves on being flagship facilities, are still below the

TABLE 5.1 HOURLY WAGES FOR MEAT AND POULTRY
WORKERS AT SELECTED NORTH AMERICAN PLANTS

Wages	Beginning Hourly Wage	Maximum Hourly Wage	Gross Annual Salary
IBP Beef, Finney Co., Kansas	$9.00	$11.20*	$18,720–$23,296
Seaboard Pork, Guymon, Oklahoma	$7.00	$10.25	$14,560–$21,320
Tyson Chicken, Robards, Kentucky	$6.80	$7.75	$14,144–$16,120
Lakeside Packers** Beef, Brooks, Alberta, Canada	$6.29	$9.80	$13,083–$20,384

Federal Assistance Eligibility (for Family of 4) in the United States, 2001

Medicaid	$17,650 ($8.49/hr.) or less
Federal Lunch Program	Free. $21,710 or less
	Reduced price: $30,895 or less

* IBP claims this is the average hourly wage for their workers.
** In U.S. dollars

Sources: Cultural Relations Board, Garden City, Kansas 2001:14; Stull 1999:2; United Food and Commercial Workers 1997; Lakeside Packers 2000:4.

levels required for one or more federal assistance programs. For example, in 2001 a family of four was eligible for Medicaid if its annual income was $17,650, which equates to an hourly wage of $8.49. A family of four was eligible for the federal free lunch program if its annual income was $21,710; for reduced-price lunch if its income was at or below $30,895. (See Table 5.1.) Not only are many eligible for federal health and school programs, but they also draw upon local charities and food banks to supplement their income. Thus, the industry offsets its costs of production and adds to the hidden cost of our "cheap food."

Reported occupational injury and illness peaked for meatpacking and poultry processing in 1990, then fell through the remainder of the decade, as they did for manufacturing in general (Table 5.2). Industry spokespersons credit advances in ergonomics—fitting the work to the worker—while others say that stiff fines for unsafe conditions and underreporting have forced the packers to improve conditions. The desire to hold workers' compensation costs in check has also been a factor. Nevertheless, the reported injury and illness rate for meatpacking was a staggering 26.7 per hundred full-time workers in 1999—three times above the average manufacturing rate. Though only half the rate for meatpacking, the rate for poultry processing was also significantly above the overall manufacturing rate.

ON THE LINE

Line supervisors and company nurses and doctors do all they can to hold down reported injuries. Take the case of Betty and Peggy (not their real names), who worked "presenting and trimming" on either side of the same USDA inspector on a poultry line in western Kentucky. As Betty described her job,

TABLE 5.2 OCCUPATIONAL INJURY
AND ILLNESS RATES FOR PRODUCTION WORKERS,
1975–1999 (SELECTED YEARS)

	Meatpacking	Poultry Processing	Manufacturing
1975	31.2	22.8	13.0
1980	33.5	22.1	12.2
1985	30.4	18.3	10.4
1990	42.4	26.9	13.2
1995	36.6	18.3	11.6
1999	26.7	14.3	9.2

Source: U.S. Department of Labor, Bureau of Labor Statistics, various years, *Occupational Injuries and Illness in the United States by Industry*, Washington, DC: U.S. Government Printing Office.

> The presenting is when you open up the bottom half of the chicken to present the guts for the USDA inspector. We reach in and we pull the guts out of them. The inspector looks at the guts, like the kidneys and things like that, to see if the chicken has a disease. And they call the birds according to what they see down into the cavity of the chicken. . . . And the trim person on the other side [of the inspector] makes the necessary marks or handles the chicken according to what the USDA says that is wrong with the bird. . . . You make different marks on, like, the chicken's back, the legs, ya know, for the people down at the end of the line to know what parts of the chicken to take off. (Stull interview, November 7, 1998)

One Sunday in October 1998, Betty and Peggy, who live 30 miles apart, each came down with severe nausea, cramping, and diarrhea. Peggy was "up all night long, hurtin'."

> I stayed on the toilet all night. I tried to call into work. I couldn't get no answer. I tried every number that I had to get ahold of someone. I couldn't get no answer. So when I went into work that morning and I went straight to that nurse's station, and I told 'em what was wrong with me. She gave me two pills to take for diarrhea, plus a tube of medicine for throwing up. I told her, "I'm not throwing up. I got blood in my stools. And I know that's not normal."
>
> And she said that everyone is coming down with a virus. So she gave me these two pills to take.
>
> "You don't think I need to see a doctor?" I said, "That's what I came in here for."
> She said, "Well, everyone is coming down with the virus. If you feel you need to go to the doctor after work, you can."
>
> So I had to go back out on that line and work in that chicken! (Stull interview, November, 9 1998)

Peggy, Betty, and four others on their line came down with what they were told was *E. coli*. By the time they were interviewed, three weeks later, Peggy's and Betty's gall bladders had been removed because of complications from their illnesses.

> I kept bleeding on that line all that day. The girls had to keep takin' my place. I had blood [running down] my leg, so that's when I come home and I had to go to the hospital. I was done dehydrated. The doctors don't understand why in the world they let me touch that meat down there, knowin' that I had diarrhea and had blood. And I told them, "I guess they didn't believe me." I didn't know what else to say. And I've been off ever since that day. And they [the company] refused to pay any kind of medical bills to me or anything.

I asked them if I could sign up for workmen's comp, and they refused to take [my application]. But the fourth day, some woman, she heard me in there talking, and I guess she realized that I'd done been down there four different times that week, and she told me she would fill one out on me. And she did. And a man come in there and looked at me real funny and said, "What's wrong with you?" I said, "I'm sick." And he said, "Well, just what's wrong with you? What do you want workmen's comp for?" I said, "I'm planning on, I think I'll be off for a while. I'm fixin' to have surgery." He said, "You don't get workmen's comp for having surgery. What's wrong with you?" And I showed him them papers and he looked at them. He said, "Don't you know that after you change a baby you're supposed to wash your hands?" I said, "Don't start with me, 'cause I haven't changed a diaper in 17 years." And he dropped his head and he walked out that door. Now, he's the plant manager!

They was really rude to me. I guess when you get sick they're done with ya. (Stull interview, November 7, 1998)

Despite lamentations about how much they spend training their line workers, plant managers and floor supervisors have little use for injured workers or those who can't "pull their count"—keep up with the rapid pace of the line: 200 chickens a minute; 1,000 hogs an hour; 400 cattle an hour.

Peggy and Betty showed up every morning at 6:30 and went directly to their lockers. Peggy remembers:

I would get my old stuff out, put my rubber boots on, and then you go form a line where they hand out your supplies and there's somebody right there that'll hand you a red smock or white smock depending on the department that you're in, and then you step to the window and she hands you your plastic—the blue gloves, the plastic apron, a pair of ear plugs and a hair net. Or a cutting glove; you need to show a cuttin' glove to get a cuttin' glove. It took 30 to 45 minutes a day just gettin' ready to, ya know, the process of getting ready and finishin' work. You can't walk outta there with blood up to your elbows, I'm not driving home like that.

And you don't get paid for that?

No.[4]

Work started promptly at 7:00. They were given a break from 9:30 to 10:00, then another, for lunch, from 12:30 to 1:00.

I don't know anyone who can eat in 30 minutes, I mean, I can't do that. I know that me and Betty worked on the same line and when the last chicken was gone we would step down off our stand and go to a wash area on the wall. We would soap our hands, our (rubber) gloves, and down the front of our aprons and throw water on ourselves to get it off. And we hang up our smocks, then we would go back to the same sink and wash our arms 'cause you're bloody up to your elbows, with chicken blood. You wash your arms down and dry 'em. And then we always went to the bathroom and I redone it again before I went to the bathroom and after I finished using the bathroom. Then by the time you get up there it's 20 minutes till, 15 minutes till 1:00, you didn't have time to go and get you enough food to eat.

What about bathroom breaks?

There is no bathroom breaks. You do not leave that line. They will relieve you to go to the bathroom, but you get in trouble for it. They say you don't, but you do. The day I was sick and needed to leave the line, like in a hurry, I waited 10 or 15 minutes before I was allowed to leave the line, before somebody come to do my job so I could leave, because you do those chickens or USDA shuts the line down. (Stull interview, November 9, 1998)

Figure 5.4 USDA inspector examing chicken entrails for disease

After lunch, the line ran without a scheduled break until quitting time at 3:30, but sometimes the day shift ran on till 4:30 or 5:00. "It just varied. When you run outta chickens you were through. We've been ready to leave the line and, 'Oops, we found another semi and a half of chickens in the back.' I'm like, 'How do you lose a semi and a half full of chickens?'" (Peggy, November 9, 1998).

Peggy and Betty were one of four teams of USDA helpers, their official job title. They sat through a week of orientation, mainly watching films. After that, "you go out on the line and you learn, ya know, you're standing there with somebody, helpin' somebody. But after orientation, you work maybe a week with somebody or until you feel comfortable that you can do it by yourself."

Betty and Peggy were the first people to touch the birds after the live hangers, who pull the birds out of the metal cages in which they travel from the broiler house. Then, in the words of anthropologist Steve Striffler (2002:306), who worked in a Tyson chicken plant in Arkansas, live hangers "grab the flailing chickens, hooking them upside down by their feet to an overhead rail system that transports the birds through-out the plant." The birds are stunned, killed, beheaded, plucked, and partially eviscer-ated—all by machines—before they come to Peggy and Betty (Griffith 1995:135).

Peggy presented and Betty trimmed 35 birds a minute—every hour and a half they switched positions to give their arms a rest from the constant motion. Peggy remembered, "Oh, your hands hurt and between your shoulder blades hurt, but they say after you're there over time, that goes away. Well, I wasn't there that long. I was there for the month and your hands do cramp." This was her third stint at the plant. The other two times she quit within two months because she didn't like her hours on third shift, 11:30 P.M. to 8:30 A.M. Betty, who had worked at the plant for two years, complains of knots in her hands and carpal tunnel syndrome, but she has

Figure 5.5 On the line at a
chicken processing plant

never gone to the doctor because she is afraid of surgery. Carpal tunnel syndrome, which is caused by fast repetitive work motions that strain tendons in the wrist and arm, results in loss of feeling in the hand and pain that can travel up the arm to the shoulders and neck. It is one of several cumulative trauma disorders common to meat and poultry line workers and others whose jobs require the same motions all day long.

Betty and Peggy are representative of both the "old" and the "new" line workers in meat and poultry processing. They were born and raised within a few miles of the plant where they were working when they became ill. Betty had worked in tobacco and other seasonal agricultural jobs for $6.00 an hour and no benefits before the plant opened. She still did in her spare time. Peggy had been a country club chef and cake decorator for a local grocery store, but she was never given enough hours to qualify as a full-time employee and thus receive health insurance and benefits. The chicken plant offered full-time work on a regular schedule and insurance.

"A LOT OF PEOPLE LEAVE"

Peggy and Betty are the kind of workers meat and poultry companies promise to hire when they tout the industry's economic benefits to government officials, economic development officers, and chambers of commerce. But there are never enough Bettys and Peggys to bring a new plant to full operating capacity, much less to keep it running. Not in an industry where workers continuously come and go. Betty and Peggy couldn't put a figure to turnover in their plant; they just know "a lot of people leave."

Industry spokespersons do all they can to avoid revealing turnover rates, but everyone agrees that employee turnover is higher than virtually any other industry (Kay 1997:31). For the beef plants in Kansas and Nebraska, annual rates average 72–96 percent for established plants; 250 percent or more for new plants (Wood 1988; Gouveia & Stull 1995:98–99). Mark Grey (1999:18–19) reported annual turnover of 120 percent at the Hog Pride (not real name) pork plant in 1997, and "on a typical day, nearly 25% of workers had been on the job for less than one month, and 60% had been employed less than one year!" After implementing a "quick-start" program designed to reduce turnover by raising wages and allowing workers to rapidly qualify for the highest pay rates for their job, annual turnover fell to 80 percent. But a third of the workers still quit in the first 30 days, before they could qualify for the program, and half were gone in 75 days.

Plant managers dream of annual turnover rates of 36–50 percent. In fact, they don't even talk in terms of annual rates of turnover. They speak, instead, of monthly rates—after all, 8 percent turnover sounds so much better than 96 percent. Besides, monthly rates more accurately reflect the constant movement of workers in and out of their jobs.

As Steve Striffler (2002:309–310) discovered while working as a breading operator—a *harinero* to his Mexican coworkers—deskilling poultry line work means that each "job involves less skill, but much more work . . . [because the company's] guiding principle is to keep the line running at all times, at maximum speed, and at full capacity." Even so, "all the workers took great pride in jobs that had, for the most part, been thoroughly degraded."

Deskilled, degraded, and stuck in dead-end jobs, packinghouse line workers are hardworking, proud, and determined to do the best they can amidst inhumane circumstances. It doesn't much matter whether you present chicken innards all day long to a USDA inspector in between machines that transform a chicken into a breaded chicken breast, halve hog carcasses with a hydraulic splitting saw, or use a knife to "drop" cattle tongues and then hang them on hooks that pass endlessly by overhead—the work will wear you down, and sooner or later you'll get fired, get hurt, or quit.

> Marcial gave his two weeks notice and worked his last day at IBP on August 6, eight years and one day after he started. When he began working on the IBP killfloor, he was Number 500 on the seniority list, when he quit he was Number 75. The woman who administered his exit interview asked why he was quitting, and he replied, "The lines go too fast, the supervisors are too mean, they push their workers too hard, and I don't like anything about working there." Startled at his candor, she looked blankly at him as he laughed. She left the space on the form for why he quit blank.
>
> Marcial took more than his two weeks vacation pay with him when he walked off the killfloor for the last time, he also took stiff wrist joints from his years chiseling meat off cow heads. His wife Mary says he "sounds like Rice Krispies" when he gets up in the morning. Marcial asked the company nurse about his joints, and she told him it was nothing to worry about, a bone specialist had told her it was just "carbon of the bones." Marcial was not surprised the nurse told him not to worry—that's her job—but "popping/cracking noises from wrists or elbows" is number 9 of the 16 cumulative trauma symptoms listed in IBP's publication on this subject (IBP 1989:13).
>
> Marcial said the killfloor has changed immensely since he helped map it in the summer of 1989 (Stull 1994).[5] Some jobs have been eliminated, and new machines are making oth-

ers easier. But the new machines are not without their price. A knocker was recently killed by the new air gun that replaced the old captive-bolt stun gun. Even Marcial's job now used a new machine. Once he got the hang of it, the machine made his job much easier than it had been before, when he used a simple sharpening steel to chisel meat off cow heads. But it took him about two weeks to get the hang of it, and during that time his wrists hurt badly.

Marcial was glad IBP was promoting more Mexicans to supervisory positions, but when asked if the company was becoming more concerned with worker safety, he replied, "No, they just want to go faster." (Stull fieldnotes, July 25, 1993)

"Getting it out the door," has always been the order of the day in meat and poultry processing, and plant managers endlessly strive to cut costs and boost worker output. But meat and poultry workers like Betty, Peggy, and Marcial are "not the hopeless, animal-like creatures described in Sinclair's novel" (Barrett 1987:9); they are active human agents in a continuing contest with management over control of their work and their workplace. They resist exploitation and oppressive working conditions in varied ways—some large, some small; some evident, some veiled; some individual, some collective.

NOTES

1. Thanks to the late Gene DeGruson (1987), Sinclair's original version of *The Jungle*, as it first appeared in *Appeal to Reason*, is once again available.

2. Since 1926, beef carcasses have been graded according to yield and quality. Yield grade measures cutability—the percentage of the carcass that can be transformed into boneless, closely trimmed retail cuts of meat. Carcasses are assigned a numerical yield grade (YG) from 1.0 (54.6 percent) to 5.9 (43.3 percent) (Boggs & Merkel 1984: 106). Quality grade (QG) is determined by the age of the animal, as determined by physiological indicators of maturity, and degree of marbling, the white flecks of intramuscular fat. Color, texture, and firmness of lean meat in the ribeye of the twelfth rib are the indicators used to assign one of eight quality grades. Quality grade determines the value of the carcass—and the cost of the retail cuts that come from it. Choice and Select are the only quality grades regularly designated for retail sale. USDA graders have only about 7 seconds to assign—by sight—both a YG and a QG to each carcass (Seibert 1989).

3. It is not our intent to trace the rise and fall of meatpacking unions—Roger Horowitz (1997) has already done a masterful job of

that in *"Negro and White Unite and Fight!": A Social History of Industrial Unionism in Meatpacking, 1930–90.*

4. On May 9, 2002, the U.S. Department of Labor announced that Perdue Farms had agreed to pay $10 million in back wages to 25,000 current and former workers for time they spent putting on and taking off their protective gear and to pay for such time in the future, estimated to total about $500 per worker per year. The same day it announced the Perdue settlement, the Department of Labor sued Tyson Foods over unpaid "donning and doffing" time. The Department of Labor contends that donning and doffing are part of work-related safety procedures, while Tyson argues that putting on and removing smocks, hairnets, and earplugs should be considered part of employees' personal time (Greenhouse 2002).

5. Because Marcial Cervantes was employed at IBP when research for "Knock 'Em Dead" was being conducted, he was identified by the pseudonym "Enrique" to protect him from possible reprisals. When he quit IBP he granted permission to use his real name, and we are pleased to now acknowledge his valuable contribution to our research.

6/On the Floor
at Running Iron Beef

THE WALKOUT

On August 27, 1992, the Running Iron Beef plant in Valley View (name of the company, its employees, and the town have been changed) announced that hours for second-shift fabrication would be changed from 1:15–9:45 P.M. to 3:15–11:45 P.M. The next day 38 workers called in sick—22 of them were then fired. This action triggered a wildcat strike in which some 200 second-shift fabrication workers walked off the job. This walkout caught both management and union officials by surprise. Running Iron was an industry leader in wages and benefits, yet striking workers complained of unfair treatment, racism, poor working conditions, an unsafe workplace, and low morale.

A settlement was reached a week later, and after serving a month's suspension the fired workers were rehired. Management agreed to make changes in the operations of its second-shift fabrication lines, adequately staff crews, work to improve communication between line workers and management, and not punish returning strikers. The company and the union formed a joint cultural diversity committee to address issues raised by the striking workers, most of whom were Mexican immigrants. Corporate executives were concerned with their "inability to recognize cultural differences and then manage them," and they wanted a researcher to identify issues of current concern to management and labor, recommend changes, and work with them to implement improvements. A year after the strike, the company's labor relations officer met with Don Stull and invited him to propose such a study. The following is an account of his research.

ANTHROPOLOGISTS IN THE JUNGLE

I asked Ken Erickson, a practicing anthropologist and a former member of the Garden City research team who speaks Spanish and Vietnamese, and Miguel Giner, an industrial psychologist and Mexican immigrant, to work with me on the project. Our proposal was accepted, and we began our research in February 1994 with a visit to Running Iron Beef's Valley View plant. Although other commitments prevented continuous fieldwork, we conducted research on and off for 8 months. We came and went in tandem to maximize our presence on site, logging a total of 75 days in the field.

The executives who hired us initially expected survey research that used a standardized questionnaire, which they viewed as "proper scientific research," but we chose participant observation as our primary method. It began with a tour of the plant one Saturday in February. By August, we could give tours ourselves—and did on one occasion. In between we went through new-hire training, talked with and interviewed managers, office staff, union representatives and stewards, and line workers. Our workdays began at 7:00 A.M. with the "morning management meeting," and often did not end until well after midnight when the second shift shut down.

We interviewed a sample of management and union officials, line supervisors and line workers, men and women, English and non-English speakers, Anglos, Hispanics, and Asians. Interviews were problem focused and questions were open ended. Notes were taken during or immediately after interviews. In a few cases, interviews were tape recorded and later transcribed.

Respondents were selected by purposive, or structural, sampling. They were chosen because of their knowledge or position (union business representative, plant manager, trainer) or to ensure that the diversity of the workplace was replicated.

We considered using formal focus groups but decided against it, fearing participants would be reluctant to "tell it like it is" unless we held numerous meetings to establish rapport. Also, pulling people off the line could cause conflict between participants and fellow workers, and it would slow production. Holding sessions before or after shifts would require overtime payments and still might cause conflict.

Instead we took advantage of naturally occurring focus groups. We attended workshops on workers' compensation held for managers by officials from the company's home office. I spent one Sunday afternoon at the union hall talking with union stewards and their families as they fried steaks and drank beer. The plant manager came late in the day, and a lively interchange took place with several workers on the plant's problems and what to do about them. On another occasion, I hosted a get-together of supervisors and foremen at a local bar to talk about their concerns. We frequently visited the home of the union's local business manager, a Mexican immigrant who had worked on the line and was respected, if not always liked, by management, union leadership, and line workers. We spent many an afternoon at the union hall, listening to workers who came to the business manager with their problems.

Our presence and the methods we employed showed that the company was concerned with improving working conditions. This was a very important message to send to men and women who are rarely afforded the courtesy of someone in an important position sitting down with them, asking their opinions, and hearing them out. As one shop steward put it at the steak fry, "Look, he's writing this down. He's listening to us."

MANAGING RUNNING IRON BEEF

For 16 hours a day, 6 days a week, thousands of animals snake along the disassembly line at Running Iron Beef, being killed, their carcasses bled, skinned, gutted, sawed, boned, cut, trimmed, shrink-wrapped, boxed, and loaded into tractor-trailers for transport to markets across the nation and around the world.

Meat&Poultry magazine

Figure 6.1 Skinning a beef carcass

Out on the floor, managerial authority is enforced through a rigid hierarchy. Job type—and status—are marked by the color of the hardhats everyone must wear: blue for managers, yellow for line supervisors, red for trainers, gray for maintenance workers, gold for union stewards, baby blue for trainees, and white for hourly line workers.[1]

For whitehats and their supervisors, the work is hard. One Mexican immigrant who worked at another plant called it *esclavitud*—slavery.

> They make you hump for your seven or eight dollars. The first 90 days it's tough till you get in shape. I'm a supervisor, and I'm not supposed to work hard, but I bet I run 10 miles a day in my job. It's no place to be if you don't like to work. (Stull fieldnotes, August 7, 1988:7)

Management controls employees in several ways: mandatory urinalysis during job application, a probation period for new hires, the ever-present threat of write-ups by line supervisors, who gets promoted and how, the very speed of the chain or line itself.

Hourly workers are assigned to their initial jobs and are on probation for 90 days. After successfully completing the probationary period, the worker is given seniority and may bid on any posted job within the same department: Slaughter; Fabrication, often called Fab; Hides; Offal; Loadout. The qualified bidder with the highest seniority wins the job.

Whether a worker is on probation or has won seniority, he is subject to strict rules and rigid sanctions. Probationary employees may be discharged without notice or recourse. Employees are written up for being late or absent without an excuse, excessive excused absences, failure to report on-the-job injuries, overstaying lunch or relief breaks, deliberate discourtesy, horseplay, substandard job performance. Workers with four such infractions within a calendar year are discharged. More serious offenses bring even quicker termination—malicious mischief that causes property damage or injury, gambling, alcohol or drug use, theft, abusive or threatening language. Fighting, even in the parking lot, results in immediate discharge—with so many knives so close at hand, it must be so.

Running Iron's Workforce

Running Iron Beef is owned by one of the world's largest food processing firms, and the Valley View plant is among the largest beef plants in the world. When we studied it in 1994, it employed more than 2,000 workers and had a slaughter capacity of some 5,000 head of cattle a day.

According to plant records, the workforce was two-thirds Hispanic (68 percent), one-fifth white (19 percent), one-tenth Asian (8 percent). Other ethnic groups were only a small fraction (5 percent) of the workforce. But overall figures are misleading: 76 percent of the plant's officials and managers were white males, and 7 percent were white females; 11 percent were Hispanic men, and 2 percent Hispanic women. Most personnel classified as professionals, technicians, and sales workers were also white men. White women made up 83 percent of the office and clerical staff. The majority of those classified as (unskilled) laborers were Hispanic men (61 percent), followed by Hispanic females (13 percent), then white males (12 percent).

Managers at Running Iron Beef averaged 20 years with the company, ranging from 2 months to more than 40 years. Hourly workers averaged only 3.5 years with the company. Fifty-five percent of the hourly workers had been with the company less than 2 years and averaged only a little more than 1 year of service; the other 45 percent averaged better than 6 years, including some who had been at the plant since it opened more than a decade earlier.

Non-Hispanics appeared disproportionately among those with more than 2 years of service. They were more likely to work on first (day) shift and hold positions that demanded less stamina and physical exertion. Hispanic hourly workers were apt to be short-term employees and work in more physically demanding jobs that were subject to higher rates of injury and turnover. They also lacked suitable job alternatives and were likely to leave the plant for varying intervals of rest and rehabilitation, only to return at some later point. In fact, of hourly employees who had been hired during the previous two years, 1 in 5 was a rehire.

Managers must supervise not one but two workforces. One force has much in common with the managers: they are native-born Americans, mainly Anglo American, with many years of experience in the industry. The other workforce—the majority of hourly workers—is decidedly different: they are likely to be new to the industry and may well be new immigrants to the United States, with little or no command of English and poor understanding of the culture and expectations of native-born Americans. It was this cultural divide that Running Iron's executives found so vexing, and it was to our team that they turned for help recognizing these cultural differences and finding better ways to manage these workers.

Labor Issues

The problems that daily beset Running Iron's multicultural and multilingual workers were revealed by the death of Agustin's grandmother.

> Agustin's grandmother died in Mexico last week. His mother panics in times of crisis and has convulsions, so Agustin needed to get to the airport in a hurry to catch a plane to Mexico for the funeral. He had to get permission to leave and then drive 200 miles to make his flight. He couldn't find his regular foreman, and when he did find someone—a trainer—to ask for a leave, that person sent him to Personnel. They told him he had to go back to his foreman to get final approval. Agustin couldn't wait any longer; he told someone he'd be back on Tuesday and left.
>
> When he came back to work on Tuesday, as he said he would, he was fired because he had left without permission. Agustin understood . . . that sometimes Mexicans say they have a family emergency in Mexico and then take off for a month or so, but he said he'd be back on Tuesday, and he was. He was told he had to have documentation of his grandmother's death, which he took to mean a death certificate, but in small-town Mexico, you have to send to the capital for a death certificate, and that may take a month or more. They generally don't have announcements in the paper and don't have programs at the funeral: "They just bury people," said Jose, the union local's business manager and an immigrant from Mexico. But while someone in authority might have told an Anglo that something simple like an announcement was enough, no one told Agustin, and he did not know to ask. The union steward ran into him as he was coming off shift and said he'd try to help. Agustin kept asking, "Why are you doing this?" This impressed the Anglo steward, who kept telling Agustin that he is a steward and that is what they're supposed to do. So the steward came to the union office to get Jose to intercede on Agustin's behalf. He made it clear that Agustin was a good worker; he came to work, did his job. Jose didn't see it as a problem; he would talk to Personnel and get them to let Agustin come back to work pending receipt of a death certificate. Then if one was not forthcoming, he could always be terminated. (recounted by the union steward and recorded in Stull fieldnotes, June 7, 1994:14-25)

Agustin's dilemma is emblematic of some of the most serious problems at Running Iron Beef:

1. *Passing the buck.* No one in authority wants to make the final decision because then he can be held accountable. Any of several people could have given Agustin permission to go to the funeral, but if something went wrong they would get yelled at. As Ray, who was among those listening to the story, said, "The motto of most supervisors is, 'Not heard, not seen, not in trouble.'"

2. *Mistrust of Mexicans.* There is widespread belief among non-Hispanics that you can get any kind of verification you want in Mexico. Racism also played a part in this case, according to the steward. He felt that had it been him, or another Anglo, there would have been no problem getting off for the funeral.

3. *Cultural and linguistic problems.* Agustin does not speak English or know the American system. Distressed over his grandmother's death and in a hurry to catch his plane, he did not ask what he needed to do to verify the funeral. Even in calmer circumstances, he might not have understood proper procedures, but no one volunteered

to help him or explain things until he got back and had the good fortune to run into the helpful steward.

4. *Relations between supervisors and employees.* The consensus among longtime line workers is that if you let yourself get pushed around, you will. Employees who stand up for themselves may make their supervisors angry, but after a time they'll get the respect and the proper treatment they want.

5. *Longevity.* The longer you've worked at the plant the more likely supervisors are to cut you some slack. Seniority is the formal aspect of this factor; longevity is the informal aspect—the former is codified, the latter not. Both are important.

While this incident reveals certain widespread problems at the plant, the concern and efforts on the part of the Anglo union steward show that many people try to understand and learn from one another. He came to the Mexican union business manager, Jose, who understood both the workings of the plant and the cultural practices in rural Mexico, to ask him to intercede for Agustin. Such cultural brokers often facilitate cross-cultural communication and are indispensable in the everyday workings of the plant.

CORPORATE AND WORK CULTURES
AT RUNNING IRON BEEF

Running Iron strives to instill the values of quality, safety, and productivity in its employees, and these values as well as other aspects of its corporate culture are documented in mission statements, training manuals, and on signs throughout the plant. Running Iron's corporate culture is embodied in documents, beginning with the *Employee Handbook*, and is transmitted to new employees in training and orientation. Corporate culture is reinforced or modified through interaction with supervisors and fellow employees and through continuing education, such as workshops. But in the plant itself, corporate culture must make room for what is often called *work culture* (Alvesson 1995).

One or more work cultures exist in any corporation and take shape wherever employees share common tasks over time. Work cultures may be dominated by a particular occupation (accounting), or they may be grounded in the collective experience of men and women who work day in and day out at a certain job or in a particular location (Slaughter, Fabrication). The work cultures out on the plant floor are intertwined with the national cultures of a multicultural and multilingual workforce, and these may run counter to the goals of Running Iron's corporate culture.

Every culture has a limited number of *themes* that control or stimulate behavior. Whether these themes are declared or implied, tacitly approved or openly promoted, they find their expression in behavior. The importance of a theme can be measured by its frequency, the breadth of its distribution, the intensity of reactions to its violation, and the factors that limit its frequency, force, and variety (Opler 1945).

The dominant themes of Running Iron's corporate culture manifest themselves in the answers managers give when asked about corporate goals, policies, and procedures. These themes permeate the company's publications, manuals, organizational charts, plant maps, slogans, advertising materials. They reveal themselves in the structure of corporate and plant computer databases and in stories recounted by employees. Because Running Iron is a large organization, no single individual knows all aspects of its corporate culture. And in some situations, the same individual may say different things about the corporate culture. In this way, Running Iron is truly a society in miniature, with specialists who control various aspects of corporate activities and knowledge, and with ideal cultural patterns that may bend according to local needs.

Most managers would agree that *safety, quality, productivity,* and *loyalty* are key themes at Running Iron. They permeate its official documents and behavior and represent the company's core values.

Safety

"Safety First" appears on bulletin boards and walls throughout the plant. Safety is highlighted and reinforced in celebrations and rituals; it is prominent in corporate and plant competitions, awards, training meetings, and paperwork. Supervisors who ignore requirements to turn in their records of safety meetings are rebuked on bulletin boards and in company memoranda. Injured employees may be called before plant managers to explain how they were hurt and suggest ways to prevent such occurrences.

Quality

According to the company's human relations manual, every task "we don't do right the first time, we must redo . . . at a cost." The word *quality* appears on the company's logo and throughout its publications—even on its promotional coffee mugs. Company trainers and their training materials say that product quality is essential to profitability, which in turn means continued employment for workers and managers alike.

Productivity

At Running Iron, quality and productivity must be measured against costs to the company. Productivity is measured in output and valued as return per head. Labor costs per head must be kept to a minimum, as well as lost time due to injuries and down time due to equipment failures. When a new project is proposed, formal documentation must be submitted to justify initial and long-term costs to the corporation. Output from the previous day is reported at each morning's management meeting, and goals are set for the coming day.

Loyalty

Employees must work for Running Iron for 6 months before they are eligible for benefits. Although it does not appear in company symbols or publications, loyal service to the corporation is rewarded. Seniority determines rights to a job, and senior employees acquire the least demanding jobs. Employees are recognized in the corporate magazine when they reach service milestones, such as 5 or 10 years on the job. Reassignment rather than termination is the likely punishment if a senior employee is unable to fulfill job expectations. Quit twice and you won't be rehired.

Top management strives for safety, quality, productivity, and loyalty through efforts to reduce workers' compensation costs; identify and eliminate factors contributing to high risk for injury or illness in certain jobs; reduce turnover and unplanned absenteeism; and maintain a high level of production. They see many factors standing in the way of these goals: language and cultural difference; poor communication, including uneven and inadequate interpretation and translation; the union; failure of employees to "buy into the quality process"; inadequate or irrelevant training; "Corporate's" lack of awareness and unresponsiveness to individual plant needs and concerns; and the constant pressure to "get the product out the back door."

These same themes underlie the everyday culture of work on the floor and the workers who perform it. But how line workers interpret these themes and put them into practice is not always in concert with managers. Discrepancies between what workers perceive as corporate ideals and the reality of daily management practices can create serious conflict, especially where management and labor don't share the same language or the same expectations of one another.

Real Work Culture: Safety

Safety is always written first on the "to-do" list used by maintenance supervisors to guide their daily work in Slaughter. But as they come and go from their office, they discuss work priorities, allocation of time and effort, and strategies to solve current problems. They don't talk about safety, except to jokingly say, "Safety second!"

Line workers bitterly complain that management is unresponsive to requests to fix broken equipment or unsafe work areas. "Nothing gets fixed until someone gets hurt" is an oft-repeated refrain. Workers say many people in positions of authority "pass the buck" to avoid making decisions for which they will then be held accountable. That "they only fix it after someone gets hurt" is borne out by management's regular discussion of problems *after,* rather than before, they result in injuries.

Safety, quality, and productivity are three principal goals of Running Iron Beef, "but sometimes safety and product quality take a back seat to production," as one longtime worker put it. In some circles, people say that "if you get injured at Running Iron, you're gonna get fired" (Workshop leader, Stull fieldnotes, March 23, 1994:3).

"In the first 45 days they can fire you for any reason, and the union can't do anything," said one goldhat.

> Trainers are not supposed to be in the line, but they get put in the line if they're short-crewed. Put them in the line and injuries go up because foremans push new hires like everybody else.

> The company tells us to tell them if things are wrong. You tell them and you tell them and you tell them, and nothing happens. Pretty soon, you just don't give a shit.

> And if you report something to the USDA [federal meat inspectors who work on the plant floor], the company gets mad. (Stull fieldnotes, June 12, 1994:4)

Policies and recommendations on safety are often in apparent conflict with the needs of line supervisors and general foremen to keep production rates up. Superintendents and supervisors "don't want to see the chain shut down," and they may ignore calls for changes. Workers often say that "not enough attention is paid to safety until someone is hurt." For example, in July a worker in Fab got his finger

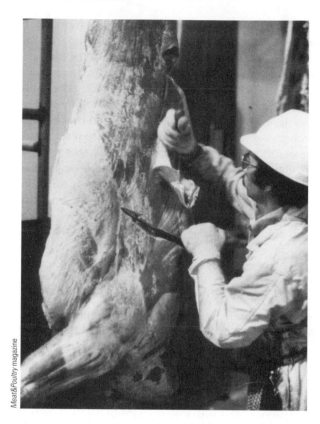

Meat&Poultry magazine

Figure 6.2 Despite many technological advances, the knife and the meat hook remain the basic tools in modern meatpacking plants. Note the worker's chain mail apron.

chopped off in a machine—the guard on this machine had been missing for 4 weeks, but nobody turned it in (Stull fieldnotes, July 18, 1994:12).

Managers often view injured workers as malingerers who want to work the system to their advantage. The case of Eusebio, who had a shoulder strain, was brought up at upper management's morning meeting. He got a lawyer to help him get a job change. According to the bluehat reporting on this case, "It doesn't matter what he does, he hurts. When he drives to work it hurts. He has the perfect lawyer answers to everything. 'Yes, I'll do whatever you want, but it hurts.'" These comments reflect a prevalent view among managers that malingerers hire lawyers who encourage them to claim to be hurt so they may split the injury settlement. While this may be true in some cases, this attitude allows them to avoid facing the fact that injuries wreck the health of many workers (Stull fieldnotes, June, 9, 1994:1).

This attitude is common among managers who remember the old days when you "worked through" pain and injury. Old-timers often swap war stories and show each other their scars. They reminisce of the days when injured workers got patched up by their supervisors with Superglue and electric tape, then were sent back to the line and told to "work through it." Such stories are a matter of pride in the industry, and though the tellers make the point of how things have changed, they seem almost nostalgic for the days when it was a rough and ready business (Stull fieldnotes, August 8, 1994:6). Their nostalgia for the old days is no doubt influenced by their current responsibility for daily production quotas.

Real Work Culture: Quality

People who work at Running Iron but have worked somewhere else say Running Iron treats its workers better than other packers but works them harder and expects them to do a better job in terms of product quality. The expectation is that treating workers better and stressing product quality will equate to loyalty to the company, but that is not always the case. (Manager, in Stull fieldnotes, June 6, 1994:4)

When asked what he would do to bring workers' comp costs down, if money were no object, this same manager said he would slow down the line and maintain adequate crews (Stull fieldnotes, June 6, 1994:3). But money is always an object, and turnover and injury remain the most enduring dilemmas facing the meatpacking industry (Stull and Broadway 1995).

Hourly employees take pride in their work and consider themselves profession-als. Like upper and middle management, they too are concerned with safety, product quality, and productivity. They respect experience and actively seek advice from old-timers. Where there are close relationships with supervisors, there is intense loyalty to the job and to the boss. Some workers will even transfer to work under a supervi-sor they respect and trust. Workers see Running Iron's interests as their own and rec-ognize that if the plant doesn't make money, they're out of a job. But the comprehensive ideal of quality—doing the job right, following measurable specifi-cations, and maintaining good relationships on the floor—is not always reflected in the day-to-day reality in the plant. On a daily basis, "hitting the numbers" matters more than product quality—or safety (Stull fieldnotes, July 20, 1994:6).

Equity and Quality

Fairness, or equity, is a recurrent theme in worker complaints. Supervisors are often accused of setting bad examples by enforcing rules they themselves do not follow: "If we can't do it, then neither should they." If quality is a corporate value, workers argue, then supervisors and workers should be held to the same standards. This is not always the case.

An Anglo yellowhat (supervisor) in his 40s came into the Fab foremans' office about 7:15 A.M. and said someone on the floor was not wearing a company-issue hairnet. The worker, a Latina, was wearing a hairnet, but it was not one of the company's white ones. He told her she had to wear one of company issue, and she became upset. An Anglo female union steward (goldhat), who was in the office at the time, said a hairnet is a hairnet, and what does it matter what kind it is. The yellowhat replied that the "regs" require a company-issued one. The goldhat asked to see the regs, politely but firmly, and with a clear tinge of hostility. The yellowhat left and returned with them, then read the regulation to the stew-ard. The regulations explicitly require company issue. The union steward responded that this has never been posted and is news to her. The yellowhat replied that it has been com-pany policy since 1988 or 1989. The situation worsened when a Chicana yellowhat walked in the room sporting a brown nonissue hairnet.

This incident set off a minor crisis as several women with nonissue hairnets got upset because they now have to change their net, and they claim their own (which must be paid for out of pocket) works just as well. The Chicana yellowhat voiced the objections of many women. She has long, "heavy" hair, and she claims her net has bigger, stronger net-ting, and is better.

Another union steward in the room remained seated at the long counter with the comput-
ers, egging the female goldhat on. "Tell [the yellowhat] to fuck himself," he said while the
yellowhat was gone to get the regs. He claimed the yellowhat is essentially a light-duty
person who has nothing better to do than go around the floor once or twice a month and
hassle people about chewing gum, their hairnets, and the like. Jose, the union business
manager, had arrived by this time. He remained calm: If the policy says company issue,
then so be it. But the female goldhat was not satisfied; she asked for a copy of the regs and
said she'd bring it up at the next union meeting.

This incident. . . . reveals how little things become big things, and how the union and
line management figuratively and sometimes literally "bump chests." Management wants
everyone wearing the white company issue because (1) they can be easily seen from a distance; and (2) they know they are of sufficient quality. Some workers don't like them for
essentially the same reasons. It appears to be women who are bucking the system on this.
Young women often do their best to look good on the floor by wearing makeup, matching
attire, attractive headscarves. By using their own brown or black hairnets they can cover
up the fact that they are wearing a hairnet, which is seen as unbecoming. Those with long
hair think the stronger ones they get on their own work better. They want to go beyond
"sufficient" to "quality," yet they are reprimanded for adhering to one of Running Iron's
basic principles.

The female goldhat didn't help matters either. She sees herself as the defender of "the
people" and is anti-management, and probably anti-company. She's been hurt on the job and
the case is in a protracted settlement phase; she believes the company tried to deliberately
screw her. The male goldhat egged her on when the yellowhat was out of the room, but kept
quiet when he came in. The union business manager, on the other hand, tried to be a mediator and realized that there was little to be done, and probably little reason to fight this fight.
Nevertheless, the Chicana yellowhat and others ended up being hassled because this
became a big issue, and now they are resentful, probably on several counts—of the worker
who got caught, of the "asshole yellowhat," and of the company for a dumb and inflexible
policy. This incident was seen as just another example of management wanting to make its
work easier at the expense of the worker. (Stull fieldnotes, June 7, 1994:1–2)

Line workers say that management is hypocritical—they say one thing in private,
another in public; they are also inconsistent—one yellowhat tells you one thing,
another something different.

One foreman will tell you this, one that, but they all have the same authority, so you can
get written up even if you are following orders, merely by one foreman chewing your
ass for doing what another told you to do. They try to buffalo everybody out there, and if
you stand up to them they try to get rid of you. (Recently fired worker, in Stull fieldnotes,
June 12, 1994:3)

Management talks a good line about quality, but the reality on the floor leads workers to distrust what they have heard. In the work culture of Running Iron, quality is
not second—it is a distant fourth.

Real Work Culture: Productivity

Workers and management alike value efficient, timely production. Workers complain
when the line runs fast, but seasoned workers also brag about their ability to "pull
count" (to keep up, to pull their weight). Workers must learn their jobs quickly, and

Meat&Poultry magazine

Figure 6.3 Hog carcasses are smaller and more uniform than those of cattle, allowing workers to process more than twice as many animals per hour.

be able to do them right, to make it on the line. They must "hang with it"—if they can't, they'll soon quit or be fired. Meatpacking is a tough business; as the safety director at another plant put it, "We don't change their diapers for 'em."

It is the line supervisors, the yellowhats, who must keep the lines running smoothly and efficiently. From the plant manager to hourly workers and everyone in between, line supervisors are seen as the key to good working conditions—or bad. Responding to management's demands, they push productivity into first place in what is valued in the real work culture of the floor.

Like industry management in general, Running Iron supervisors come up through the ranks. This helps them earn the respect of those who work under them, since workers don't respect those who haven't "earned their spurs" and look down on those who can't pull count on their own lines. But this also means that they learn to manage people from the way they were supervised, even though they go through management training. Supervisors catch all the flak when things go wrong and then all the fancy training goes out the window. "As they say in this business, 'Shit flows downhill.' If things are going well, the supervisor job is a pud. But as a company gets larger and more complex, it gets harder to manage" (Plant manager, Stull fieldnotes, June 6, 1994:5).

Lead people (assistants to the line supervisors) are often promoted to supervisors, and that is good, according to the plant's management. But "we do nothing to prepare them." Some supervisors are good ("new school"), some bad ("old school"). The bad ones cling to the "Big Stick approach"—"Do the job my way or there's the door" (Yellowhat, in Stull fieldnotes, March 16, 1994:8). The Fabrication floor supervisor told of one line supervisor who stood out on the floor and wadded up a written request for time off two weeks down the road, then loudly declared, "No fucking way," would he give the person time off. This yellowhat has since been fired.

Supervisors and foremen usually come up through the ranks, but despite experience and good work habits, they often lack "people skills." College trainees, on the other hand, often lack sufficient experience and empathy with line workers. As a result, supervisors frequently resort to the Big Stick with their people, especially when things go wrong: "Two days out on the floor with those hardheads and everything they learned in training goes out the window" (Floor supervisor, Stull fieldnotes, March 23, 1994:4–5). The Big Stick still rules.

Hourlies say, "We're not encouraged to do a good job, just get the product out the door."

> The same old pressures remain. . . . The company is too protective of management. Fred and others at the top get told about problems and agree something needs to get done, but nothing does. Their excuse is "I forgot"—and they probably did. They shouldn't be burdened with the petty stuff, but those under them don't do their jobs. Porfirio, a whitehat, says that "they only listen when you've got them by the balls. They don't give a shit about the people." Management is buddy-buddy with one another: "Kiss their ass and you get a good job; otherwise, forget it." Management continues to put productivity above all else. They turn up the chain speed, people can't do their job right and this causes "leakers" [poor seals on cuts of meat]; they then have to be rebagged. Increased speed doesn't therefore translate into more product—or better product. In the long run it reduces both productivity and quality, and, of course, it reduces safety. (Stull fieldnotes, June 7, 1994:17)

Line workers often believe that managers do not value their expertise and fail to listen, even when hourlies have good ideas, because "we're just peons." Over and over workers asked for respect. They want to be treated like professionals, "which we are," said one longtime meatpacker.

Communication and Trust: Productivity

Workers want to have input into and be informed of decisions that affect their jobs and work space. They want supervisors, maintenance workers, and engineers to ask their opinions on how things can be improved. Paradoxically, they may be reluctant to express their views if asked: seeking their opinion is often seen as a mere formality designed to rubber stamp plans already formalized. Workers are not used to being consulted and may be reluctant to express themselves on issues of productivity, quality, or safety. They don't always feel commitment to the company or ownership of what is being done and just want to put in their hours and go home. The deafening noise on the floor and the relentless speed of the chain make it difficult to discuss issues fully, and meeting space is limited. Line supervisors rarely hold meetings with their crews, and when they do occur they usually revolve around what the crew is doing wrong. "Regular" meetings on safety and quality are held sporadically as time permits; they are hurried and often concerned with other matters, usually production.

Related to accountability and productivity is trust: hourlies don't trust managers to treat them fairly and with respect; managers expect hourlies to manipulate the system and abuse it. Anglos are especially skeptical of the motives of Mexicans who ask for leaves or report illness or injury. In such an environment, it is unlikely that communication will take place, with or without a common command of one national language.

Real Work Culture: Loyalty

The value placed on longevity at Running Iron Beef has some interesting corollaries. On the one hand, it means that many people in management have worked their way up. They almost all know what it is like to hang with it and pull their count. But because of the sharp distinctions between workers and management, exacerbated by language and cultural differences, the way Running Iron rewards and recognizes seniority masks problems. Because supervisors are provided separate spaces, they become isolated from workers. When workers and management share the same language and culture, this is not such a problem. But losing touch with workers who are significantly different raises the specter of serious misunderstandings.

Upper management shares a restroom with USDA inspectors. In Fab, a restroom upstairs is used by management, safety, and maintenance staff. Downstairs, supervisors are provided with their own locker rooms and separate toilets. These facilities are clean and tidy. The restrooms provided for hourly workers are dirty and unpleasant, with toilet paper littering the floors around the stalls. The sad state of the hourly workers' restrooms is inescapable evidence that management never goes there.

Their condition is not simply a matter of litter. It stems in part from differences in the national cultures of Mexico and the United States. In Mexico, septic systems rather than centralized wastewater processing are the norm. Most of these cannot tolerate waste paper, and nearly all private bathrooms in Mexico contain a lined trash receptacle next to the stool. Some Mexican workers continue this practice. Absent this, people place paper on the floor next to the stool where it is later picked up and disposed of. A sign in the Fab restroom showed this to be a problem that Running Iron was aware of. The sign, in Spanish, asked people to please dispose of toilet paper in the stools. But this was never mentioned in training, and the sign was barely visible above the stalls.

CULTURAL AND LANGUAGE DIFFERENCES

Cultural differences between managers and line workers are exacerbated by language differences. "Interpretation is a problem on the line. You need something done, you need it done now. It is not a problem in the office; you can always get someone. But on the line, yes, it is a problem" (Fab supervisor, Stull fieldnotes, July 21, 1994:5).

"I have three Vietnamese who speak no English," one Anglo yellowhat who speaks only English told us. "One job has a Spanish and a Vietnamese who argue all the time. Neither of them speaks English." When communication between them is needed, he must get double translation.

Despite interpretation and translation difficulties, managers and hourlies were continually bridging language and cultural barriers in innovative ways. In the process, they built trust and reconciled differences between the ideal and real cultures in the plant. When we asked supervisors and workers what made a good supervisor, respect and trust were more important than bilingualism. Line workers and supervisors agreed that lacking a shared national language was a barrier to effective work, but it was not an insurmountable one. When there were immediate problems to be solved, even where languages differed, managers and workers were at their very best.

Randy, the maintenance man, who speaks only enough Spanish to greet or cuss out a friend, provided an example of an effective response that involved three language groups:

As he walks past the tripe room, a Vietnamese guy catches Randy's eye and signals "broken" by making like he is breaking a twig and making a face. . . . Randy does a quick right face and steps over to a conveyor that usually carries tripe. There stood a Mexican white-hat, and Randy greeted him in perfect colloquial Spanish, "Eh, Fernando, ¿que pasó hombre, como 'sta?" He went straight to work [fixing the conveyor that] was off the tracks. (Erickson fieldnotes, August 8, 1994:13)

While cultural and language differences between ethnic groups should not be ignored, neither should they be exaggerated. At the same time, cultural differences between managers and hourlies are to be found in the plant, and these differences are at the root of certain problems.

Our research demonstrated that the knowledge and experience of hourly workers is critical to productivity, quality, and safety. Take, for example, the squeegee operator whose job is to mop up blood and grease from the killfloor. This is arguably the simplest job on the floor, the one that requires the least amount of skill, but squeegee operators must know their tools and how to effectively use them. Without the right kind of squeegee, the operator can't do his job properly, and if he doesn't do it right, others will slip and fall, perhaps seriously injuring themselves.

Supervisors must appreciate the specialized knowledge of their crew members if the workplace is to function smoothly and efficiently. Unfortunately, line supervisors often lack adequate knowledge of the craft skills needed to perform the jobs they supervise. Equally troublesome is an absence of shared knowledge about the craft of supervision itself. As a result, new supervisors are often improperly socialized, which in turn prevents them from effectively training new hires on their crews. For example, knife sharpening is a crucial skill on the floor, and very difficult to master—dull knives contribute to cumulative trauma disorder and fatigue. A good supervisor, said one Mexican whitehat, is one who knows how "to speak to the people and help them, and sharpening is the most important." A Spanish speaker praising an English-speaking supervisor said, "He comes to see what I need, to see if my knife is sharpened" (Giner fieldnotes, August 8, 1994:3). Despite the critical importance of knife care, supervisors had different techniques for the care and use of knives and the steel used to keep them sharp. One worker simply said, "I've seen a lot . . . of supervisors that can't keep a knife sharp." This translates into inconsistency in how yellowhats train their new hires in the most important "trick of the trade."

Line supervisors hold the key to productivity, quality, safety, and loyalty out on the floor through their actions and their example. They can inspire their crews to work hard and well, or they can contribute to low morale, elevated turnover, and increased injury. While line workers and managers agree that line supervisors are vital to good working conditions—or bad—there is no shared view, no consensus, about what makes a good supervisor, or what makes good supervision at Running Iron Beef.

OUR FINAL REPORT AND ITS IMPACT

Eight months after our first tour of Running Iron Beef's Valley View plant, we submitted our final report. It concluded that the company's ideals of safety, productivity, quality, and loyalty were widely shared by its multicultural and multilingual workforce, but how managers and workers interpreted these ideals and put them into practice on the plant floor often differ—and when they do, conflict is the likely outcome.

Figure 6.4 Confusing signs can be found in any language in a meatpacking plant. Michael Broadway photographed this sign at IBP's Dakota City, Nebraska, beef plant.

Running Iron Beef has two workforces, not one, and managers and line workers are mirror opposites in language and culture. Despite constant and often intimate daily contact, relations between ethnic groups are often framed by stereotypes. For example, most Asian and Mexican hourly workers have a basic formal education, and some are medical doctors, engineers, and teachers—but management treats them as if they were all uneducated.

Translation of English to Spanish presented an urgent problem at Running Iron. While many documents were translated, from the *Employee Handbook* to informal signs and postings, most are done by Mexican Americans whose literacy in Spanish was inadequate. Badly translated signs are not just annoying to Spanish-speaking employees, they compromise company efforts to get workers to "buy into the quality process." A glaring example was the *Employee Handbook,* which opens with the word *Welcome.* In the Spanish version the word for "welcome," *bienvenidos,* is misspelled as "Bienveido"! Handwritten notes and announcements prepared by line workers were at times more professional and more motivational than those prepared by the company.

Despite many good efforts, safety does not appear to be a primary concern out on the Slaughter and Fabrication floors. Orientation and training sent clear messages to workers that discouraged them from reporting safety violations and problems. In the end, productivity—"hitting the numbers"—was the ultimate, and only true, goal at Running Iron Beef. Nothing was allowed to get in the way of "getting the product out the door."

Our report did more than point out these problems, of which company executives were well aware long before we came on the scene. It presented a series of recommendations on how to improve relations between plant managers and their multicultural workforce, address recurrent complaints by hourly workers, and improve training for supervisors and new hires.

In February 1995, a year after we began our study, we met with the executives who had commissioned it at corporate headquarters. At that meeting, we were asked to propose ways to resolve major problems identified in our report. Three months later we submitted a proposal for a pilot training program for Running Iron Beef supervisors. We never heard from Running Iron Beef again.

The working conditions that led to the wildcat strike at Running Iron Beef in 1992 are found throughout the meat and poultry industry. Managers will tell you they care about their workers and they spend huge sums on training, but they will also tell you high rates of employee turnover and excessive rates of occupational injury and illness are the price of doing business. Despite what managers say, solutions to the problems that continue to plague Running Iron Beef—and the rest of the industry— are no mystery. Pay a fair wage. Provide better and longer periods of training for supervisors and line workers. Adequately staff work crews. Vary job tasks to relieve muscle strain. Provide longer recovery periods for injured workers. Most of all, slow down the chain.

The executives who hired us to help them "recognize cultural differences and then manage them" knew what we would find. They had heard recommendations like the ones in our report many times over. But as Andy Adams (1903:52) said of his days driving cattle up the Western Trail in the 1880s, "Men were cheap, but cattle cost money." The men who sit in the corporate boardrooms that control today's meat industry, and those who do their bidding in the massive factories that turn cattle into meat, know the truth of those words. And so, as long as men are cheaper than cattle, little will change.

NOTE

1. Although the color of the hardhat worn by the floor supervisor, the general foreman, line supervisors, maintenance workers, or quality control officers varies from company to company, hourly line workers are always whitehats.

7/Garden City, Kansas:
Trophy Buckle
on the Beef Belt

THE WORLD'S LARGEST BEEF PLANT
AND BEEFPACKING'S GOLDEN TRIANGLE

In January 1952, Earl C. Brookover, Sr., opened the first commercial feedyard in southwest Kansas. In December 1980, IBP opened the world's largest beefpacking plant 10 miles west of Garden City, near the hamlet of Holcomb. In the time between these signature events, southwest Kansas emerged as beefpacking's "Golden Triangle," and Garden City became the "trophy buckle on the beef belt."

Innovations in irrigation technology and the development of hybrid grain sorghum (milo) as a cheap source of cattle feed in the late 1950s helped catapult southwest Kansas to preeminence in commercial cattle feeding. By 1980, Kansas was feeding more than 3 million cattle a year, and 2 million cattle were being fed within a 150-mile radius of Garden City (Krause 1991:5; Austin 1988a:10A).

An abundance of fed cattle and water from the Ogallala Aquifer attracted beef processors who were abandoning their aging plants in large midwestern cities and moving closer to their source of animals to reduce costs. In 1964, a cattlemen's co-operative opened Producer Packing Company in Garden City, and in 1969 National Beef built a plant in Liberal, 65 miles to the south on the Oklahoma line. In 1980, Excel Corporation opened a plant in Dodge City, 50 miles east of Garden City. In 1983, Val-Agri purchased the idled Producer Packing plant on the eastern edge of Garden City and quickly doubled its capacity. (The Val-Agri plant was later sold to ConAgra.) The industry's expansion in southwest Kansas was completed in 1992, when Farmland Industries purchased National Beef's Liberal plant and the old HyPlains Dressed Beef plant in Dodge City and doubled its slaughter capacity. By the 1990s, southwest Kansas contained the largest concentration of beefpacking plants in North America. The five plants in the Golden Triangle had a combined slaughter capacity of 23,500 head a day and employed more than 10,000 workers (Dhuyvetter, Graff, & Kuhl 1998).

Don Stull

Figure 7.1 Brookover Feed Yards, Garden City, Kansas

THE FASTEST GROWING TOWN IN KANSAS

When IBP opened its Finney County plant in 1980 and Val-Agri began operations in 1983, area unemployment hovered around 3 percent. With virtual full employment, it was apparent that most of the 4,000 workers needed to run these plants would have to come from elsewhere. Fortunately for the packing plants, the early 1980s were a time of increased immigration and refugee flows to the United States. Southeast Asian "boat people" were being resettled across the country, and many of these new-comers lacked the English-language abilities necessary to compete for skilled jobs. Meatpacking offered them entry-level employment and a chance for a new life in America—a function the industry has performed for immigrants since the days of Upton Sinclair's *The Jungle*. Job seekers flocked to Garden City.

Fueled by its expanding beefpacking industry, Garden City grew from around 18,000 people to more than 24,000 between 1980 and 1990. Most of this increase occurred in the first half of the decade, as Garden City became a modern-day boom-town and the fastest growing city in the state. Not only was Garden City's popula-tion exploding, it was also rapidly becoming more diverse. Of its 6,000 newcomers, approximately one-third were Southeast Asian refugees, primarily Vietnamese. Many had been initially settled in Wichita, sponsored by officers at McConnell Air Force Base. When Wichita's light aircraft industry laid off workers during the reces-sion of the early 1980s, some sought work in Garden City. At the same time there was increased pressure from the federal government to get refugees off welfare. Another one-third of the newcomers were Mexicans, who came north to escape eco-nomic hardship and runaway inflation in their homeland.

Figure 7.2 The world's largest beef plant. Cattle pens are in the foreground.

While Southeast Asians were new to southwest Kansas, immigrants were not. Those who first settled Garden City a century earlier included Protestants, Catholics, and Jews from northern and eastern Europe, as well as midwestern farmers and Texas cowboys. By the turn of the twentieth century, Mexicans were immigrating to southwest Kansas to work on the Santa Fe Railroad. Soon they were joined by Japanese and Russian Mennonites, who labored alongside them in the emerging sugar beet industry. The beginning as well as the end of the twentieth century were times of rapid growth and ethnic transformation in Garden City—but this time social scientists were part of Garden City's latest immigrant wave.

THE CHANGING RELATIONS PROJECT

Removal of immigration quotas that discriminated against non-northwest Europeans in 1965 altered U.S. immigrant flows. Since implementation of the 1965 amendments to the Immigration and Nationality Act, migrants from the developing world have become the primary source of U.S. immigrants, and in the process have changed the composition of American communities. Immigration, both legal and illegal, accounted for up to one-third of the nation's population increase in the 1980s, and the 1990 census recorded nearly 20 million foreign-born residents in the United States—a decade later this number reached 31 million (Bach 1993:1; Stull 1990: 303–304; U.S. Census Bureau Public Information Office 2002).

Responding to the reemergence of immigration as an important national concern, the Ford Foundation commissioned a project called "Changing Relations: Newcomers and Established Residents in U.S. Communities" to investigate how new immigrants and established residents had adjusted to one another. After a national competition, the Changing Relations Project Board selected interdisciplinary teams to conduct ethnographic research for 2 years in five metropolitan areas: Philadelphia, Miami, Chicago, Houston, and Monterey Park, California. The sixth site—Garden City, Kansas—was selected to represent the small towns of America's heartland (see Lamphere 1992).

Alejandro Portes and József Böröcz (1989) argue that the modes of incorporation of new immigrants into host societies are largely determined by (1) conditions of exit, (2) class origins, and (3) the contexts of their reception in host communities and societies.

The circumstances that inspire emigrants to leave their homes for a distant land— and their economic and educational backgrounds—are beyond the control of the receiving community. But the reception a community offers to newcomers is not. According to Portes and Böröcz (ibid.:620), the context of reception for new immigrants is determined by governmental policy, labor market demand, the presence or absence of preexisting ethnic communities, and public opinion.

Immigration policy—and its enforcement—is established by the federal government and is thus beyond local control. Work in meatpacking and related jobs has fueled Garden City's growth and rapidly changing ethnic composition. Hispanics had been a significant presence in Garden City since the beginning of the twentieth century, but by 1980 the descendants of those earlier immigrants had become Mexican Americans and were culturally differentiated from newly arriving Latino immigrants. Fewer than 100 Southeast Asians called Garden City home in 1980, and most Garden Citians were ill prepared for the sudden arrival of hundreds of Vietnamese refugees.

Federal immigration law, the labor needs of meatpacking plants headquartered in distant cities, and the ethnic makeup of the community were beyond the influence of the average Garden Citian in 1980. But the fourth factor that contributes to the context of reception—public opinion—was not.

Clergy, educators, social service providers, law enforcement officials, and local journalists have struggled to provide a positive context of reception for Garden City's newcomers, whatever their backgrounds. It has not been easy.

Two decades of sustained growth have combined with high population mobility and dramatically increasing ethnic and linguistic diversity to present what are remarkable challenges: housing shortages, soaring school enrollments, rising rates of crime and social problems, insufficient medical services, and an overburdened road system. But Garden City has met these challenges head on and emerged as an exemplar for cities and towns throughout North America that are facing rural industrialization, rapid growth, and increasing ethnic and linguistic diversity.

In the decade since the Changing Relations Project, Garden City has been the subject of intense focus by journalists, essayists, filmmakers, and social scientists who have been drawn by the apparent paradox of a small town smack dab in the middle of the country that has become a magnet for immigrants. Even more interesting has been how Garden City, overwhelmingly Anglo and agrarian twenty years ago, has apparently accommodated an astonishing influx of newcomers in such a short time—and done so with great success.

We submitted our final report to the Ford Foundation—and to the people of Garden City—in February 1990 (Stull et al. 1990). Over the next decade we studied the impact of meat and poultry processing on a half-dozen communities across North

America. In the course of our studies, we developed a good idea of what happens to communities when a packinghouse comes to town (Broadway 1990; Broadway & Stull 1991; Gouveia & Stull 1995; Stull & Broadway 1990; Stull, Broadway, & Erickson 1992). But what about the long haul? Do the transformations we had documented time and time again continue unabated? To answer this question, we came once again to "the Garden," where it all began—for us, at least.

We spent the week of July 23–30, 2000, in a rapid appraisal of the changes in Garden City over the 1990s. Over the course of that week, we collected numerical data and interviewed experts in key sectors—schools, crime and law enforcement, social and health services, business and the economy, agriculture and cattle feeding, the environment. We revisited and re-interviewed a number of people who had played a major role in our initial research, and our every request was met with the kindness and hospitality for which Garden City is known.

WILL IT EVER SETTLE DOWN? GARDEN CITY, 1980–2000

Social and Economic Change, 1980–1990

Garden City's sudden population growth at the beginning of the 1980s created an immediate demand for low-cost housing. In June 1980, as construction of the IBP plant was in full swing, housing became so critical that city officials held a press conference to ask home owners to make sleeping quarters available to the many workers unable to find accommodations (Reeve 1996:219). In fall 1981, a year after the plant opened, IBP surveyed more than 600 employees and found that 5 percent were living in motels or cars, while 33 percent felt they were paying excessive rent. IBP used this survey to convince local officials to rezone land on the eastern edge of town for a mobile home park. East Garden Village grew to more than 500 units and housed nearly a tenth of the town's population.

A rapidly growing young population increased Garden City's school enrollment by more than 2,000 students between 1980 and 1990. Local voters responded by approving bond issues to build three new elementary schools and expand existing facilities. Minority enrollments doubled, and bilingual and English as a Second Language (ESL) programs greatly expanded.

A rapidly rising population, coupled with the high population mobility characteristic of packinghouse towns, contributed to the steady rise in property and violent crimes during the 1980s. Domestic violence was behind most of the increase in violent crimes (Broadway 1991a).

Against this backdrop of social upheaval, employment rose by more than 75 percent from 1980 to 1990. Beef processing led the way in job creation, followed by eating and drinking establishments and general merchandising. Seventeen new restaurants opened along with 39 new retail outlets, many in a new shopping center anchored by JC Penney and Wal-Mart. However, many of these newly created positions rely upon part-time employees and pay poorly. As a result, despite the creation of more than 5,000 jobs, the county's per capita income and average wage per job actually fell relative to the state's average from 1980 to 1990 (see Table 7.1).

Demand for social services grew along with the area's population. Church volunteers founded Garden City's Emmaus House in 1979 to provide temporary shelter and hot meals for indigents, drawn by the construction of IBP and a regional power

TABLE 7.1   FINNEY COUNTY WAGES AND
INCOME AS A PERCENTAGE OF STATE TOTAL,
1980, 1990, AND 1997

	1980	1990	1997
Average wage	92.5	86.6	86.5
Per capita personal income	91.7	87.1	85.0
(Kansas = 100)			

Source: Kansas Center for Community Economic Development, 1999,
Kansas County Profile Report, Finney County, Policy Research Institute,
University of Kansas, various years.

plant. During the 1980s the number of persons sheltered and fed increased by 250 percent. From 1986 to 1990 the number of food stamp recipients increased by more than 1,100 persons, or 90 percent. (Official USDA records for Finney County are illegible prior to 1986.)

The increase in low-wage jobs offering few if any benefits strained the health care system. In 1990 Finney County ranked in the worst 10 percent of Kansas counties for births to single teens, births lacking early prenatal care, and children lacking adequate immunization (Hackenberg & Kukulka 1995).

Garden City's rapid growth in the 1980s was based upon a low-wage economy. Rapid growth and increasing ethnic and linguistic diversity placed significant demands on the community and strained existing resources and the abilities of social, health, and law enforcement providers to meet rapidly rising community needs.

Social and Economic Change, 1990–2000

Even as much of western Kansas lost population, Finney County—and the rest of southwest Kansas—continued to grow in the 1990s. From 1990 to 2000, Finney County grew by 22.5 percent (to 40,523). This rate of growth was slower than the 39 percent increase of the preceding decade, but still it ranked second among the state's 105 counties (*Garden City Telegram* 2001a:A6).

Meatpacking fueled the county's continued growth. Meatpacking has long depended on immigrant workers, but its reliance on Hispanic workers surged in the 1990s. Figure 7.4 reveals the shifting ethnicity of Finney County's IBP and ConAgra facilities, which by 2000 were overwhelmingly Hispanic (Cultural Relations Board 2001:14). As the proportion of Hispanics increased in the packinghouses, so did their share of the overall population—from 14.5 percent in 1980 to 43.3 percent in 2000 (Hackenberg & Kukulka 1995:194; *Garden City Telegram* 2001b:A1, A5).

Education and Schools

Official enumerations have been criticized for undercounting minorities, and we believe school enrollment figures provide a more accurate portrait of Garden City's changing ethnic makeup. Enrollment in the Garden City public schools (USD 457) increased by 1,044 students (15.5 percent) from 1990 to 1999, resulting in serious overcrowding at the high school. Built for 1,500 students, its enrollment has aver-

Figure 7.3 A guest relaxes on the lawn of Emmaus House, Garden City, Kansas.

aged more than 1,900 for several years. But unlike the 1980s, when Garden City voters approved bond issues to build three elementary schools, proposed bond issues to fund the construction of a new high school were defeated in 1998 and again in 2000 (Cultural Relations Board 2001:3).

More significant has been the dramatic shift in the ethnic and linguistic composition of the student body (Table 7.2). So called minorities have become the majority in the public schools, up from 39 percent in 1990 to 63 percent in 1999. Hispanics overtook non-Hispanic whites to become the majority ethnic group, comprising 57 percent of the pupils in the Garden City public schools in 2000, up from 31 percent in 1990. In some elementary schools more than 90 percent of students are Hispanic. During that same decade, non-Hispanic whites declined from 63 to 37 percent. The number of students of Asian descent declined as well, from 5 percent to 3 percent of the total student body—the result of out-migration and overall growth in school enrollments.

Best estimates place the number of Vietnamese families in Garden City at about 250. Half are said to live in trailers and the others in homes throughout the community. Some are still coming to town as a result of family reunification, but those numbers are small, and only four arrived in town as refugees through the first half of 2000. Although most Vietnamese work at IBP, a growing number are entering white-collar jobs (tax preparers), skilled trades (plumbing), and small businesses (dry cleaning, retail stores).

In the 1999–2000 school year, seven languages were spoken in the Garden City public schools, and some older students enter school without literacy in their native language. The number of students who are non-English speakers or limited-English

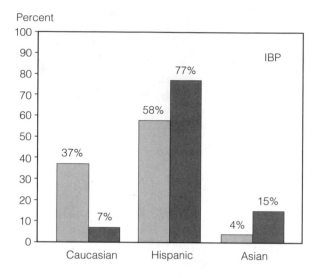

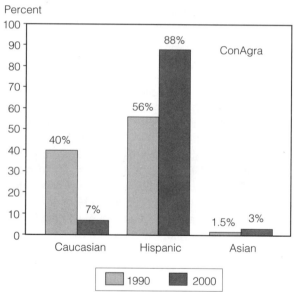

*Figure 7.4 The changing ethnicity of Garden City beefpacking
workers, 1990 and 2000 (Cultural Relations Board 2001). In 2000,
IBP's workforce numbered 3,000 employees (300 management,
2,700 workers) and ConAgra's workforce totaled 2,295 employees
(230 management, 2,065 workers).*

speakers more than tripled over the course of the 1990s to stand at 1,700—22 percent
of the student body. Signs are in English, Spanish, and Vietnamese in all school
buildings, and in Lao in some buildings. There are Spanish translators in all buildings, and some schools have Vietnamese translators.

The school district has responded to these challenges. In 2000, the district had 78
teachers and a school psychologist who spoke Spanish and 2 teachers who spoke

TABLE 7.2   STUDENTS IN THE GARDEN CITY
PUBLIC SCHOOLS BY RACE, 1989–1999

Year	White No.	White %	Hispanic No.	Hispanic %	Asian No.	Asian %	Total
1989	4,222	64.0	1,908	28.9	359	5.4	6,591
1990	4,220	62.6	2,109	31.3	315	4.6	6,736
1991	4,210	60.3	2,310	33.1	341	4.8	6,974
1992	4,096	57.7	2,492	35.1	373	5.2	7,092
1993	4,050	55.8	2,680	36.9	377	5.2	7,264
1994	3,847	52.7	2,932	40.1	378	5.2	7,303
1995	3,661	49.5	3,245	43.9	328	4.4	7,394
1996	3,439	46.6	3,472	47.0	302	4.1	7,383
1997	3,313	44.2	3,701	49.4	320	3.8	7,490
1998	3,196	41.8	3,986	52.1	291	3.8	7,645
1999	3,080	39.6	4,303	55.3	260	3.3	7,780

Source: Garden City, Kansas, Public School District (USD 457)

Vietnamese; 165 others were taking college Spanish classes (Cultural Relations Board 2001:4). According to the school superintendent, 250 of the district's 600 teachers are certified in ESL. To deal with the continued influx of non–English-speaking migrants, the school district joined with Garden City Community College and the county to establish the Finney County Community Learning Center. Since 1999 it has provided a number of vital services, including adult basic education, ESL, family literacy, preschool, and workforce development. Its intake center offers "survival" English-language instruction for adults and students in grades 5–12, as well as community information relating to housing, health, and schooling procedures. Most of the intake center's 115 clients in its first year were from Mexico, followed by El Salvador, Somalia, and Guatemala.

High student turnover is a persistent problem. An average of 35–45 percent of the students are not enrolled for the entire year, and in some elementary schools yearly turnover exceeds 100 percent. Dropout rates have fallen, however, from a high of 16 percent earlier in the decade to 8 percent in the 1999–2000 school year.

Despite a high percentage of immigrants among the student body, reading levels for the high school are at the state average and writing is above average. In 2000, for the first time, an immigrant student who began in the ESL program was inducted into the National Honor Society. Four out of 5 of the high school's graduates receive some postsecondary education—about 50 percent go to Garden City Community College.

The community college, the school district, and IBP have created a joint program to train maintenance workers. Using funds from the Migrant Education Program, liaisons between the school district and both IBP and ConAgra have been hired to orient parents and help families with housing and other non-educational needs.

Crime and Law Enforcement

Crime rose in Garden City throughout the 1980s and into the 1990s. It then declined during the second half of the decade (Table 7.3). This would suggest that Stan Albrecht (1982) was right when he hypothesized that social disruption in rural

TABLE 7.3   REPORTED CRIME INDEX OFFENSES,
GARDEN CITY, 1990–1999

Year	Personal[1]	Property[2]	Total	Offenses/10,000 Persons[3]
1990	187	2,039	2,226	922
1991	226	2,468	2,694	1,101
1992	229	2,272	2,501	1,007
1993	199	2,217	2,416	986
1994	176	2,772	2,948	1,140
1995	204	2,445	2,649	981
1996	174	2,560	2,734	959
1997	153	1,798	1,951	656
1998	175	2,004	2,179	729
1999	130	2,255	2,385	788

[1]Includes murder/manslaughter, rape, robbery, aggravated assault
[2]Includes burglary, theft, auto theft, arson
[3]Rate computed on the basis of population projections provided by Garden City Planning and Development Department
Source: Garden City Police Department Master Activity Reports, 1990–1999

boomtowns is temporary and declines as newcomers develop neighborhood, friendship, and community ties.

But there is another plausible explanation for the decline in crime—that the increasing proportion of non-English speakers chose not to report crimes because of language and cultural barriers. (It is worth noting that while the chief of police is fluent in several languages, dispatchers and most officers speak only English.) This alternative explanation is, in fact, suggested by police records on crimes reported (Figure 7.5).

Although the number of crimes reported rose and fell over the decade, the figure is almost identical in 1990 and 1999, despite a 22.5 percent population increase. Arrests peaked in 1997, but they are still 32 percent above the 1990 figure. Nontraffic-related law enforcement activities increased by 61 percent. However, traffic accidents fell by 34 percent, and driving under the influence arrests fell by 45 percent. Given the significant population increase over the decade and the demographic profile of the community, these figures are surprising.

Whether crime rates will rise or fall in the future is uncertain. Nevertheless, the law enforcement center, new when we began our research in the late 1980s, is now inadequate, and its jail has been expanded from 50 beds to 200. Graffiti, relatively rare a decade ago, is now a common sight. Gangs were just making their appearance during our initial research. According to the chief of police, there are now 13 active gangs, totaling about 400 members, ranging in age from early teens to mid-twenties. Gangs are ethnically based rather than territorial, and most members are Hispanics. There is some intercity crossover between Garden City and Dodge City, but there does not appear to be any connection to gangs in large urban areas.

Growth in the Garden City Police Department has not kept pace with the community. The department has added 8 officers since 1990, an increase of 13 percent, for a total of 63 sworn personnel. Finding bilingual personnel is a serious problem. The department calls on a pool of local translators for Spanish and Vietnamese. For

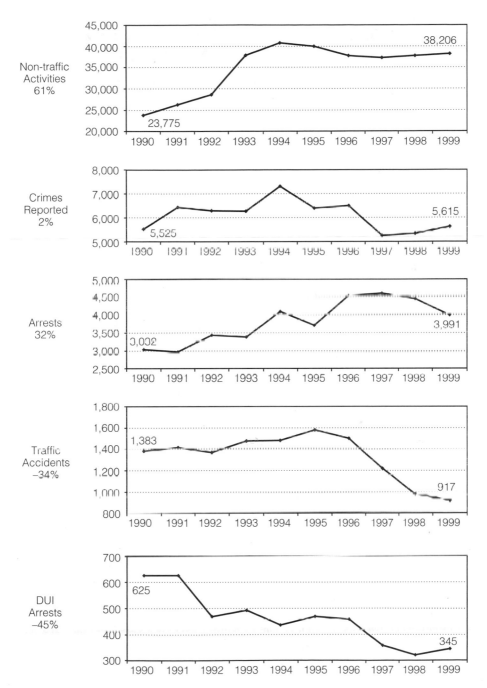

Figure 7.5 Garden City crime statistics, 1990–1999 (Garden City, Kansas, Police Department)

Don Stull

Figure 7.6 Gang graffiti under the Arkansas River bridge, south of Garden City, Kansas

"exotic languages"—Somali, Russian, Mayan, German—they use AT&T's translation service. Since the early 1990s, the police department has offered scholarships to minority students who major in criminal justice at Garden City Community College. Thus far, only two students have completed the program, and both have been hired. While there has been an increase in applications from and hires of minority persons, retention is the department's primary problem, regardless of ethnic origin. Officers do not receive formal cross-cultural or foreign language training, but they do receive sensitivity training, which includes a booklet on basic Spanish for new officers.

Housing

Housing is perhaps the single greatest concern in communities experiencing rapid growth due to rural industrialization. It remains a serious concern in Garden City. According to the U.S. Census, there were 8,072 housing units in Garden City in 1990; a Community Development study identified 9,574 units in 2000. This 19 percent increase did not keep pace with population growth, however. Not only is housing tight in Garden City; often it is unaffordable. The Garden City Cultural Relations Board (2001:8) defines affordable housing as anything costing between $80,000 and $95,000, although it admits that such a price range is "of little assistance to beef processing employees."

In July 2000, the city manager told us that only 3 percent of the city's housing stock was listed as for sale, and most of that was "upscale." Rental units are also scarce: 40 percent of the city's housing units were rentals, 60 percent were owner occupied. The primary source of low-cost housing in Garden City has always been mobile homes, but the largest mobile home park—East Garden Village—is nearing capacity on the number of approved lots (560). The newest source of affordable

Dor-Stul

Figure 7.7 Children playing on a street in East Garden Village, Garden City, Kansas

housing is to be found in Prairie Wind, a subdivision of doublewides to the north of East Garden Village.

But the tight housing market is not all bad. In our initial study, we concluded that scarce housing served to disperse newcomers throughout the community (Stull et al. 1990:34). Comparing school district enrollment records for 1990 and 1999, we found that the percentage of so-called minorities has dramatically increased in virtually all of the district's elementary schools (Figure 7.8). If elementary school enrollments serve as a valid proxy for residential patterns—and we believe they do—then housing segregation is not a problem for Garden City's minority members. On the other hand, if minority status is also a proxy for social class and economic status—and we believe it is—then economics plays a key role in what part of town people live in.

Social and Health Services

Welfare reform cut the number of food stamp recipients in Finney County in half—from a January 1993 high of 2,722 to a low of 1,334 in January 1999 (Betts-Freeland, personal communication, July 19, 2000). But this figure is misleading. The number of children in the county who receive free or reduced-price lunches rose to an all-time high of 48 percent by fall 2000. In fact, overall demand for social services from nongovernmental agencies continued to rise during the 1990s. Between 1990 and 1997 the number of food boxes distributed by Emmaus House and the number of people it fed increased by 70 percent (Table 7.4).

Access to health care continued to be a major issue. Finney County continued to rank in the worst 10 percent of Kansas counties for children lacking immunization, teen pregnancies, and lack of early prenatal care (Kansas Department of Health and Environment 1999). Almost half (49 percent) of Finney County births in 1999 were

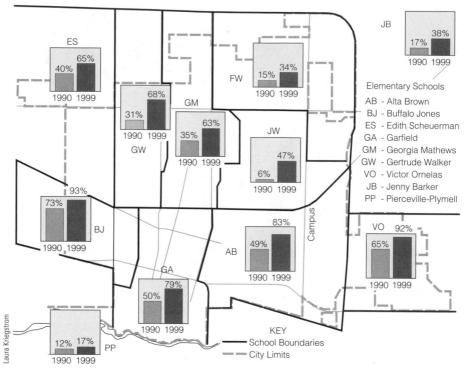

Figure 7.8 Percent of minority students in Garden City elementary schools, 1990 and 1999 (USD 457)

to mothers without a high school education, compared to 18 percent for Kansas as a whole (Kansas Action for Children 2000).

United Methodist Western Kansas Mexican-American Ministries Care Centers and Health Clinics, Mexican-American Ministries (MAM) for short, is the region's primary health care provider for persons without medical insurance. (St. Catherine's Hospital in Garden City also provides care for persons without health insurance through its emergency room—it must, by law.)

Founded in 1987, MAM recorded 6,000 primary care medical visits in 1990, by 1995 the number had increased to 17,652, and by 2000 it reached 22,207—an increase of 270 percent for the decade (Figure 7.9). It serves persons regardless of ethnic, religious, or language background, and all services are provided in both Spanish and English—two-thirds of its clients need language translation. Needless to say, increases in funding and staff lag far behind demand for their services.

TWENTY YEARS AFTER THE PACKERS CAME TO TOWN

Garden City and Finney County now have more than 20 years of experience with the beefpacking industry. The social and economic upheaval that attended the opening of IBP in 1980 and the reopening of what became ConAgra in 1983 is but a distant memory. Indeed, Garden City is the grande dame of meatpacking communities. Towns such as Lexington, Nebraska, Guymon, Oklahoma, or Brooks, Alberta, look

TABLE 7.4   EMMAUS HOUSE MEAL STATISTICS,
1990–1997*

Year	Food Boxes	Number of People Fed
1990	6,185	25,245
1991	7,183	30,638
1992	8,500	36,567
1993	8,373	33,805
1994	9,709	39,529
1995	10,611	42,251
1996	12,136	50,441
1997	10,496	43,006

*Emmaus House had a new director in 1998 and changed the system of data
collection, so the subsequent years are not comparable.

Source: Emmaus House, Garden City, Kansas

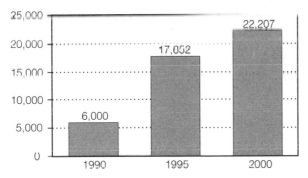

*Figure 7.9 Garden City Mexican-American Ministries,
number of persons served, 1990, 1995, and 2000 (Garden
City Mexican-American Ministries)*

to her and ask, "Will it ever settle down?" Based on its experiences throughout the
1990s, Garden City's answer appears to be, "No, not really. But there are some hope-
ful signs. And there is much that communities can do."

Population growth definitely slowed during Garden City's second decade as a
meatpacking town, but it was still surpassed by only one other county—a sprawling
well-to-do residential area of Kansas City. And after rising steadily until the
mid-1990s, the crime rate turned downward—but the causes of this decline are
unclear. The issues that challenged Garden City in the 1980s remain—overcrowded
schools, inadequate and unaffordable housing, unequal access to health care and social
services.

The meatpacking industry does little to offset the problems it brings to host communities, and only grudgingly does it offer assistance. When it does, the support is
minimal and largely symbolic. Industry executives know the challenges communities face, and they know how to use community goodwill to their own advantage.

There is a clear linkage between meatpacking's work environment and recruiting
practices, the steady flow of new immigrants in and out of host communities, and the

elevated social problems these communities face. Effective federal mandates exist to ensure food safety and purity, but government regulations designed to ensure worker safety and legal status have fallen far short of the mark. Meatpacking has embraced tax incentives to employ disadvantaged groups (what used to be called Targeted Job Tax Credits, for example). Incentives—and stiff penalties for noncompliance—could also be used to reduce turnover and improve working conditions. Unfortunately, high rates of injury and turnover have characterized the meatpacking industry for well over a century. These problems—and their root causes—will likely endure.

At the beginning of the twenty-first century, Garden City is a vibrant multicultural community. Its emerging Latino and Asian business communities have enriched the economy and society of southwest Kansas. Entering Garden City from the east along U.S. Highway 50, a visitor is immediately aware of its diverse population. On the edge of town is a Salvadoran restaurant and dance hall; nearer town, and adjacent to East Garden Village, is a mini-mall that includes Long's Billiards and La Panaderia Real. U.S. Highway 50 becomes Fulton Street in town, and the stores and restaurants that line this major thoroughfare further testify to Garden City's cosmopolitan nature—Kieu's Market, El Remedio, Pho Hoa, El Zarape, the Grain Bin. Thumbing through the Yellow Pages confirms this windshield ethnography—of the 68 restaurants listed, 20 are Asian or Latin American. Glancing at the names on virtually any page of the telephone book shows the many peoples that call Garden City home—Tran, Trejo, Trieu, Turner, Unruh, Urrutia.

But the ability of the community to meet newcomers' needs is constrained by the persistence of a low-wage economy and the employment practices of the packers. And despite a decade of concerted effort by local government and nonprofit agencies to resolve the problems we identified at the close of the Changing Relations Project, most remain unabated. Until the meatpacking industry recognizes its responsibility to the communities that are home to its facilities, these communities will continue to struggle. The struggle may be valiant, as it has been in Garden City, but it will be unlikely to do much more than hold the line.

GARDEN CITY'S FUTURE

On Christmas night 2000, the ConAgra plant burned, putting most of the plant's 2,300 employees out of work. ConAgra promised to announce whether it would rebuild in Garden City by April 1, 2001. The citizens of Garden City, and the plants workers, are still waiting to learn its fate. Meanwhile, ConAgra sold its red meat division in 2002.

No matter what becomes of the ConAgra facility, southwest Kansas will remain the nation's center of cattle feeding and beefpacking for many years to come. And Garden City will remain the preeminent community in the region. But other livestock-based agro-industries are entering the area. In 1995 the first large-scale dairy in southwest Kansas began operating in Syracuse, 50 miles west of Garden City, and by 2000 there were 14 large dairies, milking 45,000 head. Sixty thousand "wet cows" (cows in milk production) are needed to support a cheese processing plant, and predictions are that it is only a matter of time until one is built in the area.

In January 1996, Seaboard Corporation opened a pork processing plant 100 miles south of Garden City in Guymon, Oklahoma. Some of the hogs slaughtered in Guymon are grown in southwest Kansas. While the arrival of dairies is welcomed by

Figure 7.10 A multicultural mini-mall on the outskirts of Garden City

many, controversy has surrounded the appearance of large-scale confinement hog operations. It is unlikely that pork production will expand.

The dairy industry is in the process of relocating from the West Coast, and southwest Kansas seems to be one of its newest destinations. If mega-dairies emerge as serious rivals to cattle feeding, as some predict, there will be definite changes in the economy and demography of the region.

Economic opportunity has always drawn people to southwest Kansas. Since it was first settled in the 1870s, the region has been dominated by a series of economies. As each preeminent economy waned, another succeeded it. In the 1890s, sugar beets supplanted the open-range cattle kingdom. In the 1960s came the ascendancy of irrigated feed grains, followed closely by cattle feeding. In the early 1980s, when oil and gas prices plummeted and American agriculture was in crisis, beef-packing came to town. Will dairies and the processing plants that serve them emerge to compete with cattle feeding and meatpacking as the next dominant economy in southwest Kansas? We must wait and see.

What we can say, however, is that the people of southwest Kansas have built a resilient economy based on adding value to agriculture and livestock production. It has stood them in good stead throughout the past century, and if they are careful to preserve and protect their most important resource—water—it will likely carry them through the next one as well. We have learned much from the people of Garden City—and been inspired by them. By offering to its new immigrants a positive context of reception, Garden City has shown other communities how to meet the challenges of rapid growth and rural industrialization. We are confident that Garden City will continue to point the way—and we will be there to learn its lessons.

8/Don't Shoot
the Messenger:
Technical Assistance
to Packinghouse Towns

The Garden City Changing Relations Project final report concluded with 15 recommendations to the people of Garden City—four concerned education, and the remainder dealt with community issues such as housing, health care, day care, and social services (Stull et al. 1990). In collaboration with the school district, we organized the Multicultural Action Committee (MAC), an advisory board representing public school teachers, city government, Garden City's three main ethnic groups, and service organizations. We worked with this committee to fine-tune our recommendations and present them to appropriate institutions and agencies.

Our report was soon put to local use: social service agencies used our findings to obtain external funds; the school district revised policies and procedures on curriculum, bilingual and ESL instruction, extracurricular activities, community outreach, personnel training, evaluation, and retention with our recommendations in hand; the city commission established a cultural relations board with wide community and ethnic representation; and local law enforcement aggressively sought minority personnel. Perhaps the most lasting legacy of the Changing Relations Project in Garden City is the Five-State Multicultural Conference. Held each spring, this conference grew directly out of the heightened awareness of Garden Citians that theirs was a cosmopolitan community—one that had much to learn from its rich cultural and linguistic diversity, and much to teach others.

As we carried out our research in Garden City, we wondered whether what we were finding there was also happening in other packinghouse towns. We soon had the chance to find out. Late in 1988, IBP announced plans for a new beef plant in Lexington, Nebraska, some 250 miles northeast of Garden City. It was to be the first beef plant built in the United States since the one near Garden City had opened in 1980. Lexington established a Community Impact Study Team (CIST), which visited packing towns and sponsored public forums. A CIST representative visited us in Garden City in January 1989. The following April we addressed a public forum in Lexington. We followed up with a report on changes Lexington might expect, provided materials from our Garden City research, and fostered interchanges between public and private agencies in both communities.

CIST included leaders in business, government, social services, health care, education, media, and the church. In December 1989, CIST completed its data-gathering mission, disbanded, and issued an exit report. By then the community was mobilizing to meet anticipated needs. Efforts influenced by our input included organization of a countywide ministerial association, which contributed to several community preparedness activities, and an interagency council intended to develop and implement an integrated strategy to deal with growth. When CIST disbanded, we began to identify and work with key agencies and individuals.

Of the original Garden City team, we were the only ones to take up work in Lexington, and we were joined by Lourdes Gouveia, a bilingual Latina sociologist from the University of Nebraska at Omaha. In the summer of 1990 we collected baseline data on welfare caseloads, school enrollments, crime, and characteristics of newcomers. We conducted participant observation and interviews with civic and religious leaders, service providers, IBP officials, cattle producers and feeders, proprietors of local businesses, and "everyday citizens." We arranged for ongoing collection of data from the school district, Nebraska Department of Social Services, Lexington Housing Authority, Nebraska Job Services, City of Lexington, and the police and sheriff's departments. Our status as outside experts, and our early and ongoing presence, fostered a working relationship with the city manager and others who were guiding community responses to the changes taking place in Lexington.

The nonprofit Community Services Center sponsored public forums and community leadership workshops. Following our advice, and working with the ministerial association, it purchased a building and opened a shelter for low-income newcomers in January 1991. Known as Haven House, and patterned after Garden City's Emmaus House, it provides short-term housing, meals, and social service referrals for newcomers. The Salvation Army selected Haven House as a national pilot project, and for the first time funded and staffed a food program in a facility it neither owned nor operated.

We conducted intermittent fieldwork in Lexington through 1992 and monitored developments for several years thereafter. We reported on our research in the press, public forums, publications, and a 1996 report to the community (Broadway 1991b; Broadway, Stull, & Podraza 1994; Gouveia & Stull 1995, 1997; Hackenberg et al. 1993).

THE PLIANCY FACTOR

Members of our team have taken what we learned first in Garden City and then in Lexington to other communities and have worked with them to try to modify and mitigate the negative consequences that attend the meat and poultry industry. In doing so, we have sought to apply what Allan Holmberg (1958:14) called the *pliancy factor:* "When a generalization on behavior is communicated to people who are also its subjects, it may alter the knowledge and preferences of these people and also their behavior."

Three factors limit the pliancy of communities that host meatpacking plants: the nature of the industry, the timing of interventions, and the approach to development taken by the community.

Figure 8.1 *Haven House, Lexington, Nebraska*

Elsewhere we have argued that "communities . . . cannot alter the nature of meat-packing, its relative low pay, hazardous work conditions or recruiting practices" (Broadway 2000:41). That packing plants bring to their new homes significant levels of growth, turnover, and social problems is not only predictable, it is apparently inevitable. At least it has been in North America.

Companies do not usually announce plans for a new plant until a final decision has been reached, and they play competing towns against one another. If plans become public too soon, opposition often surfaces, especially now that our research and that of others offers clear evidence of packing plants' consequences for host communities. How then are small communities best able to respond to the challenges posed by meat and poultry processing plants?

COMMUNITY DEVELOPMENT MODELS

Many communities, rural and urban alike, pursue economic development without considering larger issues of community development. They equate development with jobs and see economic development as the sole means for community maintenance and improvement. But unless economic development results in an improved quality of life, it can actually be detrimental to community development. Jobs, like lunches, are rarely free. Certainly not in an age when corporations expect public subsidies and tax holidays; when companies threaten to leave host communities for greener pastures unless taxpayers dig ever deeper into their pockets. And low-wage jobs and the transient work forces they often create, coupled with corporate tax holidays, can harm the quality of life in a community.

Most members of host communities have little, if any, say in whether a processing plant comes to town. But the chorus of "jobs, jobs, jobs," sung in unison by the packers' front men and local boosters gives way to the "slaughterhouse blues" (Broadway 2000) once people realize that all those new jobs will bring significant social and economic costs—and that most will be filled by immigrant workers.

It is then that those in positions of leadership, and oft times citizen groups, start to look beyond the narrow confines of economic development schemes to broader issues of community development. For community development to take place, problems must be identified, competing courses of action considered, resources recognized and mobilized, and strategies implemented. While communities and their goals differ widely, Flora et al. (1992:251ff) identify three general models of community development: self-help, technical assistance, and conflict.

The *self-help model* emphasizes process—community members working together to arrive at group decisions and then taking actions to implement them. Broad-based participation in the decision-making process and subsequent actions are needed for this model to succeed. Interest and motivation on the part of a wide spectrum of community members are essential, and decision making must be participatory and democratic. Unless the process itself is institutionalized, the effort will fail, since community involvement is a primary goal of this approach.

In contrast to the self-help model, *technical assistance* is task oriented. Local people are seen as consumers of development, not its architects. Community needs are couched in technical terms that call for expert advice. Development is defined as the achievement of predetermined outcomes, and efficiency in reaching those outcomes is the measure of success. Cost-benefit analysis is the common language of this approach. State and local governments emphasize recruitment of new employers as the primary vehicle for development. Throughout rural North America, industries that add value to local commodities are targeted, especially where jobs and population are in decline.

The *conflict model* is like the self-help approach in bringing community members together to discuss their problems, develop local leadership, and devise and implement strategies to achieve agreed-upon goals. It differs from self-help by seeking to redistribute power and in the strategies used to achieve this general goal. This is usually the only model available to citizen groups who oppose government-sponsored development schemes, and it has frequently been employed by groups fighting proposed packinghouses and concentrated animal feeding operations.

In testing the pliancy factor through research and technical assistance to packinghouse communities in the United States and Canada, our goal has been to develop what Fred Gearing (1979) called *alongside-of* relations among social scientists, community members, and the institutions they represent. We have met with varying degrees of success.

HOPE FOR THE BEST AND PREPARE FOR THE WORST

The trade-off between economic development and its accompanying social costs is clearly evident in the efforts of the western Canadian province of Alberta to attract investment in its beef industry. To entice potential investors, the province's economic development publications proclaim that Alberta has the lowest overall taxes in Canada, wage costs much lower than in the United States, and the lowest workers'

Michael Broadway

Figure 8.2. Members of the team Michael Broadway assembled to advise Brooks on community impacts from IBP's expansion of the Lakeside Processing Plant: Don Stull; Mark Grey, Professor of Anthropology, University of Northern Iowa; Penney Schwab, Executive Director, United Methodist Western Kansas Mexican-American Ministries and Health Clinics; and Amy Richardson, District Administrator, Nebraska Department of Social Services

compensation premiums in Canada (Alberta Economic Development 1998). Government funds are available to assist developers. In the 1980s, when Cargill built its beef processing facility at High River, about 30 miles south of Calgary, the provincial government provided $4 million (Canadian) for the construction of a wastewater treatment plant. It also provided $16 million (Canadian) in grants and loans to Lakeside Packers of Brooks, 110 miles southeast of Calgary (Broadway 2001).

Many Albertans were pleased when IBP purchased Lakeside Packers in 1994 and announced it would double the slaughter capacity and add a boxed beef plant. Fewer cattle would be shipped to the United States and more valued-added processing would be completed in the province.

When we visited Brooks in September 1996, many of the town's 10,000 residents were unsure what to expect after Lakeside began hiring the first thousand workers for its newly expanded beef processing plant. As a guide, we detailed the social and economic impact of meatpacking plants on small towns in the United States at a public forum. Many in the audience, including the former owner of Lakeside, were skeptical: "Surely, the same things would not happen in Canada." The local newspaper editor, who proudly traces his family roots to the town's early pioneers, openly wondered whether the plant would even open. Nevertheless, we outlined a set of recommended community responses to the challenges posed by packinghouses based upon two basic premises: (1) social changes are inevitable; and (2) communities need to embrace the changes (see Table 8.1).

TABLE 8.1   LIKELY SOCIAL IMPACTS OF A MEATPACKING PLANT
AND RECOMMENDED COMMUNITY RESPONSES

Impact	Response
1. Influx of visible minorities and an increase in language and cultural differences	1a. Establish cultural awareness workshops, a diversity committee, and provide ESL services
2. Increase in demand for low-cost housing	2a. Disperse new rental accommodations throughout the community
3. Increase in crime	3a. Establish a community liaison office
4. Increase in homeless persons	4a. Provide a homeless shelter
5. Increase in demand for social services	5a. Create an interagency service-provider group
6. Increase in demand for health care	6a. Hire additional health care professionals and assure the provision of translators

Source: "The Impact of Meatpacking Plants on Small Towns: Lessons to Be Learned from the U.S. Experience," workshop presented by Michael Broadway at Heritage Inn, Brooks, Alberta. September 12, 1996.

We stressed that it would be residents and their elected officials who determined how Brooks responded to the challenges of rapid growth, and we believed that some of the worst community outcomes we had encountered in the United States could be avoided with appropriate planning. Housing shortages in Garden City had been alleviated by the construction of large trailer courts, which served to marginalize newcomers and stigmatize them (Benson 1990). Moreover, the concentration of highly mobile persons in trailer parks prevented the development of a sense of a community, and trailer parks became "high crime" areas. To prevent the repetition of these circumstances in Brooks, we recommended dispersal of affordable rental housing throughout the community (Table 8.1, Response 2a).

To deal with an expected influx of poor people looking for work, we strongly advocated establishing a homeless shelter (Response 4a). Providing shelter, food, and assistance to indigents requires careful coordination between voluntary and governmental agencies (Response 5a). Given the diverse nature of Canada's immigrant stream, we had no way to predict which immigrant groups would end up working in the plant and which language proficiencies would be needed by teachers and other service providers. But once it became apparent where the immigrants were coming from, we proposed that cultural awareness workshops be held for service providers and that Brooks recognize newcomers' contributions by celebrating ethnic holidays and hosting international festivals. To achieve these outcomes, we advised establishing a diversity committee made up of representatives from local government, business, and immigrant groups, which could identify the problems newcomers were experiencing and devise culturally appropriate solutions (Response 1a).

Lakeside's recruitment of young adult single males assured an increase in crime and alcohol-related incidents. But some criminal activities may be prevented if the community is able to establish clear expectations for behavior and communicate them to newcomers (Response 3a). Although Alberta has a government-funded health care plan for all its citizens, Brooks, like most small towns in rural areas, suffers from a shortage of physicians and nurses. The influx of workers and their families would add to the demand for health care, and we recommended that more health care professionals be hired and professional translators be provided for newcomer clients (Response 6a). Implementing such a recommendation is problematic, since Alberta already has programs to encourage physicians and nurses to settle in rural areas. But heavy patient loads, long and unpredictable hours, and the absence of support staff make recruitment difficult.

Finally, based upon the Lexington experience, we recommended formation of a community impact study team (CIST), which would consist of representatives from Lakeside, government, and social service providers. Its mandate would be to share information about the newcomers, identify problems in the delivery of services to them, and where necessary formulate or coordinate a response. This recommendation was unofficially adopted by the town council during our visit, and a member of the council was appointed to chair the study team.

We left town believing we had laid the foundations for a proactive response to the challenges posed by Lakeside's expansion. But it was not to be. A follow-up visit, 3 months after Lakeside began hiring, found a skeptical community—they had been promised social upheaval and none had occurred! Unfortunately, they were only experiencing the calm before the storm.

A small pool of surplus labor and high turnover led the company's human resources manager to conclude in late March 1997 that "we've pretty much exhausted the local labor supplies." And so Lakeside began recruiting nationally, beginning in Newfoundland and Nova Scotia, where the collapse of the Atlantic cod fishery had produced unemployment levels of 30 percent and more in coastal communities (Broadway 2001).

The company established on site housing for recruits. The housing was designed to provide temporary accommodation, with rent increasing the longer a person stayed. Renters were also provided with meal vouchers for use in the plant's cafeteria. These "benefits" were then deducted from workers' paychecks. When they received their first checks after two weeks on the job, many new hires had little to show for their efforts.

The restructuring of Canada's meat industry in the late 1990s, with plant closures in cities and the construction of large plants in rural areas, attracted media attention. A Canadian television producer found an article by Michael Broadway on the Canadian meat industry in a Lexus Nexus search and called to find out what I knew about the Lakeside plant. I said I was conducting a longitudinal study of how Brooks was dealing with the social and economic changes accompanying the plant's expansion and would be going there in January 1998. The producer asked whether I would mind meeting with him and a reporter during my visit. I said "No."

When I returned to Brooks I found it in the throes of many of the predicted social changes. The town council was upset that Brooks was attracting unwanted national attention and that I was providing the media with data on the extent of social change. Within a week, my working relationship with the town council was severed by the city manager in an e-mail message accusing me of publicly stating that "the town has its head up its ass." Worse was to follow.

A report to the Brooks Community Impact Study Team (Broadway 2001), prepared with the assistance of local social service providers, documented that since the plant expanded in 1996, the town had experienced: a 15 percent rise in population; housing shortages; an influx of immigrants from as far away as Iraq, Somalia,

Michael Broadway

Figure 8.3 *Housing for workers on the grounds of IBP's Lakeside beef plant in Brooks, Alberta*

Bosnia, and Cambodia; a 200 percent increase in the budget of the Salvation Army for indigent care; a 70 percent jump in the reported crime rate; a 38 percent upswing in the use of the emergency room at the local hospital; and an astounding jump of 820 percent in the demand for one-time transitional assistance payments (welfare) from the Alberta Department of Family and Social Services.

The Brooks CIST dismissed the report in a press release, noting, "It is unfortunate that media attention is drawn to our area because of the meatpacking plant, which in actuality, has caused minimum impacts to our community" (*Brooks Bulletin* 2000).

This view is not shared by many who work diligently "on the front lines." On my last visit to Brooks, I met with a former member of the town council and initial chair of the community impact study team, who told me, "You've been right about everything" (Broadway fieldnotes, October 9, 2001).

COMMUNITY STUDY TEAMS: THE IDEAL AND THE REAL

Brooks is not the only town we have encouraged to follow Lexington's example and form a community impact study team (CIST). Such teams usually include prominent citizens selected from the clergy, business, government, and providers of health care, education, and social services. The packers rarely participate in a meaningful way.

Impact study teams gather information and provide forums for public discourse. Members from the Garden City Changing Relations Project team have provided outcomes data in other communities and put counterparts in contact with one another. In Brooks and elsewhere we have brought along experienced service providers to

offer advice in public forums and focused work groups. Such "lateral learning" (Flora et al. 1992:319) is key to successful responses by host communities.

But the packers know the value of lateral learning, too. Not until the deal is done, the ink is dry, and the first spade has been turned on the site of the new plant do we usually ride into town, brandish our articles and reports from other communities, and tell people the horse is out of the barn and they're in for one rough ride. We may raise doubts—and serious ones—in the minds of many, but we are poor competition for the packers' "spin doctors." And we have no corporate jets or expense accounts to underwrite trips to other communities that host company plants.

Impact study teams are vital as a community prepares for the onslaught of change that accompanies a new plant. But having a study team does not guarantee a community will be successful in resolving difficult and often intractable problems. In Brooks, team members were divided between those who thought its function should be information sharing and those who wanted it to have a policy-making role as well. Divisions were so great that an outside mediator was brought in to see if some common ground could be found between the competing perspectives. Resolution proved impossible, and some social service providers began to meet outside the team and coordinate their own policies (Broadway 2000:44–45).

At one time, social scientists believed in a rural-urban continuum, where small towns, like tribes, were characterized by consensus. We know better now. Citizens of host communities are no more of one mind on economic development than on anything else. What Harvey Molotch (1976) called the *growth machine*—a coalition of individuals and groups that realize economic gain from community growth—thrives when a meatpacking plant comes to town, even as other aspects of the community suffer.

Just as the local growth machine looks to the packers to infuse its economy with new jobs and tax revenue; local communities have looked to us for magic bullets to dispel the negative consequences associated with hosting a meatpacking plant. Although we try to develop a collaborative, alongside-of relationship with communities suitable to a self-help model, most local officials adopt the technical assistance model and assign us to the role of outside expert. They want us to provide them with quick fixes for the problems looming on their horizon. Unfortunately, most of the problems packinghouse communities face are long-term and intractable, and broad-based citizen efforts often falter in the face of what one Garden City agency director calls "change fatigue."

Only rarely do community members have the chance to consider and debate whether they want a meat or poultry plant in their town. In those instances, we have been invited by citizen groups to present our findings, and in several cases plant proposals have been defeated (see Crews 2001a).

Communities have welcomed many of our suggestions, and implemented a number of them, such as establishing homeless shelters, adopting housing codes and zoning ordinances, and creating diversity committees and citizen advisory boards to local governments and agencies. And we have been able to develop lasting collaborative research relationships with local institutions, such as Garden City's Mexican-American Ministries.

As applied social scientists with a longstanding commitment to providing assistance to those communities where we carry out our research, we wish we could speak

with authority and confidence of a set of principles and methods that consi
produce desired outcomes. But we have no magic bullets—just warnings that
want to hear. And while we nod knowingly as community members tell us our p
dictions came true, we are invariably humbled and disappointed by the rigidity of th
industry and the inability of local communities to do more than mitigate its social and
economic costs.

WHAT CAN HOST COMMUNITIES DO,
AND WHEN MUST THEY DO IT?

Initially, rural communities are ill prepared to cope with the problems meatpacking
and its immigrant workforce bring, since they are usually strapped for resources. And
they give new industries tax incentives in exchange for the jobs they promise, further straining already meager resources. Local and state governments are usually
eager to provide for increasing demands on physical infrastructure, such as roads and
sewer systems. Providing for increasing demands on social infrastructure—social
services, health care, education—is another matter. Much of this task falls to nongovernmental organizations, churches, and volunteer groups.

While details may vary, packinghouse towns all face similar economic, social,
and environmental dilemmas. Some have only begun to experience the impact of the
industry and its workforce, while others have grappled with these challenges for
many years. Next we review four positive steps communities use in mitigating the
negative impact of meat and poultry processing plants.

1. Look to Other Communities for Guidance and Assistance,
and Utilize the Expertise of Experienced Practitioners

Special funds of knowledge already exist, and practitioners experienced in dealing
with an array of concerns are to be found in meatpacking communities near and far.
Agencies and individuals that exemplify "best practices" should be identified and
called on for guidance. Health care is a good place to begin.

Headquartered in Garden City, Kansas, Mexican-American Ministries operates
full-time primary-care centers in Dodge City, Liberal, and Ulysses, and offers part-
time care at smaller sites. MAM, as it is often called, serves the unemployed and
underemployed, the uninsured and underinsured, the undocumented, and others
unable to access mainstream medical care. MAM services include physical exami-
nations and health screening; prenatal and postnatal care; preventive care; treatment
of illness and injury; health education; laboratory tests; prescription assistance; man
agement of chronic conditions; and referrals (see Hackenberg & Kukulka
1995:200–202).

Penney Schwab, MAM executive director, and her staff have nearly 2 decades of
experience in providing effective and appropriate health care and related services to
low-income persons of diverse linguistic and cultural backgrounds in several communities. They possess an unparalleled font of knowledge upon which other communities can draw—and often have.

2. Broaden Local Community Participation

Broad-based community participation in the planning process is essential. In reality, participation in planning and development activities in most communities is uneven, and unless great care is taken some constituencies will be excluded from the process. It is especially important not to restrict minority or newcomer interests to a single committee or advisory board.

A number of packinghouse communities have had success with citizen advisory committees to their police department, city government, school board, and helping agencies. Mark Grey was a member of the Garden City research team, and he has gone on to study and work with packinghouse towns across Iowa. He recommends the creation of "diversity committees," representing a broad array of community agencies and constituencies, including service clubs, helping agencies, institutions of higher education, news media, labor unions, and representatives of major employers. Such committees should be careful to include longtime residents and newcomers from every major ethnic group. Grey (1998:15–16) points out that:

> These committees not only encourage communication between newcomers and the community, but they also can respond constructively to incidents that may heighten distrust.
> . . . (They) can coordinate services and avoid duplication of service and save precious resources. They also can identify barriers to existing services and help newcomers overcome these barriers. Just as important, these committees can identify unmet needs and create ways to address them.

3. Invest in Communication

Throughout North America, the making of our meat and poultry increasingly falls to new immigrants with limited English-language skills. On the other hand, the plants where they make it are located in rural communities where the vast majority of established residents are monolingual English speakers.

Effective translation and interpretation are pressing needs in packinghouse communities, but these services are usually provided by persons with no training in these areas, and, as often as not, with poor writing or verbal skills in one or both of the languages in question. Volunteers, children, support staff pulled off their jobs in an emergency—these are the language brokers, the intermediaries between cultures, who are most often called upon. Private individuals can limp along "knowing enough to get by" in Spanish, which has become the dominant language on the floor of many meat and poultry plants, or learning a few polite phrases in Vietnamese or other newcomer languages. But the police, health care providers, schools, and social service agencies need bilingual professional staff.

Recognizing the need for bilingual staff and filling that need are different matters, however. Bilingual professional staff in any field are in short supply, and they can demand premium wages. Isolated, rural communities find it exceedingly difficult to attract such persons, and packinghouse towns like Brooks, Guymon, and Garden City must compete with cities near and far that are eager for persons with the same skills.

Higher salaries and signing bonuses have been used in some locales, but they cause resentment among coworkers who do not qualify for these enhancements.

Small towns usually cannot compete with larger communities for such persons, and even when they can, newcomers often don't stay long.

"GROW-OUR-OWN" PROGRAM   The Garden City School District has implemented a program to "grow its own" bilingual teachers. Bilingual high school graduates are eligible for scholarships to Fort Hays State University, a two-hour drive from Garden City, if they agree to return to teach for a certain time after receiving their bachelor's degrees. This program does not produce a large number of bilingual teachers, but the ones who do complete the program are likely to remain in Garden City because they have family ties to the community and "know what they are getting into."

There are also adults, some with college degrees, living in packinghouse towns who would be eager to return to school to obtain the necessary language or occupational skills to qualify for positions in local agencies. For example, native Spanish speakers might be offered scholarships in law enforcement or nursing if they agree to serve for a specified time.

TRANSLATION   Garden City, Dodge City, and Liberal, Kansas, each have community colleges, and Brooks has a branch of Medicine Hat College. Tyson's Robards, Kentucky, plant is within a 30-minute drive of two community colleges. Foreign language instructors at these colleges or local secondary schools could be enlisted to translate signs, newspaper advertisements, and forms. They could also "back-translate" materials in existing foreign languages to ensure translations are correct. Presently, much translation in U.S. processing plants and host communities is provided by Mexican Americans with little or no formal training in Spanish. Mexican Americans may speak Spanish, but often they do not write or read the language well. Limited literacy is also a problem for many native English speakers, and back-translation can help in English usage as well.

All printed matter intended for wide distribution or long shelf life should be professionally translated and back-translated. Documents should be translated by a competent translator from English to all other languages spoken by significant numbers of workers or community residents. A second competent translator should translate the document back into English without referring to the original English version. Then a *third* person, a literate English speaker familiar with the intent of the document, should review the back-translation and note problems. The marked-up back-translation should be returned to the original translator for final revision and publication.

REACHING NON-ENGLISH SPEAKERS   School announcements going home to parents, signs in offices and businesses serving the general public, and public announcements in the local media should speak to every major language community in town. The public library should add significantly and regularly to its books and periodicals in these languages.

Brochures welcoming non–English-speaking newcomers and introducing them to local laws, expectations, and services in their native languages can provide an important tool in fostering cross-cultural communication. Such materials may already exist in other communities, and whenever possible should be adapted for local use.

- STOP -

Deposite el Correro Aqui
Xin Bo Thu Vao Day
Deposit Mail Here

Fuera del Pueblo   Para Garden City
Thu Guicac Noi Khac   Thủ Gui Trang Dia Phòng
Out of Town   Garden City

LAST PICKUP 5:40 PM

Michael Eroaeway

Figure 8.4 Signs in Spanish, Vietnamese, and English at the Garden City, Kansas, Post Office

Cultural brokers emerge to provide essential cross cultural links anywhere two or more ethnic or language communities intersect. These natural brokers should be identified and utilized whenever possible. The role of cultural broker can also be formalized. A good example comes from Storm Lake, Iowa, a pork packing town.

> Storm Lake police sought to overcome communication barriers . . . through the creation of two community service officer positions. One position was created for a native Lao speaker and the other for a native Spanish speaker. In both cases, these were community outreach officers who wore uniforms, but did not carry guns. Their primary purpose was to establish relations between the newcomer communities and the police and other local services. Because both officers were native speakers and members of the cultural groups they worked with, they were able to establish an immediate rapport. These officers often prevented crime by communicating the community's expectations for behavior. (Grey 1998:21–22)

Storm Lake's police department also worked to prevent officer bias and discrimination by banning derogatory language about ethnic groups. Officers also received training in the cultures of newcomer groups (Grey 1998:22).

4. Recognize and Respect Cultural Differences and Similarities

Culture refers to the collective knowledge and patterns of behavior socially learned and shared by a group of people (Peoples & Bailey 1999:17). Cultural systems take hold in and subsequently shape the behavior of many different types of social groups: nations, organizations, occupations, families, and interest groups. Various cultural

Don Stull

*Figure 8.5 Children from many cultural backgrounds enjoy the Beef Empire Days parade.
Beef Empire Days is held each June in Garden City, Kansas.*

forms coexist in the same space, and people belong to more than one cultural group-
ing at the same time, making the relationship between coexisting cultural systems
complex.

National cultures, the ideas and behaviors people share because they were born
and raised in a particular country or region, are the most obvious. Several national cultures are invariably represented in packinghouse towns, and the towns rapidly become
multicultural and multilingual. This is something their citizens can be proud of.

Distinct cultures also spring up around certain occupations, and these work cultures often transcend the boundaries between national cultures. Although it has
become the hog capital of the Southern Plains, the heritage of Guymon, Oklahoma,
is rooted in the cattle kingdom. Ranching, and the way of life on which it depends,
is also the heritage of many of Guymon's newcomers, Anglo and Hispanic alike. As
such, it offers an important common ground. Rodeo is part of the ranching heritage
of both Mexico and the United States; in fact, the word comes from the Spanish
rodear, to go around, or to round up cattle. Many of the terms Anglo stockmen and
cowboys use on a daily basis are derived from Spanish: *bronco, buckaroo, chaps,
dally, hackamore, lasso, lariat, latigo, remuda.* The involvement of Mexican immigrants in Guymon's Pioneer Days, Garden City's Beef Empire Days, or any of the
rodeos to be found in packinghouse towns everywhere from Dumas, Texas, to
Brooks, Alberta, can make these events more inclusive and more entertaining to
everyone.

Work is what brings people to packinghouse towns—and what keeps them there.
Meatpacking has always had a tradition of hard, dangerous work and insular corporate cultures, characteristics that are unlikely to change. These industry characteris-

tics must be considered in whatever efforts the community undertakes. Shift work is a good example. Turnover is normally higher on the second (night) shift, which means that new workers are more likely to be placed on the second shift. Night work disrupts sleep patterns and daily routines for workers. It can also disrupt families, showing up in indicators such as "latchkey kids" and increased marital discord. Family stress, in turn, contributes to employee turnover.

Shift work is a fact of life for meat and poultry plants and for many other employers as well. Service providers, both in and out of government, must accommodate it. Schools must keep work schedules in mind when arranging parent-teacher conferences; service providers must extend their hours; translators must be available to meet the needs of second-shift workers. Health care providers can provide evening office hours to avoid the more costly practice of clients using the emergency room for routine medical care.

Awareness of, and accommodation to, the needs and cultures of newcomers is necessary if packinghouse towns expect to deal successfully with the challenges they presently face. But meeting the needs of newcomers is not *sufficient*. Planners, policy makers, and service providers must not lose sight of the concerns and the needs of long-established residents. Such forgetfulness—or the appearance of it—is a real danger for communities like Brooks, Guymon, Lexington, and Garden City, which are being stretched to the limit in developing and implementing the services needed by incoming groups.

THE WAY FORWARD

Planning is essential to development. When it involves a broad section of the community, and when it is done in a collaborative and participatory manner, planning can create a collective vision. But planning takes time, and consensus is hard to achieve. Plans can be goals in themselves—the final product of an exercise involving professional planners, often brought in from outside. Planning can also be used to exclude segments of a community and limit community choice.

Community development can mean many different things, and the indicators of its success can vary widely—job creation, population retention, increasing the tax base, cleaning up the environment. Different definitions of what is desired will influence the strategies a community chooses. And efforts to influence one outcome—job creation, for example—may have serious consequences for others.

Regardless of the goals desired—or the development models adopted—two factors are important to any effort at community development: (1) communities need to look beyond their boundaries for sources of information—they need to be open to lateral learning; and (2) they need to plan for the future.

Communities are dynamic—they change or they die. But the nature of that change determines the health of communities. Development is more than annual outputs, the number of new jobs, and multiplier effects. It is more complicated than economic forecasters and town boosters are often willing to admit. Planners and politicians should consider not only the benefits of economic development, but also its costs—not just what must be given away to attract new industry, but more important, what that industry will cost the people of the host community and the state or province after it arrives. If we wish to preserve what we cherish most about our communities, we must place economic development within the larger context of community development. And we must look to other communities and their experiences for signposts toward successful development.

Vibrant local communities are central to the future of rural North America; so are industry and government. Industry has a responsibility to communities that host its facilities—providing jobs is not enough, especially when those jobs come with significant social and economic costs. Government should do more than lure new business with tax holidays. It should make funds available to rural communities to meet their needs, especially those places facing rapid growth and increasing ethnic and linguistic diversity. Grants are needed for transitional and low-cost housing. Continuing funding is necessary to offset additional drains on the institutions that provide health care, public education, and law enforcement.

Host communities have an obligation as well. If they want new jobs, and the added business and tax revenue that come with them, they must provide a suitable environment for the workers who will fill those jobs.

Local governments must be willing—and able—to expand physical infrastructure and provide adequate and affordable new housing. They also must attend to increased demands on social infrastructure and ensure adequate and culturally aware services. Schools must provide for expanding enrollments; they must educate diverse student bodies and reach out to parents. Religious leaders must provide guidance during times of rapid change. Charitable and other nongovernmental organizations must find ways to stretch their budgets even more, to serve larger clienteles with various and often disparate needs. The media should inform, not inflame. And community members, old-timers and newcomers alike, must learn tolerance, flexibility, and openness to change.

When leaders think first of the community and its overall interests—and when planning and decision making are participatory—towns prosper. When economic interests are first and foremost—and when decision making and planning are concentrated—growth benefits only a few, and community welfare is threatened. The choices we make today shape our communities tomorrow.

9/Not in My Backyard:
Community Opposition to the Meat and Poultry Industry

Confined Animal Feeding Operations (CAFOs) have become a national issue. A new hog plant in Utah will produce more animal waste than the animal and human waste created by the city of Los Angeles, 1,600 dairies in the Central Valley of California produce more waste than a city of 21 million people. The annual production of 600 million chickens on the Delmarva Peninsula near Washington, D.C., generates as much nitrogen as a city of almost 500,000 people.

With this emotionally charged salvo, the Board of Directors of the National Catholic Rural Life Conference called for an immediate moratorium on large-scale livestock and poultry animal confinement facilities on December 18, 1997. The church is not alone in its condemnation of the environmental and social consequences of what has come to be called "factory farming." The Consumer Federation of America, the Humane Society of the United States, and EarthSave have joined with the National Family Farm Coalition and the National Farmers Union, with the Delmarva and Georgia Poultry Justice Alliances and the National Contract Poultry Growers Association, to call for increased regulation of pork and poultry production (National Catholic Rural Life Conference 1997). Leading this unlikely coalition is the Sierra Club, "the largest and oldest grassroots environmental organization in the world," which has named "protect[ing] America's water from factory-farm pollution" as one of its four national priorities (Sierra Club n.d.:2).[1] According to a 1999 article in *Sierra,* the magazine of the Sierra Club:

> Farms have now replaced factories as the biggest polluters of America's waterways. . . . A December 1997 report prepared for Iowa Senator Tom Harkin (D), who sits on the Senate Committee on Agriculture, says that animal waste is the largest contributor to pollution in 60 percent of the rivers and streams classified as "impaired" by the Environmental Protection Agency. . . . The United States generates 12.4 billion tons of animal manure every year—130 times more than the annual production of human waste. (Silverstein 1999:3)

Most of this waste is generated by the use of concentrated animal feeding operations (CAFOs) to raise cattle, hogs, and poultry. The technique was pioneered by the poultry industry, and today most chickens are raised inside massive houses. For every pound of gain, a chicken produces approximately half a pound of dry waste (Poultry Water Quality Consortium 1998). Mixed with the rice hulls or wood chips that are used to line the floors of chicken houses, this waste is called *litter.*

Properly handled, poultry litter is the most valuable of livestock manures (Rasnake, Murdock, & Thom 1991:1). It is high in nitrogen, phosphate, and potash, and is well suited to hay and corn, which require high nutrient levels and a long growing season that allows litter decomposition and nutrient release (Rasnake 1996:1–2). Best of all, it is often free for the taking from growers, who must regularly remove and dispose of it.

WESTERN KENTUCKY'S TOUR DE STENCH

Broiler houses produce somewhere between 140 and 200 tons of litter each year (Rasnake 1996:1; Stull 2000:157); breeder houses, where eggs are produced to supply the broiler houses with chicks, generate about 80 tons of litter a year. At this rate, the 567 broiler houses and 68 breeder houses that supply the Tyson Foods plant near Robards, Kentucky, annually produce somewhere between 84,820 and 118,840 tons of chicken litter. Spread on fields at the recommended rate of 4 tons per acre, and multiplied by 4 (the number of poultry processing plants in the state), enough litter is produced to fertilize somewhere between 132 and 186 square miles of Kentucky every year (640 acres per square mile).

Having an abundance of free fertilizer would be good news for farmers, except for the fact that chickens, and the litter they produce, smell. And disposing of 400,000 tons of chicken litter every year would be a simple matter if it were spread evenly across Kentucky's 39,732 square miles. But it is not. Poultry processing is concentrated in the western half of the state, and poultry houses are located within a 60–70 mile radius of the plants they supply.

At first, rural western Kentucky's residents welcomed the poultry industry. It promised new jobs, increased revenues, and new markets and premium prices for their corn. But they didn't reckon with the smell. For poultry companies and their growers it was the smell of money. But for many who live near chicken houses, which are built in complexes ranging from 2 to 16 houses, it has become the stench of environmental and cultural degradation.

A full year before the Tyson plant, originally built by Hudson Foods, opened on July 9, 1996, area residents were raising concerns (*Sebree Banner* 1995). Within a year of the plant's opening, neighbors of broiler houses were protesting odor, flies and other vermin, ground water pollution and potential health risks, increased and overweight traffic and resulting road damage. Coalitions of property owners went to court to block construction of broiler houses in three counties. The Fiscal Court of Webster County, the county with the largest number of chicken houses, mandated that poultry houses be at least 600 feet from homes—11 days later the poultry company filed suit to block enforcement of the ordinance (Gilkey 1997). Neighbors turned against neighbors, and some chicken houses were vandalized (McKinley 1998:A1). The "chicken war" was in full swing (Whittington 1997). Meanwhile, more poultry houses have appeared, their neighbors have continued to complain, and chicken houses remain at risk for vandalism (Associated Press 2002).

Don Stull

Figure 9.1 An anonymous combatant issues a call to arms in western Kentucky's "chicken war," McLean County, Kentucky, 1998.

Taking up their cause has been the Sierra Club, which hired Aloma Dew in 1999 to work full-time on its campaign against poultry CAFOs in Kentucky. She has forged alliances with grassroots organizations, organized conferences on the environmental and socioeconomic consequences of industrial agriculture, and collected money for CAFO opponents who fell on hard times.

She has led an annual Tour de Stench to raise awareness of the problems associated with CAFOs in western Kentucky. The tour is designed to raise general awareness of the "problems of health, environment, water and quality of life related to concentration of poultry CAFOs" (Anonymous 2001:1). In all these efforts she has defended the rights and livelihoods of Kentucky's farmers, even those who have chosen to become poultry growers. In a 1999 interview she said, "The farmer is the victim too. Nobody wants to make life harder on farmers. . . . These corporations are not farmers. They don't care about farmers. They care about the bottom line" (Hutchison 1999:A2).

Nevertheless, chicken farmers, commonly called growers, are part of the poultry industry, and their livelihood is increasingly bound to it. Although most farmers consider themselves stewards of their land, they are often bitterly opposed to environmentalists and their causes. One western Kentucky grower put it this way:

> There are some treehuggers, and the funniest thing is that the firebrands and the treehuggers are mostly above-middle-class housewives with nothing to do on their hands. . . .
> These people were socially involved, and they were trying to do the right thing. . . . But

Figure 9.2 At a stop on the Tour de Stench, a mother and her young children extol the "pleasures" of having broiler houses, which can be seen in the distance, for neighbors.

they don't know what the hell they're talking about. . . . And they're stirring these people up, and they're benefiting from it. . . . I would rather be an active environmentalist than an environmental activist. Yeah, there are concerns. You can't be running around doing Chicken Little all the time, too. And that's what these people are doing. (Stull interview, November 24, 1998)

Of more immediate concern to growers than so-called treehuggers are their neighbors, who, like them, are country people and often farmers themselves. A grower with four broiler houses characterized his circumstances as follows:

I've had some that supported me, and I've had some that didn't want 'em. I've had some that was really, really against 'em. For the most part, I think there's nine households around mine, and two of 'em was against 'em and seven of 'em didn't care. . . . My dad was gonna put four [broiler houses] up and put 'em by mine. And that's when they really got to squealing about it. Didn't like it . . . so we decided to move his down here behind this house. . . . They haven't really given me a whole lot of trouble but I know they didn't like 'em and they didn't want 'em. But now they'll tell you that they're not nearly what they thought they'd be. (Stull interview, November 19, 1998)

THE SIERRA CLUB TAKES ON BIG CHICKEN

On April 22, 2002—Earth Day—the Sierra Club sued Tyson Foods and four of its largest western Kentucky growers, who operate complexes ranging from 16 to 24 broiler houses, citing their operations for emitting excessive levels of ammonia and dust under the federal Superfund law, the Clean Air Act, and the Community-Right-to-Know Act (Lucas 2002b:A1; Lovan 2002:A1).

Responding to the lawsuit, Tyson issued a statement regretting the Sierra Club's "attempts to politicize agriculture." "In its misguided lawsuit it wants the public to believe the 7,500 independent farmers who grow chickens for Tyson Foods around the country are running 'factories' and not chicken farms" (Tyson Foods 2002d).

But, the Sierra Club, through its attorney, argues otherwise:

> This is all about massive concentrations of chickens. It's not about family farmers. Due to this massive concentration, it is triggering both the reporting requirements for hazardous substances under our toxics laws, and triggering the permit requirements for dust emissions under the Clean Air Act. These emissions—and the reason they are required to report them—are because they threaten public health. (Bruggers 2002:1)

Three of the 4 farms named by the Sierra Club, including the "Tyson Children" partnership, are owned by out-of-state interests. But most of those who operate chicken houses in western Kentucky are indeed local farmers who saw poultry as a means to diversify and augment their farm operations at a time when it is increasingly difficult to make a living. As one tobacco farmer with four broiler houses explained:

> I just thought it might be a pretty good deal to make some money on the side. In contrast, tobacco, they're always on it about "stop smoking" and maybe suing the tobacco companies and all that, and I didn't know how long tobacco was gonna be around. (Stull interview, November 19, 1998)

THE FUTURE OF FARMING IN WESTERN KENTUCKY

Tobacco, long Kentucky's principal cash crop and vital to its economic welfare and culture, is in sharp decline as an agricultural commodity. Between 1998 and 2001, the value of the state's tobacco crop fell from about $900 million to about $400 million, the result of a reduction of almost 80 percent in the quotas that dictate how much burley tobacco each farm can grow (Lucas 2002a:A7).

State and local leaders have argued that poultry is a good alternative to tobacco (Stull 2000.159). And chickens have enabled some young farmers to stay on their land and others to augment what is an increasingly precarious economic existence. But Big Chicken, like Big Tobacco, is under attack—for how its birds are grown, for the environmental consequences of the waste they produce, and for the antibiotics that have long been part of the ration fed to its birds. And like Big Tobacco, Big Chicken is bowing to increased public pressure. Tyson, Perdue, and Foster Farms, which produce one-third of the chicken eaten by Americans, recently claimed they have ceased or greatly curtailed the use of antibiotics in chicken feed (Burros 2002:1).

Kentucky's farmers are in a bind. In this most tobacco-dependent state, about half of Kentucky's farms either produce tobacco or have allotments for it (Lucas 2002a:A7), and until recently 60,000 Kentucky farmers averaged $12,000 income per year from tobacco (Apple 1998). But as tobacco allotments are slashed, small producers can no longer count on "tobacco keeping their corn crop going" in what has proved to be a sustained period of depressed grain prices. Tobacco growers, like producers of other farm commodities, are finding they must "get big or get out." Tobacco is also being "chickenized." Traditionally sold at auctions around the state, two-thirds of Kentucky's tobacco crop is now sold under direct contract (Lucas 2002a:A7).

Poultry and tobacco growers know that "tobacco's not going to be here forever," but they also know that chicken

> ain't gonna replace tobacco [because] it can't be as widespread . . . [because] you can start for nothing with tobacco. And if you want to quit today, you can quit today. [But] you can't build these [chicken] houses hardly and start from scratch and live and scramble and get along . . . and get these chicken houses paid for. (Stull interview, November 11, 1998)

Doubts about the benefits of the poultry industry for western Kentucky are growing, and some of the growers who were so enthusiastic back in 1998 have already sold their operations. Others find themselves like the pullet grower who spoke at the Sierra Club conference on CAFOs in Murray, Kentucky, on November 5, 2000. He had grown for Seaboard (now ConAgra) for 11 years, ever since they built the first poultry plant in the state. He figured that he and his wife earn only 81 cents an hour for their labor. He wants to get out of his contract, but he can't because he can't get out of debt. "We're just white Mexicans," he lamented (Stull fieldnotes, June 26, 2001:4–5).

A FIGHT LOST, A FIGHT TO BE WON: BIG PIG IN ALBERTA

Kentuckians could not keep CAFOs out of their state. Elsewhere in North America the fight continues. In western Canada, a bountiful supply of feed grains and sparse rural population have combined with an aggressive business recruitment strategy, "The Alberta Advantage," to make Alberta a battleground between CAFO developers and opponents.

In 1997 and 1998, 471 permitting requests for CAFOs were submitted to rural Alberta municipalities. About half the applications were for hog confinement facilities, one-third for cattle feedlots, and the rest for poultry and dairy operations. Sixty percent of the proposals were for new operations, and the remainder sought to expand or replace existing ones. Those who oppose confined animal feeding have a difficult task: 438 of the 471 applications were approved (Alberta Agriculture, Food and Rural Development 2002).

One such proposal came from Taiwan Sugar Corporation (TSC), a state-owned transnational company based in Taipai with operations in Vietnam and Australia. In early 2000, it proposed to build a facility capable of producing 150,000 hogs a year in Foremost (pop. 531 in 2001).

Foremost is surrounded by farms and ranches in the County of Forty Mile, in the southeast corner of the province. The county covers almost 3,000 square miles but is home to only 3,000 souls, making it a seemingly ideal location for a CAFO. But just in case TSC's permit was denied, the company simultaneously applied to Flagstaff County, 100 miles southeast of Edmonton. Flagstaff, like Forty Mile, serves a farming and ranching area with a declining and aging population (pop. 3,697 in 2001).

Responsibility for approving CAFOs rested with local municipalities at the time of TSC's application. The provincial government encouraged local governments to incorporate the 1995 Code of Practice for the Safe and Economic Handling of Animal Manure into their land use bylaws. The code set standards for the amount of land base required for manure disposal, lagoon construction, minimum distance separation requirements, and other mitigating measures.

TSC appeared before the County of Forty Mile Municipal Planning Commission in June 2000 to argue that its $42 million (Canadian) investment would create 54 new jobs, provide local farmers with a market for their grain and a source of free manure, and supply Alberta's packers with hogs. Opponents raised concerns about the CAFO's environmental impact and disputed its classification as a farm, which would save the company $250,000 a year in property taxes. More than two-thirds of Forty Mile's registered voters signed a petition opposing the plan. The petition and a summary of scientific research on the environmental impact of hog CAFOs were presented at the planning commission's hearings. A month later the commission denied TSC planning permission because of the potential for manure to contaminate surface and groundwater, as well as the negative effects of odor from the barns on adjacent property values (Duckworth 2000). Taiwan Sugar appealed the decision (which was later denied) and announced its intention to construct a similar operation in Flagstaff County.

LET THE MATCH RECOMMENCE

Round 1: The Proposal

To grow out 150,000 hogs a year, TSC proposed to place 7,200 sows in 14 barns in 5 sites near Hardisty in Flagstaff County. Each barn would be constructed so manure would fall through slatted floors to be pumped to a nearby lagoon. The lagoons would be covered with a negative air-pressure cover to reduce odor and would be lined with high-density polyethylene. Beneath the plastic would be a compacted clay liner and leak-detection system. Each lagoon would be emptied once a year, allowing for any necessary liner repairs. The manure would be spread over 29,400 acres and injected into the soil to reduce runoff and odor. The entire operation would consume an estimated 45 million gallons of water a year, provided from wells at one or more of the development sites.

Flagstaff County Development Authority approved the proposal in September 2000 after determining it met requirements for operating a CAFO, as outlined in the county's land use bylaws. In undertaking the review, the county development officer later testified that the county had:

> sought to address concerns with respect to odor control, manure storage systems, surface water management, dead animal disposal, pest management, road upgrade, manure management, including soil sampling and tests and land base requirements, record keeping, water sampling and minimum distance separations [and concluded that the development is] compatible with existing land uses in the area.[2]

Round 2: The Appeal

The development authority's decision was immediately appealed by 18 landowners and the Flagstaff Family Farm Promotional Society. The society based its appeal on the grounds that: (1) the lagoons were improperly sited with respect to local groundwater conditions; (2) the development lacked a land base large enough for safe manure disposal; and (3) the barns constituted a danger and/or an annoyance to adjacent landowners, which was a violation of the land use bylaw. The following month Flagstaff County's Subdivision and Development Appeal Board met to hear the case.

The appeal board consisted of five local farmers. Its chair was a retired provincial government employee with strong ties to the ruling provincial Progressive Conservative Party. Taiwan Sugar, the appeal board, the development authority, and appellants were each represented by legal counsel. Over the course of 4 days in October 2000, the board listened to more than 920 pages of testimony from engineers, pork industry lobbyists, soil scientists, planners, environmentalists, Taiwan Sugar executives, provincial and county government officials, local citizens, former residents of the area, and Michael Broadway. Legal counsel on both sides agreed that the appeal board's function was to sift through the presented evidence to determine whether the proposal conformed to Flagstaff County's Land Use Bylaws and Municipal Development Plan. Much of the testimony presented at the hearings dealt with the technical aspects of the proposal, such as lagoon design and hydrogeological conditions in the vicinity of the barns. But many local residents "deemed to be affected" used the hearings to speak out against their elected officials for their role in recruiting TSC.

Round 3: Opening Salvos

Most of the 98 people who spoke at the hearings were against the proposal. A petition presented to the board with 1,222 signatures of local ratepayers also opposed the project. Wendy Mazure, a local farmer whose family homesteaded in the area in the early 1900s, told the board:

> We expect that our government will act in the best interest of our society rather than those of a foreign corporation. . . . We would be much happier if Alberta's own pork producers were allowed to produce the pork required by Taiwan Sugar rather than selling out our environment, our industry and our community to a foreign corporation.

For Lorraine Davidson, another local farmer, the development was "about the coming home of 'The Alberta Advantage.'" Her mother-in-law, Faye, agreed:

> I have viewed with disbelief that our Alberta government would invite a foreign government treasury into compete against our pork producers. . . . This is not just a move by a foreign government to use our country as a cesspool, while they run the money home to Taiwan. . . . It is an assault by corporate hogs on private hog producers.

Taiwan Sugar executive, Danny Huang, responded, "We are just invite[d] by your people to come over here. I think we have come over here to make friend, not to fight against people or make your people fight together or against each other."

Deep community divisions were also noted by a United Church minister, who characterized the divide as "a conflict between agribusiness and agriculture . . . a clash between those who live here and those who just want to do business here. . . . What is value added to one is devaluation to the other."

Round 4: Factory Farms versus Agriculture

Under Flagstaff County's Municipal Development Plan (MDP), "agriculture and providing services to the agricultural community are regarded as the most important forms of development in Flagstaff County." TSC's counsel, citing the MDP, argued that when farming is practiced in accordance with generally accepted practices in any provincial regs . . . these activities may occur 24 hours a day, 365 days a year; and the noise, odors, dust and fumes by the activities will be allowed. . . . What this section is saying is inherently farming can be a nuisance but it takes priority.

Opponents cited a different section of the MDP: "Landowners should be able to act as they please on their own land as long as or provided neighboring landowners, business people, residents and future neighbors are not harmed." The provision that any development must not have any harmful effects on neighbors was echoed in the land use bylaws, which gave the county's development authority power to reject any proposal that constitutes "a danger or annoyance to persons."

Round 5: Economic Benefits

The director of Alberta Pork, a marketing organization, supported TSC's proposal because it would increase the supply of hogs and allow packing plants to add "that second shift that they require to make them more cost efficient and globally competitive." An eleventh-grader testified that for teenagers, "jobs are few and hard to come by in a small town," but the barns represented an "opportunity to make money." The jobs would be "perfect for any person who has any interest at all in agriculture." A formal endorsement of the project was provided by the chairman of the Hardisty Economic Development Committee, who noted that "although they did not go looking for TSC," the project offered an opportunity to revitalize "the local economy which is presently quite dismal." This view was reinforced by a consultant, who estimated that the 54 full-time jobs provided by TSC would generate 26 others. Based upon a study of land sales in a nearby county, he concluded that "a well managed intensive livestock operation will not decrease land values in the proximity in which it is located."

Some local farmers noted that if TSC purchased 45,000 tons of feed grain a year, inventories would fall and thereby boost prices. Farmers would also benefit by having the manure from the barns spread on their land for free, a value they estimated at $25 an acre. Danny Kroetsch, a farmer with a 240-sow farrow-to-finish operation supported the proposal for a different reason:

> People have asked me if I think I will be squeezed out because of the size of TSC. No. In fact I view them as a plus for me and all hog producers because of their knowledge of the Japanese market. These people know that market . . . and that can only be seen as a benefit.

But based upon U.S. studies, opponents argued that the community would end up absorbing the costs of the operation without receiving any economic benefits. Housing property values would decline in the vicinity of CAFOs, and most of TSC's purchases would occur outside the region—a view that was reluctantly conceded by a TSC consultant who acknowledged that the larger the CAFO operation, the more it spent outside the region. The negative economic consequences of the project were supported by a representative of Canada's National Farmers Union, who noted that while the development would create jobs and a market for feed grains, corporate hog barns "provide significantly fewer of these benefits than the family farms they displace," and "employ fewer people per hog and spend less in their communities than family farm hog producers." The representative concluded, "Transferring hog production from local farm families to corporations such as Taiwan Sugar, Smithfield, and Maple Leaf facilitates and accelerates the extraction of wealth and capital from rural areas."

Round 6: Environmental Issues

Lori Goodrich, president of the Flagstaff County Family Farm Promotional Society, summarized the society's concerns:

> No one person can tell us that 150,000 pigs will not create odors. No one person can tell us that they will not contaminate our waters. No one person can say that unlined concrete lagoons under the barns will not leak. No one person can tell us that manure pipelines through culverts and across land will not break or separate. It has happened. Don't tell us our land values won't decrease. Who the hell will live beside stinking hog farms?

TSC responded that the sites exceeded the code's recommendation for minimum distance separating CAFOs and neighboring developments and that the covers on the lagoons would substantially reduce the odor.

Both sides agreed that the lagoons met the code's construction standards, but they differed on the suitability of the proposed sites. A hydrologist, testifying for the appellants, argued that none of the sites were "suitable" in view of the potential for leaks and resulting groundwater contamination, since there was no hydrological data indicating the water table level or movement of groundwater. TSC's experts acknowledged that some of the barn sites were in hydrogeological "high risk areas," but if a leak were to occur in the primary liner it would be detected by monitoring wells and contained by the clay liner, giving them sufficient time to empty the lagoon and make any necessary repairs.

Local farmers were also concerned about the amount of water the project would use and its impact upon aquifer levels. Lana and Barry Love noted that their well levels had dropped for the last 3 years, and TSCs extraction of another 124,000 gallons a day would only compound the problem. TSC responded that it was only proposing to use four times as much water as the Hardisty golf course uses to water its fairways and greens and that "in terms of groundwater supply and availability we are not asking to use that much."

TSC estimated it would generate 41.3 million gallons of liquid manure. But each side disputed the amount and suitability of the land base identified for manure disposal. An agrologist hired by the appellants analyzed the 29,400 acres identified in the proposal for manure spreading and suggested that less than a third of the acreage was suitable, due to slope and soil characteristics that increased potential for runoff and water contamination. Henry Hays, a fifth-generation farmer, voiced the fears of many local people about this aspect of the proposal: "A vast area northwest and west of our house is slated for pig manure. Spring runoff brings water from this area through two County culverts to sloughs adjacent to our house, will pig manure residue end up in our basement?"

TSC said it would comply with the 1995 Code of Practice for the Safe and Economic Handling of Animal Manure: prior to spreading manure, the soil would be sampled to determine the amounts of phosphorous and nitrogen extractable by the crops (to prevent excess amounts running off that would pollute streams and rivers);

manure would be sampled for nutrient content and the application rate adjusted accordingly; and any abandoned wells would be capped. An agrologist would supervise the application and verify compliance with appropriate setbacks from wells, water courses, and property lines. Each landowner would receive a report summarizing the soil sampling plan, the manure content, and application rates. The report would also be provided to Flagstaff County.

THE DECISION AND ITS AFTERMATH

In reaching its decision, the board acknowledged that "we are to apply the Land Use Bylaw and any other planning instruments, such as the Municipal Development Plan, as we find them, having regard to proper planning considerations" (Schorak 2000:17). But after reviewing the evidence and applying the standard, the board disregarded the petition, the concerns expressed over the future of family farms, the potential economic impact of the project, its effect on land values, and the national origin of the developer. Instead, it concluded that "the Land Use Bylaw does contemplate that intensive animal operations may be allowed within the agricultural dis trict. . . . Based upon the evidence which was before us, the development should be allowed subject to (certain) conditions" (Schorak 2000:19). Among the conditions added to the permit were requirements that TSC pay for persons, appointed or approved by the county, to monitor compliance with the code of practice, and that in the event of any breach of the permit, the county could issue a stop order and close the operation.

The conditions added to the permit failed to allay the concerns of many local people, and following announcement of the board's decision its chairman was besieged with "hundreds" of angry phone calls from residents protesting the decision (MacArthur 2000). The Family Farm Promotional Society was left with one option, to appeal the decision to the Alberta Court of Appeal.[3]

The opposition mounted against TSC is one of numerous battles fought against CAFOs across Alberta. The manager of the Alberta Pork Producers Association expressed the industry's frustration with the planning approval system at the TSC hearings:

> We believe that agriculture must be allowed to do business in rural areas. We're getting a little frustrated with some of the antics in some of the counties that have occurred . . . so we'd like to see the province come in and induce an act and some regulations and put out some standards that we can work with.

The provincial government's efforts to attract CAFO investors and value-added processing to the province have also been frustrated. To resolve this situation, it established a committee to examine how to remove the "uncertainty and controversy" surrounding the approval of CAFOs. It issued its report in April 2001 and recommended that the responsibility for approving CAFOs be *taken away* from local municipalities and given to a provincial government board. The board would have responsibility for reviewing applications, issuing approvals, monitoring, and enforcing provincewide standards.

Seven months later the provincial legislature gave Alberta's Natural Resources Conservation Board the responsibility for regulating CAFOs. It also gave the board power to overturn existing bans on CAFOs previously enacted by local municipalities

(MacArthur 2001). The standards to be used in judging a project's suitability are contained in the 2000 Code of Practice for Responsible Livestock Development and Manure Management developed by Alberta Agriculture, Food and Rural Development.

The pork industry welcomed the change in the approval process. But the president of the Alberta Association of Municipal Districts was disappointed, noting that "land use decisions are properly decided at the local level." After all, communities have to live with the decisions. Lisa Bechthold, a rancher who successfully organized the opposition to TSC in the County of Forty Mile, viewed the new system as a "way to ram the livestock industry down our throats" (Duckworth 2001).

NOT IN MY BACKYARD, REPRISE

Opposition to the meat industry is not restricted to its environmental impact. Public forums, the Internet, books, and journal articles have assured the widespread dissemination of research results on the social and economic impact of meat processing facilities. Sudden population growth, housing shortages, rising social service demands, and increases in crime have become ammunition for those who oppose new plants.

In the late 1990s, Seaboard Corporation began actively searching for a site for its second hog processing facility. It initially considered Garden City and Great Bend, Kansas, and St. Joseph, Missouri. Don Stull outlined the likely impacts of a hog processing plant at public forums in Great Bend and St. Joseph, and his publications played an important role in the debate in Garden City. After strong opposition surfaced in these three communities, Seaboard finally chose Moore County, in the Texas Panhandle, 75 miles southwest of its other plant in Guymon, Oklahoma. A Seaboard spokesman explained that the primary reason for its decision to build in Texas was the "tremendous support and encouragement from the people of Moore County and especially Dumas" (*Kansas City Business Journal* 2002). Dumas (13,747 pop. in 2000) already had a beef processing plant that employs 2,300 workers.

Excel and the Iowa Cattleman's Association have proposed a cooperative venture to build a $100 million beef plant in the state. A statewide survey by Iowa's economic development department found widespread public support for the project, but only 22 percent of survey respondents stated they would welcome a new beefpacking plant in their community. In fact, Des Moines, Iowa Falls, and Cambridge rejected it (Crews 2001a:26).

If corporations wishing to open processing plants are to avoid opposition, they must address the impact of their plant's operations on the host community. Gold Kist, a poultry processor heavily reliant upon Latino labor, has gained recognition for its innovative community relations efforts. The company works with local housing authorities to establish living arrangements for newcomers, develops ESL courses for employees and their children, promotes recreational opportunities, and works with local churches to provide a welcoming environment for Latino workers and their families (Crews 2001a). Without such attention to community issues, corporations are unlikely to find many local residents willing to put the "welcome mat" out for them.

NOTES

1. The other three are to "protect wildlands; challenge sprawl; [and] end commercial logging in our national forests."

2. All the quotations dealing with the public hearing are from the official transcripts taken at the Subdivision and Development Appeal Hearing by Snow's Court Reporting, Edmonton, Alberta.

3. Three months after the hearing, an Alberta Appeal Court judge agreed with the society's argument that the proposal violated the code in terms of its manure management plan and failure to identify the water table at the lagoon and barn sites. In November 2001, a three-judge panel conducted a full hearing on the appeal.

On December 9, 2002, the Alberta Court of Appeal ruled in favor of the appellants, canceled the planning permit, and referred the matter back to Flagstaff County's Subdivision and Development Appeal Board. In the aftermath of the decision, the Flagstaff Family Farm Promotional Society issued the following statement: "We hope that Taiwan Sugar Corporation will uphold their promise and if the courts turn them down they will leave" (County of Flagstaff Family Farm Promotional Society 2002).

10/Food for Thought

My early interest in meat began at the dinner table. Like everyone else I knew growing up during the 1960s in a small village 20 miles from the center of London, my family's meals revolved around meat. I left for school most days with a "full English breakfast" inside of me—bacon, sausage, bread, and tomatoes fried in bacon grease. Saturday lunch usually consisted of a steak and kidney pie or a casserole filled with bacon, sausage, and liver. Sundays we would dine on roast: lamb, pork, or beef. Mother served leftovers cold during the week or transformed them into shepherd's pie (ground beef covered with mashed potatoes and baked in the oven) or a lamb or beef curry. When we ate Sunday dinner at my grandparents' house, I watched my grandmother drain fat from a roast beef to make gravy and Yorkshire pudding. She poured leftovers into a bowl to cool, and the next day my grandfather would spread the solid fat onto his toast for breakfast. Occasionally he allowed his grandchildren to sample the delights of "drippings."

When I was young, my mother always took me with her when she went shopping. We walked the 15 minutes from our home to the center of our village and made the rounds of the local food stores. At the end of the High Street, across from my elementary school, stood the butcher's. In its big glass windows I could see carcasses hanging from hooks and smaller cuts of meat neatly displayed and tagged—New Zealand lamb, British beef, Wiltshire ham, Danish bacon. Inside the shop, the butcher, Mr. Groves, stood behind a long wooden table with a small glass front and narrow counter top. "How are you today Mrs. Broadway, lovely weather we are having. And what can I get for you today?"

"A pound of skirt and a quarter of kidney, please," meant our family would be eating steak and kidney pie that evening.

While Mr. Groves deftly cut through bone with a hacksaw or used a razor-sharp knife to trim fat from a skirt steak, I amused myself by making mountains with my toe out of the sawdust spread on the floor to soak up blood. Mr. Groves weighed each cut of meat my mother ordered, carefully wrapped it in white wax paper, wrote its price on the outside, and gave it to the cashier.

Mr. Groves's butcher shop had a distinct aroma—a mixture of sawdust, blood, and fresh meat. It was a wonderful smell.

By the 1980s, growing concerns over the harmful effects of red meat were transforming my family's diet. My mother had replaced steak and kidney pie with steak and mushroom pie—and the full English breakfast had become a bowl of cold cereal and two pieces of toast and marmalade. When I brought my children to see their grandparents in 1996, our visit coincided with the British government's announcement of a possible link between new variant Creutzfeldt-Jakob disease (nv CJD), a degenerative brain disease, and bovine spongiform encephalopathy (BSE)—mad cow disease. Stories about food safety filled the newspapers and airwaves, and my parents refused to serve us beef. So far, more than a hundred persons in Britain have died of nv CJD.

In 2002, Mr. Groves closed his shop. None of his children wanted to take up his trade, and with no willing buyers my parents lost their neighborhood butcher shop. Now they must travel 6 miles to the nearest supermarket to buy their meat, where they can choose from an array of neatly packaged portions in the refrigerator section of the meat department. But, if the store does not have the cut of meat they want, they are out of luck. The supermarket does not receive carcasses, nor does it employ skilled butchers to dismember them. Sadly, their grandchildren will no longer be able to gaze in wonder at sides of meat hanging in a shop window, or build sawdust mountain ranges as they listen to talk of "a small shoulder of lamb, a loin of pork, or a nice piece of sirloin suitable for roasting," or watch a butcher carefully prepare the meat for their evening meal. No, their grandchildren's meat smells of Styrofoam and cellophane.

THERE'S PLENTY MORE WHERE THAT CAME FROM

Never before have we had so much food to choose from. Most of our food is grown and processed under the control of giant transnational corporations, which search the globe for cheap and reliable sources of food and feed. The bacon a Peoria schoolboy eats for breakfast probably came from a hog raised in North Carolina on feed imported from Argentina or Canada. The McDonald's hamburger he eats at lunch might well come from cattle raised in Australia or New Zealand. The chicken fingers he eats at supper most likely came from birds grown in Arkansas on grain imported from Brazil.

Industrialized agriculture's bounty has lowered the cost of food. It has also contributed to "supersized" food portions in restaurants. In 1957, a White Castle hamburger ("The hamburger specialists since 1921") contained just over 1 ounce of cooked meat. The typical fast food hamburger today contains 6 ounces (Putnam 1999). McDonald's original hamburger, french fries, and 12-ounce cola provided 590 calories; today's Extra Value Meal—a Quarter Pounder with cheese, supersize fries, and supersize drink—is 1,550 calories (Spake 2002).

The supersizing of restaurant portions has contributed to the explosion in obesity among North Americans. In Canada, 15 percent of adults were considered obese in 2000, up from 13 percent in 1994 (Statistics Canada 2002). Sixty-one percent of U.S. adults are overweight or obese,[1] and 13 percent of children and adolescents are overweight. The percentage of overweight children aged 6–11 has more than doubled since 1980 and tripled for adolescents. An estimated 300,000 deaths a year are associated with obesity (U.S. Dept. of Health & Human Services 2001).

Michael Broadway

Figure 10.1 White Castle remains part of North America's fast food landscape.

Not only are the meals we eat out getting bigger, we also have more to choose from when we shop for food. The median number of items stocked by an American supermarket jumped from 14,000 in 1980 to 40,000 in 1999. Supermarkets are carrying more nonfood items, but there has also been a dramatic increase in the variety of foods being marketed by processing companies. In 1998 alone, in excess of 11,000 new food and beverage items were introduced in the United States—728 of them were for different types of processed meats (Gallo 1999). Some of these new products were "fist foods," meat encased in pouches, pockets, tubes, and wraps. Fist foods have become the fastest growing category of frozen and refrigerated foods in the United States (Jolley 2002).

The food we take home is more and more "convenient." But it is even more convenient to eat out. Restaurants accounted for about 25 cents of every dollar Americans spent on food in the 1950s. By 1999 they took 44 cents out of each food dollar, and their share is projected to rise to 53 cents by 2010. Of each dollar we spend eating out, a quarter goes to only 20 restaurant chains. This is not surprising, since fast food restaurants are literally everywhere—there is one fast food outlet for every 1,500 Americans (Tillotson 2002).

The traditional American dining pattern of "three square meals a day" is going the way of the traditional American family of a breadwinning father, a homemaking mother, and their children. More and more Americans are eating throughout the day, a phenomenon referred to as "grazing." Fast food chains and convenience stores have responded with "dashboard dining." Sonic Drive-In recently began packaging its french fries in round containers so they will conveniently fit in car cup holders (Jolley 2002).

"Fast food culture" has spread around the world. In Asia, for example, KFC (formerly Kentucky Fried Chicken) restaurants are common in Japan, Korea, Malaysia,

Thailand, Indonesia, the Philippines, and China. "The Colonel" is hawking his "original recipe" in every province of China except Tibet, and there are 70 KFC storefronts in Beijing alone. According to the chairman of Yum Brands,[2] which owns KFC, "one day I am certain we will have more KFCs in China than we do in the United States" (Novak 2002:4). There are more than 5,000 KFCs in the United States.

Rising levels of disposable income in developing nations are fueling increases in meat consumption. Among the world's poorest countries, meat supplies (a measure of consumption) increased in excess of 300 percent—from 12 to 49 pounds per capita—between 1961 and 1998 (Table 10.1).

Recent developments in China reflect this trend. Fueled by a rapidly growing economy, its share of world meat production soared from 11 percent in 1980 to 26 percent in 1998 (see Table 10.2). To accommodate this growth, China has increased imports of feed grains, which has caused concern about whether the world can support its burgeoning demand for meat (Brown 1995).

THERE'S NO SUCH THING AS A FREE LUNCH

Industrialized agriculture promises cheap food. But hidden costs in this production system are passed on to other sectors of the economy or externalized. Family farms, which once raised a variety of livestock and incorporated manure into their crop production as parts of a sustainable system, have been displaced by factory farms that specialize in a single commodity and depend upon large amounts of agrichemicals and petroleum. But despite, or perhaps because of, industrialized agriculture's success in producing greater quantities of food, commodity prices and farm incomes have dropped. U.S. farm income in 1999 was more than $10 billion *less* than its 1996 record of $55 billion (U.S. Census Bureau 2001). In Canada, net farm income, adjusted for inflation, dropped 24 percent between 1988 and 2002 (Canada National Farmers Union 2002.)

Population peaked for many rural counties in the Midwest—America's breadbasket—in the 1930s. Since then, the number of farms has declined by more than 1.2 million (Table 10.3). On Canada's prairies, Manitoba and Saskatchewan lost more than 25 percent of their farms between 1971 and 1996 (Bone 2000).

Small towns once were hubs for local economies, supplying local farmers and in turn depending on their business. But rural communities are being bypassed by the corporate replacements of family farms and are suffering a slow death through out-migration and falling incomes. According to the U.S. Office of Technology Assessment, as farm size increases so does rural poverty (Kimbrell 2002a). Farms that remain increasingly produce foodstuffs under contract to processors, who determine the final sale price. According to Nolan Jungclaus, an independent producer from Lake Lillian, Minnesota, who testified before the U.S. Senate Agriculture Committee on the effect of packer ownership of livestock, this process is "sucking the lifeblood out of rural communities" (*National Farmers Union News* 2002). The truth of his testimony is evident in Nebraska, home to the 3 poorest counties and 7 of the 21 poorest counties in the United States (Center for Rural Affairs 2002).

In desperate attempts to reverse their declining fortunes, local chambers of commerce or, increasingly, economic development officers in state and local governments actively recruit new businesses and industries using low or no taxes, free land,

150

TABLE 10.1 WORLD SUPPLY OF MEAT, 1961, 1980, AND 1998

Countries	Pounds per Capita			Percent Change
	1961	1980	1998	1961–1998
Low income	11.7	22.0	48.9	317.9
Middle income	50.0	74.1	87.7	75.4
High income	119.5	167.8	189.2	58.3

Source: Regmi & Pompelli, 2002

TABLE 10.2 WORLD MEAT PRODUCTION, 1980 AND 1998

Region	Percent of World Total	
	1980	1998
North America	20	18
Western Europe	22	16
Oceania	3	2
East and Southeast Asia	4	5
South Asia	3	3
China	11	26
Near East	2	3
South America	9	10
Rest of world	26	17
Total	100%	100%

Source: Regmi & Pompelli, 2002

TABLE 10.3 NUMBER OF FARMS IN MIDWESTERN STATES, 1940 AND 2000

State	1940	2000	Decline
Ohio	233,700	80,000	153,700
Missouri	256,100	109,000	147,100
Michigan	187,600	52,000	135,600
Illinois	213,400	78,000	135,400
Indiana	184,500	64,000	120,500
Minnesota	197,400	79,000	118,400
Iowa	213,300	95,000	118,300
Wisconsin	186,700	77,000	109,700
Kansas	156,300	64,000	92,300
Nebraska	121,100	54,000	67,100
N. Dakota	74,000	30,300	43,700
S. Dakota	72,500	32,500	40,000
Total	2,096,600	814,800	1,281,800

Source: U.S. Department of Agriculture (USDA), 2002

"spec" buildings, and other incentives. More and more small towns are turning to value-added processing of agricultural commodities as a means of job creation, and meatpacking and poultry processing accounted for much of the rural manufacturing job growth in the United States during the 1980s and 1990s. Take Arkansas, for example. While running for president in 1992, Bill Clinton boasted of the record number of manufacturing jobs created during his term as governor. What he failed to mention was that most of these jobs were in poultry plants. Arkansas was not alone. Poultry processing became the second fastest growing factory job in the United States and the biggest industry in the South during this period (Horowitz 1994:1; Kwik 1991:14). Beef processing became Nebraska's largest manufacturing employer and accounted for half the state's manufacturing jobs (Ackerman 1991).

But work on meat and poultry lines is physically demanding and dangerous. And packinghouses bring significant social and economic costs to host communities: declining per capita income, housing shortages, increases in population mobility, and rising demands for health care, public safety, education, and indigent care. Employers ignore the added costs that come with their workforces. These costs fall on local residents, who, in addition to paying higher taxes, give of their time and money to support food banks, homeless shelters, and other newcomer services.

Consumers benefit from cheap food, but that same food may place them at risk for food-borne illnesses. Antibiotics are an important weapon in the battle against disease. The widespread use of antibiotics to curtail illness among animals grown in confinement has been blamed for alarming increases in the incidence of human bacterial infections that fail to respond to treatment with these same antibiotics (Angulo et al. 2000). Multidrug resistance in some *Salmonella* bacteria has grown from 5 to 95 percent in the past 20 years (Young et al. 1999).

MEAT ME IN THE LEGISLATURE

Concerns first arose about using antibiotics in animal feed soon after the practice began in the 1950s. Critics feared the long-term use of these drugs to promote growth and feed efficiency posed a threat to human health. In the 1970s, the U.S. Food and Drug Administration (FDA) attempted to ban certain agricultural uses of antibiotics, but was thwarted by opposition from agribusiness and farm-state legislators. Efforts to ban agricultural use of certain antibiotics since then have proved unsuccessful.

Despite lack of legislative success, mounting medical evidence links nontherapeutic uses of antibiotics in livestock to antibiotic-resistant bacteria that make it harder to treat certain infections in humans (U.S. National Research Council 1999). These findings led to an editorial in the *New England Journal of Medicine* urging elimination of antimicrobials in animal feed (Gorbach 2001). In the same issue of the journal, researchers reported that 20 percent of ground meat samples purchased in Washington, D.C., supermarkets contained *Salmonella* and that 84 percent of the isolates were resistant to at least one antimicrobial. The American Medical Association, American Public Health Association, and American College of Preventive Medicine oppose nontherapeutic use of antimicrobials in animal agriculture. The European Union, Japan, Australia, and New Zealand have banned the subtherapeutic use of penicillin and tetracycline (Lieberman & Wooten 1998).

MEAT ME IN COURT

The poultry industry has been vertically integrated for years, and thousands of independent pig farmers went out of business after prices for live hogs plummeted in 1998 and again in 2002. Packers already own or hold contracts on about 75 percent of all hogs grown in the United States (USDA Grain Inspection, Packers and Stockyards Administration 2001). If the packers have their way, cattle will soon follow. Already, the four leading packers receive one-third of their cattle from "captive supplies" (Lenz 2002).

But just as nineteenth-century cattlemen fought to protect their ranges, so their descendants battle efforts by transnational processing firms to vertically integrate the beef cattle industry. Independent producers cite studies by agricultural economists who say packer ownership of captive supplies depresses cattle prices. Packers cite different agricultural economists who maintain that captive supplies have no impact on prices. The argument will be settled in court—with very real consequences for the future of the beef industry.

In 1999 a federal judge certified a class action antitrust lawsuit, *Pickett v. IBP,* which alleges the company used captive supplies to depress prices paid to producers. Class members include 27,000–30,000 cattle feeders who sold cattle to IBP from February 1994 to the end of April 1999 (Looker 2002). It took 5 years for a judge to certify the class action, and the case is unlikely to be tried until 2003. In the meantime, low prices will force many small cattle producers and feeders out of business.

Efforts to include a federal ban on meatpacker ownership of livestock more than 14 days before slaughter in the 2002 farm bill fell victim to claims from companies like Smithfield that such a ban would force them into bankruptcy. State bans on corporate ownership of livestock already exist in several midwestern states. Iowa's law forbids processors from owning, controlling, or operating livestock operations. Smithfield filed suit against Iowa, claiming its law is protectionist, discriminatory, and designed to force them out of the state (Fitzgerald 2002). In early 2003, a federal judge ruled in favor of Smithfield and overturned the state's ban on packers owning hogs. The decision will in all likelihood be appealed by Iowa's attorney general (Perkins 2003).

The working conditions in meat and poultry processing plants are also the subject of litigation. In 1993, 14 present and former employees of IBP's Kansas beef plants filed suit against the company, alleging it had subjected Mexican and Mexican American employees to a "hostile work environment" and "assigned the most difficult and least desirable jobs solely on the basis of their national origin." The case dragged on for years. In 1995, we were asked by the plaintiffs' attorneys to prepare depositions summarizing our knowledge of IBP's operations in its Finney County, Kansas, plant. Several years later a federal judge refused to certify a class action and required that each case be tried individually. In June 1999, on the day the first trial was to begin, attorneys for both sides settled out of court. Terms of the settlement were sealed, but the plaintiffs' lead attorney explained to Michael that "the workers received more money than they had probably ever seen in their lifetimes," and her law firm had recovered its costs. But, in her view, the amount of the settlement "was not sufficient to alter IBP's way of doing business."

Nevertheless, meat and poultry companies face a growing number of lawsuits. In 2002 alone, a half-dozen suits were filed against as many companies claiming violations of the federal Packers and Stockyards Act, the Oklahoma Business

Opportunities Sales Act, and the Texas Antitrust Act and Deceptive Trade Practices and Consumer Protection Act. In these cases, chicken and turkey growers accused companies such as O.K. Industries, Pilgrim's Pride, and Cargill with misrepresentation, fraud, and breach of contract. Growers claim their integrators exaggerated potential income and minimized total costs, including the need for constant upgrades to their houses and equipment. Plaintiffs argue that paying growers according to a ranking system is a deceptive trade practice, since the rank depends on company inputs over which the grower has no control (RAFI-USA 2002).

In August 2002, Tyson Foods announced it was "restructuring" its live swine operations and terminating its relationships with 132 contract hog producers in Arkansas and eastern Oklahoma. The hog barns were paid for with borrowed capital; now these farmers have no means to pay off their debts. Many of these growers filed suit against Tyson, asking compensation for damages caused by the financial collapse of their farming operations (*Arkansas Democrat Gazette* 2002).

The Sierra Club's 2002 lawsuit against Tyson and some of its growers in western Kentucky for violations of federal environmental law was outlined in Chapter 9. It is but one of many in the Sierra Club's *RapSheet on Animal Factories* (2002), which chronicles the "convictions, fines, pollution violations and regulatory records on America's Animal Factories." This "rap sheet" is a who's who of agribusiness giants. Smithfield was fined $12.6 million by a federal judge in 1997 for dumping slaughterhouse waste into a tributary of Chesapeake Bay. In 2001, the Waterkeeper Alliance filed suit against Smithfield for allegedly polluting waterways in eastern North Carolina in violation of the Clean Water Act and the Resource Conservation and Recovery Act. Seaboard's hog facility in Dorman, Oklahoma, has reported more than a dozen waste spills, including one of 100,000 gallons into a nearby streambed. In 2002, Cargill agreed to a $1 million fine for illegally dumping hog waste that killed 53,000 fish in the Loutre River, 75 miles northwest of St. Louis. The list goes on.

The U.S. Department of Labor fined ConAgra's beef plant in Greeley, Colorado, $1.2 million for willful and repeated violations of the Fair Labor Standards Act—a charge that has also been leveled at Excel's Beardstown, Illinois, pork plant. Tyson was repeatedly charged with violations of federal environmental and labor laws during the 1990s. In 2001, the U.S. Justice Department charged Tyson employees with smuggling undocumented workers from Mexico and Central America to work in some of its poultry processing plants. The company denies a companywide conspiracy and says a few managers acted on their own in violation of company policy (Barboza 2002).

Such cases are nothing new. In the late 1980s, the federal Occupational, Safety and Health Administration (OSHA) fined John Morrell, IBP, and Monfort for under-reporting work-related injuries at several packing plants. These fines brought unwelcome public attention, but the dollar amounts the companies actually paid were relatively small, and they were able to reduce them even further through negotiations with OSHA (Stull and Broadway 1995).

This litany of court cases and settlements suggest that for many companies, fines are just another cost of doing business. When lawyers' fees, court costs, and fines exceed the price of improving working conditions, paying a fair wage, and preventing environmental damage, meat and poultry companies may change their ways. Until then, it will be business as usual.

Criticisms of industrialized agriculture's impact on farmers, processing plant employees, local communities, and the environment are mounting (Schlosser 2001; Kimbrell 2002b). And more and more groups—from production workers and growers to environmentalists and community activists—are taking the industry giants on. But are there viable alternatives to the existing system? A quick trip around the globe provides some answers.

SUSTAINABLE AGRICULTURE IN WESTERN EUROPE

Farming in Great Britain looks much like it does in the United States: depressed commodity prices, falling farm incomes, price supports, and production increasingly concentrated in highly capitalized farms linked to food processors and supermarkets. Add to these structural characteristics the devastating effects of mad cow disease and the 2001 outbreak of foot-and-mouth disease, and the United Kingdom is faced with what the Report of the Policy Commission on the Future of Farming and Food (2002:6) called a "dysfunctional" agricultural system "detached from the rest of the economy and the environment." To address this problem, the commission recommended policies: "To reconnect our food and farming industry; to reconnect farming with its market and the rest of the food chain; to reconnect the food chain and the countryside; and to reconnect consumers with what they eat and how it is produced."

The commission advocated strengthening the connection between consumers and the food they eat by expanding and strengthening existing food assurance schemes such as the Little Red Tractor program. Started in 1999, the program covers between 60 and 90 percent of Britain's major commodities and 550 product lines. It guarantees production of covered food according to an agreed upon set of agricultural practices. Participation is voluntary and farmers pay to participate. Assurance standards exist for a variety of foodstuffs, including beef, pork, lamb, and poultry. Inspectors visit participating farms to enforce standards for animal welfare, housing, feed, and animal transportation (*British Farm Standard* 2002).

Chickens raised under this program (about 80 percent of U.K. production) are not fed antibiotic growth promoters; cattle and sheep do not receive artificial growth hormones; and all animals receive sufficient space "to perform normal patterns of behavior" (*British Farm Standard* 2002). Pigs raised outdoors must have a muddy area where they can wallow and cool themselves or be provided with shade or sprinklers. Those raised indoors must be "housed in groups so that they can see, hear and smell other animals, which encourages normal social behavior" (Assured British Pigs 2002). Britain banned the use of crates in raising pigs in 1998 (Report of the Policy Commission on the Future of Farming and Food 2002).

Such measures are part of a broader movement within the European Union (EU) to improve animal welfare and reduce the level of antibiotics in livestock production. Sweden banned growth-promoting antibiotics in its poultry industry in the mid-1980s (Humphrys 2001), and more recently the EU banned seven commonly used growth-promoting antibiotics. Germany stopped subsidies to farmers who raise livestock on slatted floors, will ban chickens raised in cages beginning in 2007, and plans to use about 20 percent of the direct farm aid it receives from the EU to promote more environmentally friendly farming. Germany's goal is to devote about a fifth of its agricultural land to organic farming by 2010 (*Economist* 2002a:52).

IT'S BETTER DOWN UNDER!

Four companies, which employed thousands of workers to slaughter and process meat in massive plants, dominated New Zealand's meat industry—until recently. Three of the four companies have been driven out of business by a "new generation" of small, technologically advanced firms that owe their success to higher worker productivity, better designed plants, lower employee turnover, and an ability to produce, market, and export high-quality, safe products.

Instead of running their lines at more than 400 cattle per hour, these new plants process about 500 head a day. Lower line speed encourages more attention to quality and safety. Cattle and sheep are cleaned to remove fecal matter and dirt before they enter the plants. Keeping plants microbiologically clean is essential to producing meat with a 4-month shelf life for export around the world. Time between stunning an animal and packaging has been reduced to only 45 minutes, which also cuts down on contamination risks. On the killfloor, more tasks are done by hand than in the larger, more mechanized plants in the United States. Yet productivity actually increases: 20 cattle can be processed per worker per day in these new plants, compared to only 12 in traditional large-volume plants.

Good pay, better training, and an environment that encourages workers to participate in the design and operation of the plants translates into low employee turnover—only about 7 percent a year, compared to about 7 percent a month in U.S. plants. Some plants play "classic rock" through radio speakers on production floors. At others, glassed-in galleries overlooking the slaughter line provide natural light and create a more pleasant work environment.

Smaller plants also benefit local economies. These new plants need fewer cattle each day, so processors can buy them from nearby farmers, who in turn support other local businesses. If all this sounds too good to be true, McDonald's, the world's largest purchaser of beef, is importing New Zealand beef to supply its stores in the southern United States (Bjerklie 2002b).

VOTING WITH YOUR STOMACH

The decisions we make about what we eat and where have significance beyond our waistlines. Eating at McDonald's or KFC supports transnational corporations and their corporate suppliers; buying locally grown food from a farmers' market and cooking it ourselves supports a more sustainable system of agriculture. Food choices have economic implications; they have moral ones as well. The National Catholic Rural Life Conference (NCRLC) has proclaimed an Eaters' Bill of Rights (2002). Each of us has the right to know how our food is grown and processed. We have a right to food that is safe, nutritious, and produced under socially just circumstances, without harming air, water, land—or people. We also have a right to know the country of origin of our food and whether it has been genetically modified.

The NCRLC advocates policies that "uphold the dignity of family farmers" and opposes the contract-grower system of agricultural production, which makes "serfs of family farmers." It encourages people to support sustainable agriculture and calls on us to purchase locally grown food, use church halls and parking lots for farmers' markets, promote cookbooks that use local produce, and celebrate special days and seasons to widen the connection between food, the land, and spirituality.

Michael Broadway

Figure 10.2 Organic farm in Westby, Wisconsin

In *Silent Spring,* Rachel Carson (1962) awakened the public to the environmental effects of pesticides and planted the seeds of an organic food movement in the United States. Two decades later, growing opposition to industrialized meat production spawned alternative suppliers, such as Coleman's Natural Products Company, Niman Ranch, Laura's Lean Beef, Applegate Farms, and Petaluma Poultry, which raise cattle and poultry on natural grains or grasses without antibiotics or growth hormones.

Founded in 1979, Coleman Natural Products was the first to brand its beef and promote it as "natural"—grown without antibiotics or growth-promoting hormones. Coleman Natural Products slaughters more than 1,000 head of cattle a week and sells its beef throughout the United States (Bjerklie 2002a). Annual sales for Laura's Lean Beef soared from $10,000 in 1985, its first year of operation, to more than $50 million in 2001. The American Heart Association certified that Laura's beef meets its criteria for saturated fat and cholesterol levels—a first for the meat industry. Laura's Lean Beef is available in 34 states, but its sales are often limited to gourmet and health-oriented food stores.

The increasing popularity of organic foods has led to the appearance of health-conscious food chains, such as Bread & Circus, Mrs. Gooch's, and Whole Foods Market. Founded in 1980, Whole Foods Market, with 133 stores across the United States, calls itself "the world's largest retailer of natural and organic foods." Its meat department assures customers that "many of the animals are raised in a free-roaming

Figure 10.3 Whole Foods Market in Minneapolis, Minnesota

setting . . . on wholesome grains and well water, instead of byproducts, hormones and steroids" (Whole Foods Market 2002). Despite their growing popularity, natural foods represent only a fraction of total food sales. In 1997, retail sales of natural foods totaled $5.5 billion. Sales are expected to reach $60 billion by 2008, but even then they will account for only 10 percent of total food sales (Grey 2000a:147).

THE MEAT AND POULTRY INDUSTRY: HISTORY REPEATED?

When Upton Sinclair wrote *The Jungle* in the early years of the twentieth century, five companies dominated America's meatpacking industry. Livestock producers complained that the beef trust conspired to set prices—a claim later supported by a report from the Federal Trade Commission:

> Five great packing concerns of the country—Swift, Armour, Morris, Cudahy, and Wilson—have obtained such a dominant position that they control at will the market in which they buy their supplies, the market in which they sell their products, and hold the fortunes of their competition in their hands.
>
> Not only is the business of gathering, preparing, and selling meat products in their control, but an almost countless number of by-product industries are similarly dominated; and not content. . . they have invaded allied industries and even unrelated ones. (cited in Skaggs 1986:105–106)

In 1919, the Justice Department indicted the five companies for numerous antitrust violations. In 1920, the five companies agreed to divest themselves of their "vertical business structures" (Skaggs 1986:107).

Now, in the early years of a new century, all that remains of these companies are their names. But in their place a new oligopoly has emerged to dominate the meat industry. In 2002, the top four companies controlled 81 percent of the beef market, 59 percent of the pork market, and 50 percent of the poultry market. Tyson and ConAgra were among the top four in all three markets; Cargill in two of the three (*Foodstuffs* 2002a).

This pattern is repeated throughout the food industry. Three firms control 81 percent of corn exports and 65 percent of soybean exports—one of these firms is Cargill. The three largest supermarket chains—Kroger, Albertson's, and Safeway—now control one-third of supermarket food sales and one-fourth of all retail food sales (*Foodstuffs* 2002b).

But in the twenty-first century, the federal governments of the United States and Canada are turning a deaf ear to concerns about monopolistic practices of the giant corporations that control our food. Farmers' and ranchers' complaints about captive supplies and packer ownership of livestock fail to resonate with urban consumers, who are far removed from the where and the how of food production. Politicians and government officials, whose constituents are increasingly urban, are more likely to curry the favor of powerful agribusiness corporations than listen to the dwindling pleas of small farmers and the small towns that depend on them.

Government in North America is ignoring the fact that our food supply system is controlled by a few corporations. The consequences for our food security, safety, and quality are significant. But viable alternatives exist. All we need do is look to what is being done in New Zealand and the European Union, and among a growing number of producers and providers in North America. Each of us chooses the food we eat, and our choices shape prevailing systems of production, processing, and packaging. The challenge for those concerned about developing a sustainable agricultural system, one that respects land, producers, harvesters, and processing workers is to show consumers the connection between the food they eat and the prevailing industrial production system. Only if we make that connection will more people demand changes in their food and how it is produced. It is to that end, that we offer this book.

NOTES

1. The Body Mass Index (BMI) is used to measure overweight and obesity. It is calculated as a weight in pounds divided by the square of a person's height in inches, multiplied by 703. Alternatively, weight in kilograms divided by the square of a person's height in meters. A BMI between 25 and 29.9 is interpreted as overweight, while 30.0 and above is classified as obese (U.S. Department of Health & Human Services 2001).

2. Yum Brands, Inc., owns KFC, Pizza Hut, Taco Bell, Long John Silvers, and A&W. It owns the most fast food outlets in the United States—more than 21,000 (Novak 2002).

References

Ackerman, Pam. 1991. All Across Nebraska, Beef Is Big Business. *Lexington* (NE) *Clipper,* May 29.

Adams, Andy. 1903. *The Log of a Cowboy: A Narrative of the Old Trail Days.* Boston: Houghton Mifflin.

Alberta Agriculture, Food and Rural Development. 2000. *Code of Practice for Responsible Livestock Development and Manure Management.* Edmonton: Alberta Agriculture.

——— 2002. *Loss and Fragmentation of Farmland.* Edmonton: Alberta Agriculture.

Alberta Economic Development. 1998. *Highlights of the Alberta Economy.* Edmonton: Alberta Economic Development.

Albrecht, Stan L. 1982. Commentary. *Pacific Sociological Review* 25:297–306.

Allen, Mike. 2002. Bush Signs Bill Providing Big Farm Subsidy. *Washington Post,* May 14.

Alvesson, Mats. 1995. *Cultural Perspectives on Organizations.* Cambridge: Cambridge University Press.

American Farm Bureau Federation. n.d. *America the Bountiful.* Washington, DC: American Farm Bureau Federation.

Andreas, Carol. 1994. *Meatpackers and Beef Barons: Company Town in a Global Economy.* Niwot: University Press of Colorado.

Angulo, F., K. R. Johnson, R. V. Tauxe, & M. L. Cohen. 2000. Origins and Consequences of Antimicrobial Resistant Nontyphoidal Salmonella: Implications for the Use of Fluoroquinolones in Food Animals. *Microbial Drug Resistance* 6:77–83.

Anonymous. 2001. Tour de Stench. April 20. Typescript, 2 pp. Authors' files.

Apple, R. W., Jr. 1998. For Tobacco Growers, a Changing Life. *New York Times,* September 14.

Ard, Owen S. 1998. *Housing Market Analysis Real Estate Consultation: Texas County Market Analysis, Texas County, Oklahoma.* Report submitted to Oklahoma Department of Commerce, January 5. Typescript, 32 pp. Authors' files.

Arkansas Democrat Gazette. 2002. Hog Growers File Suit Against Tyson. September 13.

Armour Pork Products. 2002. Perfectly Seasoned Pork. URL:<http://www.freshpork.com/products/Seasoned/index.html> (May 21, 2002).

Associated Press (AP). 2000. Kentucky Poultry Production Up 13,000 Percent. *The Gleaner* (Henderson, KY), June 25.

———. 2002. Chicken Farmers Increasing Vigilance. *Evansville* (IN) *Courier & Press.* October 22. URL:<http://myinky.com/ecp/local_news/article/0,1626,ECP_745_1494529,00.html> (October 22, 2002).

Assured British Pigs. 2002. Pork. URL:<http://www.littleredtractor.org.uk/products.asp?id-pork> (September 3, 2002).

Austin, Lisa. 1988a. Rich Potential for Kansas Carries Risk. *Wichita Eagle-Beacon,* September 11:1A, 10A–11A.

———. 1988b. Southwest Area Takes Choicest Cut of Meat Industry. *Wichita Eagle-Beacon,* September 11:11A.

Bach, Robert. 1993. *Changing Relations: Newcomers and Established Residents in U.S. Communities: A Report to the Ford Foundation by the National Board of the Changing Relations Project.* New York: Ford Foundation.

Ball, Charles E. 1992. *The Finishing Touch: A History of the Texas Cattle Feeders Association and Cattle Feeding in the Southwest.* Amarillo: Texas Cattle Feeders Association.

Barboza, David. 2002. Tyson Fosters Ties to Officials But Is Unable to Avoid Scrutiny. *New York Times,* January 1.

Barrett, James R. 1987. *Work and Community in the Jungle: Chicago's Packinghouse Workers, 1894–1922.* Urbana: University of Illinois Press.

Benson, Janet E. 1990. Good Neighbors: Ethnic Relations in Garden City Trailer Courts. *Urban Anthropology* 19:361–386.

Bjerklie, Steve. 1993. A Fine Scattering of Genes: Poultry Breeders Meet New Needs with New Birds. *Meat&Poultry* 39(2):18–24.

———. 1994. Dark Passage II: The Empire Strikes Back. *Meat&Poultry* 40(10):32–35.

———. 2002a. The Man at the Head of the Creek. *Meat Processing* 41(3):7.

———. 2002b. Peak Performance: How "New Generation" Meat Plants Forever Changed New Zealand's Industry. *Meat Processing* 41(5):30.

Blanchard, Leola Howard. 1989. *Conquest of Southwest Kansas.* Garden City, KS: Finney County Historical Society. (First published in 1931.)

Boggs, Donald L., & Robert A. Merkel. 1984. *Live Animal Carcass Evaluation and Selection Manual,* 2nd ed. Dubuque, IA: Kendall/Hunt.

Bone, Robert M. 2000. *The Regional Geography of Canada.* Don Mills, Ontario: Oxford University Press.

Bowers, Douglas E. 2000. Cooking Trends Echo Changing Roles of Women. *Food Review* 23(1):23–29.

Bowler, Ian. 1985. Some Consequences of the Industrialization of Agriculture in the European Community. In *The Industrialization of the Countryside.* Michael Healey & Brian W. Ilbery, eds., pp. 75–98. Norwich, UK: Geo Books.

———. 1992. The Industrialization of Agriculture. In *The Geography of Agriculture in Developed Market Economies.* Ian Bowler, ed., pp. 7–31. Harlow, UK: Longman.

Boyens, Ingeborg. 2001. *Another Season's Promise: Hope and Despair in Canada's Farm Country.* Toronto: Penguin.

British Farm Standard. 2002. Pork, Poultry, Beef & Lamb. URL:<http://www. littleredtractor.org.uk/products> (September 3, 2002).

Broadway, Michael J. 1990. Meatpacking and Its Social and Economic Consequences for Garden City, Kansas, in the 1980s. *Urban Anthropology* 19:321–344.

———. 1991a. *Cows, Cowboys, and Crime: A Study of Changing Patterns of Crime in a Kansas Beefpacking Town.* Paper presented at the annual conference of the Middle States Division of the Association of American Geographers, University Park, PA, October 4–6. (With Susan Roy.)

———. 1991b. Economic Development Programs in the Great Plains: The Example of Nebraska. *Great Plains Research* 1:324–344.

———. 1995. From City to Countryside: Recent Changes in the Structure and Location of the Meat and Fish Processing Industries. In *Any Way You Cut It: Meat Processing and Small-Town America.* Donald D. Stull, Michael J. Broadway, & David Griffith, eds., pp. 17–40. Lawrence: University Press of Kansas.

———. 2000. Planning for Change in Small Towns or Trying to Avoid the Slaughterhouse Blues. *Journal of Rural Studies* 16:37–46.

———. 2001. Bad to the Bone: The Social Costs of Beefpacking's Move to Rural Alberta. In *Writing Off the Rural West: Globalization, Governments, and the Transformation of Rural Communities.* Roger Epp & Dave Whitson, eds., pp. 39–52. Edmonton: University of Alberta Press and Parkland Institute.

Broadway, Michael J., & Donald D. Stull. 1991. Rural Industrialization: The Example of Garden City, Kansas. *Kansas Business Review* 14(4):1–9.

Broadway, Michael J., Donald D. Stull, & Bill Podraza. 1994. What Happens When the Meat Packers Come to Town? *Small Town* 24(4):24–28.

Brooks Bulletin. 2000. Michael Broadway Report Says Lakeside Expansion Created Social Problems in Brooks. October 11.

Brown, Lester. 1995. *Who Will Feed China?* New York: Norton.

Bruggers, James. 2002. Sierra Club Vows Suit Over Chicken Farms and Dust They Produce. *Courier-Journal* (Louisville, KY), February 5:1–3. URL:<http://www.courier-journal.com /localnews/> (February 5, 2002).

Burros, Marian. 2002. Poultry Industry Quietly Cuts Back on Antibiotic Use. *New York Times,* February 10:1, 23.

Bush, George W. 2002. President Signs Farm Bill: Remarks by the President

Upon Signing the Farm Bill. URL: <http://www.whitehouse.gov/news/releases/2002/05/print20020513-2.html> (May 21, 2002).

Canada National Farmers Union. 2002. "Free Trade": Is It Working for Farmers? Saskatoon, Saskatchewan, Canada.

Canadian Pork Council. 2002. Statistics. URL:<http://www.cpc-ccp.com /ats.html (May 22, 2002).

Canfax. 2001. Statistical Briefer. URL:<http://www.cattle.ca/CanFax/default.htm> (May 22, 2002).

Carson, Rachel. 1962. *Silent Spring*. Boston: Houghton Mifflin.

Center for Rural Affairs. 2002. Rural Schools. URL:<http://www.cfra.org.issues/rural_schools.htm> (August 8, 2002).

Centers for Disease Control. 2000. Foodborne Infections. URL:<http://www.cdc.gov/ncidod/dbmd/diseaseinfo/foodborneinfections_t.htm> (June 16, 2002).

Clemen, Rudolf Alexander. 1923. *The American Livestock and Meat Industry*. New York: Ronald Press Company.

Connor, John, Peter C. Carstensen, Roger A. McEowen, & Neil E. Harl. 2002. The Ban on Packer Ownership and Feeding of Livestock: Legal and Economic Implications. URL:<http://www.harkin.senate.gov/specials/20020313-packer-report.pdf> (June 16, 2002).

Constance, Douglas H., & Alessandro Bonanno. 1999. CAFO Controversy in the Texas Panhandle Region: The Environmental Crisis in Hog Production. *Culture & Agriculture* 21(1):14–26.

County of Flagstaff Family Farm Promotional Society. 2002. Alberta Court of Appeal Decision. Flagstaff County, Alberta, Canada.

Crews, Joel. 2001a. Not in My Backyard: Community Resistance Hinders New Plant Construction Projects. *Meat&Poultry* 47(2):24–26, 28–29, 80.

———. 2001b. Maximum Capacity: Is Chicken Consumption "Maxed" Out? *Meat&Poultry* 47(12):21–23.

Cultural Relations Board, City of Garden City, Kansas (CRB). 2001. Changing Relations: Newcomers and Established Residents in Garden City, Kansas, 1990–2000. Unpublished manuscript, 34 pp. Authors' files.

Dale, Edward Everett. 1965. *Cow Country*. Norman: University of Oklahoma Press. (First published in 1942.)

Davidson, Alan. 1999. *The Oxford Companion to Food*. New York: Oxford University Press.

Davis, David E., & Hayden Steward. 2002. Changing Consumer Demands Create Opportunities for U.S. Food System. *Food Review* 25(1):19–23.

DeGruson, Gene, ed. 1988. *The Lost First Edition of Upton Sinclair's* The Jungle. Memphis: Peachtree Publishers.

Dhuyvetter, Kevin C., Jennifer Graff, & Gerry L. Kuhl. 1998. *Kansas Beef Industry Economic Trends*. Manhattan: Kansas State University Agricultural Experiment Station.

Donham, Kelley J. 1990. Health Effects from Work in Swine Confinement Buildings. *American Journal of Industrial Medicine* 17:17–25.

———. 1998. The Impact of Industrial Swine Production on Human Health. In *Pigs, Profits, and Rural Communities*. Kendall M. Thu & E. Paul Durrenberger, eds., pp. 73–83. Albany: State University of New York Press.

Drabenstott, Mark. 1998. This Little Piggy Went to Market: Will the New Pork Industry Call the Heartland Home? *Federal Reserve Bank of Kansas City Economic Review* 83(3):79–97.

Duckworth, Barbara. 2000. Alta. Community Says No Thanks to Sow Barn. *Western Producer*, July 20.

———. 2001. Alberta's ILO Policy Gets Mixed Reviews. *Western Producer*, July 12.

Duewer, Lawrence A., & Kenneth E. Nelson. 1991. Beefpacking Costs Are Lower for Larger Plants. *Food Review* 14(4):10–13.

Durand, Brian. 1999. The Chicken or the Egg? Both Come First. *Cross & Crescent*, Summer:20–23.

Economist. 2002a. Renate Künast, Would-Be Farm Reformer. April 20.

———. 2002b. Oh, Temptation; Fast-Food Lawsuits. August 3.

Edmonds, Scott. 2002. Action Urged on U.S. Farm Subsidies. *Toronto Globe and Mail*, May 21.

Education Oversight Board, Office of Accountability. Various years. *Profiles District Report*. Oklahoma City: Education Oversight Board.

Elitzak, Howard. 2000. Food Marketing Costs: A 1990's Retrospective. *Food Review* 23(3):27–30.

Fesperman, Dan, & Kate Shatzkin. 1999a. The New Pecking Order: The Plucking of the American Chicken. *Baltimore Sun,* February 28. URL:<http://sunspot.net/content/storyserver> (March 13, 1999).

———. 1999b. The New Pecking Order: Taking a Stand, Losing the Farm. *Baltimore Sun,* March 1. URL:<http://sunspot.net/content/storyserver> (March 13, 1999).

Fiddes, Nick. 1991. *Meat: A Natural Symbol.* London: Routledge.

Fink, Deborah. 1998. *Cutting into the Meatpacking Line: Workers and Change in the Rural Midwest.* Chapel Hill: University of North Carolina Press.

Fitzgerald, Anne. 2002. Smithfield Case Sparks Questions on Farm Control. *Des Moines Register,* July 28.

Flora, Cornelia, Jan L. Flora, Jacqueline D. Spears, Louis E. Swanson, with Mark B. Lapping & Mark Weinberg. 1992. *Rural Communities: Legacy & Change.* Boulder, CO: Westview.

Foodstuffs. 2002a. Concentration in Ag Markets Continues Upward Climb. Online Update, February 15. URL: wee.nfu.org> (February 18, 2002).

———. 2002b. Five Largest Grocery Retailers Increase Control of Food Markets. Online Update, June 3. URL: <www.nfu.org> (June 4, 2002).

Foruseth, Owen J. 1997. Restructuring of Hog Farming in North Carolina: Explosion and Implosion. *Professional Geographer* 49:391–403.

Gallo, Anthony E. 1999. Fewer Food Products Introduced in Last Three Years. *Food Review* 22(3):27–29.

Garden City (KS) *Telegram.* 2001a. Hispanic Numbers Double in Decade. March 14:A1, A6.

———. 2001b. Liberal a Microcosm of Hispanics' Gain. March 16:A1, A5.

Gearing, Fred. 1979. Microanalysis and Action Anthropology. In *Currents in Anthropology: Essays in Honor of Sol Tax.* Robert Hinshaw, ed., pp. 391–408. The Hague: Mouton.

George, Susan. 1986. *How the Other Half Dies: The Real Reasons for World Hunger.* London: Penguin.

Gibson, Craig D. 1998. Managing Your Poultry Business: Impacts of Income Tax, Debt Payment, and Retirement Planning. 21-page typescript accompanying presentation at the Hopkins County Extension Office, Madisonville, Kentucky, November 9. Authors' files.

Gilkey, Sam. 1997. Mega-Livestock Issues in News Since May. *The Messenger* (Madisonville, KY), September 2:1A, 3A.

Gold, Mark. 1999. Beyond the Killing Fields: Working Towards a Vegetarian Future. In *The Meat Business: Devouring a Hungry Planet.* Geoff Tansey & Joyce D'Silva, eds., pp. 169–186. London: Earthscan.

Gollehon, Noel, & Margrite Caswell. 2000. Confined Animal Production Poses Manure Management Problems. *Agricultural Outlook* September/AGO-274:12–18.

Gorbach, Sherwood. 2001. Antimicrobial Use in Animal Feed—Time to Stop. *New England Journal of Medicine* 345:1202–1203.

Gordon, John Steele. 1996. The Chicken Story. *American Heritage* 47(5):52–67.

Gouveia, Lourdes, & Donald D. Stull. 1995. Dances with Cows: Beefpacking's Impact on Garden City, Kansas, and Lexington, Nebraska. In *Any Way You Cut It: Meat Processing and Small-Town America.* Donald D. Stull, Michael J. Broadway, & David Griffith, eds., pp. 85–107. Lawrence: University Press of Kansas.

———. 1997. *Latino Immigrants, Meatpacking, and Rural Communities: A Case Study of Lexington, Nebraska.* JSRI Research Report No. 26. East Lansing: Julian Samora Research Institute, Michigan State University.

Green, George Norris, & Jim McClellan. 1985. Sick Chickens. *Southern Exposure* 13(5):48–55.

Green, Hardy. 1990. *On Strike at Hormel: The Struggle for a Democratic Labor Movement.* Philadelphia: Temple University Press.

Greenhouse, Steven. 2002. Poultry Plants to Pay Workers $10 Million in Compensation. *New York Times,* May 10.

Grey, Mark. 1995. Pork, Poultry and Newcomers in Storm Lake, Iowa. In

Any Way You Cut It: Meat Processing and Small-Town America. Donald D. Stull, Michael J. Broadway, & David Griffith, eds., pp. 109–128. Lawrence: University Press of Kansas.

———. 1998. *Handbook for Creating Sustainable Multiethnic Food-Producing Communities.* Ames: Iowa State University Extension.

———. 1999. Immigrants, Migration, & Worker Turnover at the Hog Pride Pork Packing Plant. *Human Organization* 58:16–27.

———. 2000a. The Industrial Food Stream and its Alternatives in the United States: An Introduction. *Human Organization* 59:143–150.

———. 2000b. "Those Bastards Can Go To Hell!" Small-Farmer Resistance to Vertical Integration and Concentration in the Pork Industry. *Human Organization* 59:169–176.

Griffith, David. 1995. *Hay Trabajo*: Poultry Processing, Rural Industrialization, and the Latinization of Low-Wage Labor. In *Any Way You Cut It: Meat Processing and Small-Town America.* Donald D. Stull, Michael J. Broadway, & David Griffith, eds., pp. 129–151. Lawrence: University Press of Kansas.

Guebert, Alan. 1999. Chicken Farmers Like "Land-Owning Serfs." *The Gleaner* (Henderson, KY), March 5.

Hackenberg, Robert A., & Gary Kukulka. 1995. Industries, Immigrants, and Illness in the New Midwest. In *Any Way You Cut It: Meat Processing and Small-Town America.* Donald D. Stull, Michael J. Broadway, & David Griffith, eds., pp. 187–211. Lawrence: University Press of Kansas.

Hackenberg, Robert A., David Griffith, Donald Stull, & Lourdes Gouveia. 1993. Creating a Disposable Labor Force. *Aspen Institute Quarterly* 5(2):78–101.

Hage, Dave, & Paul Klauda. 1989. *No Retreat, No Surrender: Labor's War at Hormel.* New York: William Morrow.

Haley, Mildred, Elizabeth A. Jones, & Leland Southard. 1998. World Hog Production: Constrained by Environmental Concerns. *Agricultural Outlook* AGO-249:15–19.

Harris, Marvin. 1985. *Good to Eat.* New York: Simon and Schuster.

Healthy Choice. 2002. Dinners. URL: <http://www.healthychoice.com/ products/products-category_dinners.jsp> (June 5, 2002).

Heffernan, William D. 1984. Constraints in the U.S. Poultry Industry. *Research in Rural Sociology and Development* 1:237–260.

Heffernan, William, with Mary Hendrickson & Robert Gronski. 1999. *Consolidation in the Food and Agriculture System.* Report to the National Farmers Union. February 5.

Hefling, Kimberly. 2002. Area Chicken Farmers Concerned About Vandals. *Evansville* (IN) *Courier & Press,* September 14. URL:<http://www. myinky.com/ecp/news/article/0,1626, ECP_734_1416173,00.html> (October 22, 2002).

Hendee, David. 2002. Natural Evolution. *Meat&Poultry* 48(4):22–29.

Holmberg, Allan R. 1958. The Research and Development Approach to the Study of Change. *Human Organization* 17:12–16.

Hord, Bill. 2002. Cattlemen Sue Packers— "A Line in the Sand." *Omaha World Herald,* May 11.

Horowitz, Roger. 1997. *"Negro and White Unite and Fight!" A Social History of Industrial Unionism in Meatpacking, 1930–1990.* Urbana: University of Illinois Press.

———. 2002. *Making the "Chicken of Tomorrow."* Paper presented at the International Conference on The Chicken: Its Biological, Social, Cultural, and Industrial History, Yale Program in Agrarian Studies, New Haven, CT, May 18.

Horowitz, Roger, & Mark J. Miller. 1999. *Immigrants in the Delmarva Poultry Processing Industry: The Changing Face of Georgetown, Delaware, and Environs.* JSRI Occasional Paper No. 37, The Julian Samora Research Institute. East Lansing: Michigan State University.

Horowitz, Tony. 1994. 9 to Nowhere: Blues on the Chicken Line. *Wall Street Journal,* December 1:A1, A8–A9.

Hoy, Jim. 1997. The Flint Hills of Kansas. *Range* 5(2):4–7.

Humphrys, John. 2001. *The Great Food Gamble.* London: Hodder & Stoughton.

Hutchison, Slone. 1999. McLean County Residents Voice Poultry Complaints. *The Gleaner* (Henderson, KY), September 14:A2.

IBP, Inc. 1989. *Cumulative Trauma Disorders*. Dakota City, NE: IBP.

Ikerd, John. 1998. Sustainable Agriculture, Rural Economic Development, and Large-Scale Swine Production. In *Pigs, Profits, and Rural Communities*. Kendall M. Thu & E. Paul Durrenberger, eds., pp. 157–169. Albany: State University of New York Press.

Johnson, Charles. 1994. Uproar in the Chicken House. *Farm Journal*, February:AC-1.

Jolley, Chuck. 2002. The Next Big Thing. *Meat&Poultry* 48(3):14.

Kansas Action for Children, Inc. 2000. *Kansas Kids Count Data Book 2000*. Baltimore: Annie M. Casey Foundation.

Kansas Beef Council. n.d. *Compliments of Cattle*. Promotional brochure.

Kansas City Business Journal. 2002. Seaboard Picks Texas Site for Second Hog-Processing Plant. URL:<http://kansascity.bizjournals.com/kansascity/stories/2002/02/04/daily20.html> (July 31, 2002).

Kansas Department of Health and Environment (KDHE). 1999. *Kansas County Health Profile 1999, Finney County*. Topeka: KDHE.

Katz, Jeffrey P., Jason W. Maddox, & Michael A. Boland. 1998. The Structure of the Custom Cattle Feeding Industry: A Strategic Analysis with Implications for Kansas Agribusiness. *Kansas Business Review* 22(1):11–18.

Kay, Steve. 1997. The Nature of Turnover: Packers Attempt to Reverse Financial Gain. *Meat&Poultry* 43(9):30–33.

Kentucky Agricultural Statistical Service. n.d. Number of Broilers Produced in Kentucky. Typescript, 1 page. Authors' files.

Kimbrell, Andrew. 2002a. Seven Deadly Myths of Industrial Agriculture. In *The Fatal Harvest Reader*. Andrew Kimbrell, ed., pp. 3–36. Washington, DC: Island Press.

———. 2002b. *The Fatal Harvest Reader: The Tragedy of Industrial Agriculture*. Washington, DC: Island Press.

Krause, Kenneth R. 1991. *Cattle Feeding, 1962–89: Location and Feedlot Size*. Commodity Economics Division, Economic Research Service, U.S. Department of Agriculture. Agricultural Economic Report No. 642.

Kwik, Phill. 1991. Poultry Workers Trapped in a Modern Jungle. *Labor Notes* 146:1, 14–15.

Lakeside Packers. 2000. Recruitment Package, 2000. Typescript, 6 pp. Authors' files.

Lamb, Russell L., & Michelle Beshear. 1998. From the Plains to the Plate: Can the Beef Industry Regain Market Share? *Federal Reserve Bank of Kansas City Economic Review* 83(4):49–66.

Lamphere, Louise, ed. 1992. *Structuring Diversity: Ethnographic Perspectives on the New Immigration*. Chicago: University of Chicago Press.

Lappé, Francis Moore. 1982. *Diet for a Small Planet*. New York: Ballantine Books.

Lappé, Francis Moore, Joseph Collins, & Peter Rosset. 1998. *World Hunger: Twelve Myths*. New York: Grove Press.

Lappé, Marc, & Britt Bailey. 1998. *Against the Grain*. Monroe, ME: Common Courage Press.

Lawrence, John, Glenn Grimes, & Marvin Hayenga. 1998. *Production and Marketing Characteristics of U.S. Pork Producers, 1997–98*. Staff Paper No. 311, Economics Department, Iowa State University.

Lenz, Kelly. 2002. Captive Cattle Supply Larger Than Expected. *Topeka* (KS) *Capital-Journal*, January 31.

Lieberman, Patricia B., & Margo G. Wooten. 1998. *Protecting the Crown Jewels of Medicine*. Washington, DC: Center for Science in the Public Interest.

Limprecht, Jane E. 1989. *ConAgra Who? $15 Billion and Growing*. Omaha, NE: ConAgra.

Long, Victoria Sizemore. 1991. Tyson Food Empire Had Its Start Between Fruit-Hauling Seasons. *Kansas City Star*, June 25:D-30.

Looker, Dan. 2002. Battle Over Captive Beef Supplies Continues on Two Fronts. URL:<http://www.agriculture.com/default.sph/AgNews.class?FNC=DetailNews_Asearch_listAgnews_html___47623> (July 26, 2002).

Lovan, Dylan T. 2002. Group Plans to Sue Chicken Farms. *The Gleaner* (Henderson, KY), February 6:A1, A11.

Lucas, John. 2002a. Keeping Farms Afloat. *Evansville* (IN) *Courier & Press*

(Western Kentucky edition), February 18:A1, A7.

———. 2002b. Suit Targets Poultry Firm, Its Growers. *The Gleaner* (Henderson, KY), April 23:A1, A12.

Lyman, Howard. 1998. *Mad Cowboy.* New York: Simon & Schuster.

MacArthur, Mary. 2000. Alberta Mega Barn Approved. *Western Producer,* December 7.

———. 2001. ILO Board Can Overturn Local Bans. *Western Producer,* November 29.

McKinley, Morgan G. 1998. Vandalism Takes Financial Bite. *The Messenger* (Madisonville, KY), July 23:A1, A3.

MacLachlan, Ian. 2001. *Kill and Chill: Restructuring Canada's Beef Commodity Chain.* Toronto: University of Toronto Press.

Martin, Larry, Zana Kruja, & John Alexiou. 1998. *Prospects for Hog Production and Processing in Canada.* George Morris Centre, University of Guelph, Ontario, Canada.

Mills, Edwin S. 1995. The Location of Economic Activity in Rural and Nonmetropolitan United States. In *The Changing American Countryside: Rural People and Places.* Emery N. Castle, ed., pp. 103–133. Lawrence: University Press of Kansas

Molotch, Harvey. 1976. The City as a Growth Machine. *American Journal of Sociology* 82:309–330.

Moore, Anne Marie. 1984. List of Beef By-Products. Tucson: Arizona State Cowbelles. Mimeograph, 9 pp. Authors' files.

Morrison, John M. 1998. The Poultry Industry: A View of the Swine Industry's Future? In *Pigs, Profits, and Rural Communities.* Kendall M. Thu & E. Paul Durrenberger, eds., pp. 145–154. Albany: State University of New York Press

National Catholic Rural Life Conference. 1997. An Immediate Moratorium on Large-Scale Livestock and Poultry Animal Confinement Facilities. A Statement from the Board of Directors of the National Catholic Rural Life Conference, December 18. (E-mail: November 29, 2001).

———. 2002. Ethics of Eating. URL:<http://www.nrclc.com/card01 backtext.html> (August 2, 2002).

National Farmers Union News. 2002. Farmers Union Members Testify on Negative Impacts of Livestock Concentration. 49(8):3.

Nestle, Marion. 2002. *Food Politics: How the Food Industry Influences Nutrition and Health.* Berkeley: University of California Press.

Novak, David. 2002. *2001 Tricon Annual Report.* Louisville: Tricon.

Nunes, Keith. 1995. Livestock: Developing More Efficient Animals. *Meat&Poultry* 41(1):38.

———. 1999. The Jungle Revisited: How Far Has This Industry Come? *Meat&Poultry* 45(12):16–20.

Opler, Morris. 1945. Themes as Dynamic Forces in Culture. *American Journal of Sociology* 5:198–206.

Ozeki, Ruth L. 1998. *My Year of Meats.* New York: Penguin.

Peoples, James, & Garrick Bailey. 1999. *Humanity: An Introduction to Cultural Anthropology.* Belmont, CA: Wadsworth.

Perkins, Jerry. 2003. Iowa Must Allow Packers to Own Hogs, Judge Rules. *Des Moines Register,* January 23.

Pollan, Michael. 2002. This Steer's Life. *New York Times Magazine,* March 31:44–51, 68, 71–72, 76–77.

Portes, Alejandro, & Josef Borocz. 1989. Contemporary Immigration: Theoretical Perspectives on Its Determinants and Modes of Incorporation. *International Migration Review* 23:606–630.

Poultry Grower News. 2001a. Poultry Growers, Catchers Secure Big Victories. 16:7.

———. 2001b. Putting a Pencil to It. 16:12.

Poultry Water Quality Consortium. 1998. *Poultry Water Quality Handbook,* 2nd. ed. expanded. Chattanooga, TN: Poultry Water Quality Consortium.

Putnam, Judy. 1999. U.S. Food Supply Providing More Food and Calories. *Food Review* 22(3):2–12.

Raab, Amy. 1997. From Sagebrush to Slaughterhouse. *Range* 5(1):18–20.

RAFI-USA. 2002. *Allegations of Fraud and Misrepresentation.* Contract Ag Reform Bulletin No. 6, July.

Ramsey, Doug, & John C. Everitt. 2001. Post-Crow Farming in Manitoba: An Analysis of the Wheat and Hog

Sectors. In *Writing Off the Rural West: Globalization, Governments and the Transformation of Rural Communities.* Roger Epp and Dave Whitson, eds., pp. 3–20. Edmonton: University Press of Alberta and Parkland Institute.

Rasnake, Monroe. 1996. *Broiler Litter Production in Kentucky and Potential Use as a Nutrient Source.* AGR-168. Lexington: University of Kentucky, College of Agriculture, Cooperative Extension Service.

Rasnake, Monroe, Lloyd Murdock, & William O. Thom. 1991. *Using Poultry Litter on Agricultural Land.* AGR-146. Lexington: University of Kentucky, College of Agriculture, Cooperative Extension Service.

Reeve, Agnesa. 1996. *Constant Frontier: The Continuing History of Finney County, Kansas.* Garden City, KS: Finney County Historical Society.

Regmi, Anita, & Greg Pompelli. 2002. U.S. Food Sector Linked to Global Consumers. *Food Review* 25(1):41.

Report of the Policy Commission on the Future of Farming and Food. 2002. Farming & Food: A Sustainable Future. URL:<http://www.cabinet-office.gov.uk/farming> (February 1, 2002).

Richards, Scott. 1992. Poultry on the Rise. *Meat&Poultry* 38(2):58.

Rifkin, Jeremy. 1992. *Beyond Beef: The Rise and Fall of the Cattle Culture.* New York: Penguin.

Sandburg, Carl. 1916. Chicago. In *Chicago Poems.* New York: Henry Holt and Company.

Schiffman, Susan, Elizabeth A. Miller, Mark S. Suggs, & Brevick G. Graham. 1995. The Effect of Environmental Odors Emanating from Commercial Swine Operations on the Mood of Nearby Residents. *Brain Research Bulletin* 37:369–375.

Schlosser, Eric. 2001. *Fast Food Nation: The Dark Side of the All-American Meal.* New York: Houghton Mifflin.

Schorak, Paul. 2000. *Decision of the Subdivision and Development Appeal Board of Flagstaff County:* Re: Development Permit No. 00-25. Sedgewick, Alberta, Canada.

Sebree (Kentucky) *Banner.* 1995. Tuesday Meeting Held to Clarify Construction of Area Chicken Houses. July 20:1–2.

Seibert, Gale. 1989. Class Lecture for Meat and Carcass Evaluation, Garden City

(Kansas) Community College, January 31. Authors' files.

Shatzkin, Kate, & Dan Fesperman. 1999a. Some Growers Happy with "the Real Good Money." *Baltimore Sun,* February 28. URL:<http://sunspot.net/content/storyserver> (March 13, 1999).

———. 1999b. Ten Ways to Show Who's Boss. *Baltimore Sun,* February 28. URL:<http://sunspot.net/content/storyserver> (March 13, 1999).

Sierra Club. n.d. *Corporate Hogs at the Public Trough: How Your Tax Dollars Help Bring Polluters into Your Neighborhood.* San Francisco: Sierra Club.

———. 2002. *The RapSheet on Animal Factories.* San Francisco: Sierra Club.

Silverstein, Ken. 1999. Meat Factories: Hellish Hog Plants, Lakes of Sewage, and Lifeless Waterways—Are Cheap Bacon-Burgers Worth It? Reprinted from *Sierra,* January/February. 9 pp.

Sinclair, Upton. 1962. *The Autobiography of Upton Sinclair.* New York: Harcourt, Brace, & World.

———. 1985. *The Jungle.* New York: Penguin. (First published in 1906.)

Skaggs, Jimmy M. 1986. *Prime Cut: Livestock Raising and Meatpacking in the United States, 1607–1983.* College Station: Texas A&M University Press.

Smithfield Foods, Inc. 2002. Financial History. URL:<http://www.smithfieldfoods.com/invest/finhis.html> (May 23, 2002).

Snow, Richard F. 1996. Letter from the Editor: Chicken Feed. *American Heritage* 47(5):5.

Spake, Amanda. 2002. A Fat Nation. *U.S. News & World Report* 133(7):40–47.

Statistics Canada. n.d. Canadian Statistics. URL:<http://www.statcan.ca/english/Pgdb> (July, 26, 2002).

———. 2002. Canadian Community Health Survey. *The Daily,* May 8.

Stentz, Zack. 1995. Too Much Poultry? *Meat&Poultry* 41(4):22–24.

Stinnett, Chuck. 1994. State May Get Another Poultry Plant. *The Gleaner* (Henderson, KY), May 19:A1.

———. 1996a. Chicken Litter. *The Gleaner* (Henderson, KY), August 24:A9.

———. 1996b. Poultry Company Chief: Production Here to Escalate. *The Gleaner* (Henderson, KY), October 24:A1, A10.

Strange, Marty, & Chuck Hassebrook. 1981. *Take Hogs, for Example: The Transformation of Hog Farming in America*. Walthill, NE: Center for Rural Affairs.

Striffler, Steve. 2002. Inside a Poultry Processing Plant: An Ethnographic Portrait. *Labor History* 43:305–313.

Stromquist, Shelton, & Marvin Bergman. 1997. *Unionizing the Jungles: Labor and Community in the Twentieth-Century Meatpacking Industry*. Iowa City: University of Iowa Press.

Stull, Donald D. 1990. "I Come to the Garden": Changing Ethnic Relations in Garden City, Kansas. *Urban Anthropology* 19:303–320.

———. 1994. Knock 'Em Dead: Work on the Killfloor of a Modern Beefpacking Plant. In *Newcomers in the Workplace: Immigrants and the Restructuring of the U.S. Economy*. Louise Lamphere, Alex Stepick, & Guillermo Grenier, eds., pp. 44–77. Philadelphia: Temple University Press.

———. 1999. *An Assessment of Seaboard's Impact on Guymon and Texas County, Oklahoma*. Submitted to Texas County Turning Point Partnership: Department of Anthropology, University of Kansas, Lawrence.

———. 2000. Tobacco Barns and Chicken Houses: Agricultural Transformation in Western Kentucky. *Human Organization* 59:151–161.

Stull, Donald D., Janet E. Benson, Michael J. Broadway, Arthur L. Campa, Ken C. Erickson, & Mark A. Grey. 1990. *Changing Relations: Newcomers and Established Residents in Garden City, Kansas*. Final report to the Ford Foundation's Changing Relations Project Board, Binghamton, New York, February 5. Institute for Public Policy and Business Research Report No. 172. Lawrence: University of Kansas.

Stull, Donald D., & Michael J. Broadway. 1990. The Effects of Restructuring on Beefpacking in Kansas. *Kansas Business Review* 14(1):10–16.

———. 1995. Killing Them Softly: Work in Meatpacking Plants and What It Does to Workers. In *Any Way You Cut It: Meat Processing and Small-Town America*. Donald D. Stull, Michael J. Broadway, & David Griffith, eds., pp. 61–84. Lawrence: University Press of Kansas.

Stull, Donald D., Michael J. Broadway, & Ken C. Erickson. 1992. The Price of a Good Steak: Beef Packing and Its Consequences for Garden City, Kansas. In *Structuring Diversity: Ethnographic Perspectives on the New Immigration*. Louise Lamphere, ed., pp. 35–64. Chicago: University of Chicago Press.

Sullivan, John, Utpal Vasavada, & Mark Smith. 2000. Environmental Regulation and Location of Hog Production. *Agricultural Outlook*, September/AGO-274:19–23.

Symes, David, & Terry Marsden. 1985. Industrialization of Agriculture: Intensive Livestock Farming in Humberside. In *The Industrialization of the Countryside*. Michael Healcy & Brian W. Ilbery, eds., pp. 99–120. Norwich, UK: Geo Books.

Tauxe, Robert V. 1997. Emerging Foodborne Diseases: An Evolving Public Health Challenge. *Emerging Infectious Diseases* 3:425–434.

Taylor, David A. 2001. From Pigsties to Hog Heaven? *Environmental Health Perspectives* 109(7):A328–A331.

Thu, Kendall, Kelly Donham, Randy Ziegenhorn, Stephen Reynolds, Peter S. Thorne, Peryasamy Subramanian, Paul Whitten, & Jason Stookesbury. 1987. A Control Study of the Physical and Mental Health of Residents Living Near a Large Swine Operation. *Journal of Agricultural Safety and Health* 3:13–26.

Thu, Kendall, & E. Paul Durrenberger, eds. 1998. *Pigs, Profits, and Rural Communities*. Albany: State University of New York Press.

Tillotson, James. 2002. Our Ready-Prepared Ready-to-Eat Nation. *Nutrition Today* 37:36–38.

Troughton, Michael J. 1986. Farming Systems in the Modern World. In *Progress in Agricultural Geography*. Michael Pacione, ed., pp. 93–123. London: Croom Helm.

Tyson Foods. n.d. Tyson's Live Production Teams Span Nine Counties. In Growing the Future. 12-page advertising insert in several Western Kentucky newspapers, July 1999.

———. 2002a. Tyson Meal Kits. URL:<http://www.tyson.com/chicken/products/default.asp?category= MealKits.> (May 22, 2002).

————. 2002b. Tyson Foods to Discontinue Fluoroquinolene Use in Broiler Flocks. URL:<http://www.tysonfoods.com/corporate/news/viewNews.asp?article=941> (July 26, 2002).

————. 2002c. 2001 Investor Fact Book. URL:<http://tsysonfoodsinc.com/IR/publications/factbook/factbook01/factbook01.pdf> (July 31, 2002).

————. 2002d. Statement of Tyson Foods, Inc. Regarding Sierra Club Lawsuit. URL:<http://www.tysonfoodsinc.com/corporate/news/viewNews.asp?article=966> (August 2, 2002).

Ulack, Richard, Karl Raitz, & Gyula Pauer. 1998. *Atlas of Kentucky.* Lexington: University Press of Kentucky.

Union of Concerned Scientists. n.d. Antibiotic Resistance. URL:<http://www.ucsusa.org/food/0antibiotic.html> (June 16, 2002).

United Food and Commercial Workers. 1997. Articles of Agreement between United Food and Commercial Workers and Hudson Foods, Inc., Henderson, Kentucky, April 21, 1997 to April 20, 2001. 48 pages. (Hudson Foods was purchased by Tyson Foods in 1998, but the contract remained in effect.)

U.S. Census Bureau. 1990. *Social and Economic Characteristics, Kansas, 1990.* Washington, DC: U.S. Government Printing Office.

————. 2001. *Statistical Abstract of the United States, 2001.* Washington, DC: U.S. Government Printing Office.

U.S. Census Bureau Public Information Office. 2002. Number of Foreign Born Up 57 Percent Since 1990, According to Census 2000. URL:<http://www.census.gov/Press-Release/www/2002/cb02cn117.html> (July 12, 2002).

U.S. Department of Agriculture (USDA). 2002. *Agricultural Statistics 2002.* Washington, DC: U.S. Government Printing Office.

USDA Grain Inspection, Packers and Stockyards Administration. 2001. *Assessment of the Cattle and Hog Industries, Calendar Year 2000.* Washington, DC: U.S. Government Printing Office.

USDA National Agricultural Statistics Service. 1999a. *1997 Census of Agriculture: North Carolina State and County Data, Part 33.* Washington, DC: U.S. Government Printing Office.

————. 1999b. *1997 Census of Agriculture: United States Summary and State Data Volume 1, Geographic Area Series Part 51.* Washington, DC: U.S. Government Printing Office.

————. n.d. Published Estimates Data Base. URL:<http://www.nass.usda.gov:81/ipedb/report.html> (Accessed May 21, 2002).

U.S. Department of Health & Human Services, Public Health Service, Office of the Surgeon General (USDHHS). 2001. *The Surgeon General's Call to Action to Prevent and Decrease Overweight and Obesity.* Washington, DC: U.S. Government Printing Office.

U.S. National Research Council. 1999. *The Use Of Drugs in Food Animals: Benefits and Risks.* Washington, DC: National Academy Press.

University of Kentucky College of Agriculture, Cooperative Extension Service. 1994. Important Notice. February 7. Typescript, under signature of various county extension agents for agriculture. Author's files.

Van Arsdall, Roy N., & Henry C. Gilliam. 1979. Pork. In *Another Revolution in U.S. Farming?* Lyle P. Schertz, ed., pp. 190–254. Washington, DC: USDA.

Vialles, Noelie. 1994. *Animal to Edible.* Cambridge: Cambridge University Press.

Ward, Fay E. 1989. *The Cowboy at Work: All About His Job and How He Does It.* Norman: University of Oklahoma Press. (First published in 1959.)

WATT Poultry USA. 2000. Industry at a Glance. January:18C.

Webb, Walter Prescott. 1981. *The Great Plains.* Lincoln: Bison Books, University of Nebraska Press. (First published in 1931.)

Whittington, Janet. 1997. "Chicken War" Is Heating Up. *The Messenger* (Madisonville, KY), August 19:1A, 3A.

Whole Foods Market. 2002. Products: Meat. URL:<http://www.wholefoodsmarket.com/products/meat.html> (September 11, 2002).

Williams, William H. 1998. *Delmarva's Chicken Industry: 75 Years of Progress.* Georgetown, DE: Delmarva Poultry Industry.

Wing, Steve, Dana Cole, & Gary Grant. 2000. Environmental Injustice in North

Carolina's Hog Industry. *Environmental Health Perspectives* 108:225–231.

Wing, Steve, & Susanne Wolf. 2000. Intensive Livestock Operations, Health, and Quality of Life Among Eastern North Carolina Residents. *Environmental Health Perspectives* 108:233–238.

Wood, Anita. 1988. *The Beef Packing Industry: A Study of Three Communities in Southwestern Kansas.* Final Report to the Department of Migrant Education. Flagstaff, AZ: Wood and Wood Associates.

Yeoman, Barry. 1989. Don't Count Your Chickens. *Southern Exposure* 17(2):21–24.

Young, Richard, Alison Cowe, Coilin Nunan, John Harvey, & Liz Mason. 1999. *The Use and Misuse of Antibiotics in U.K. Agriculture.* Bristol, UK: Soil Association.

Zane, J. Peder. 1996. It Ain't Just for Meat; It's for Lotion. *New York Times,* May 5:E5.

Index